J. M. Barrie

(photograph by G. C. Beresford)

PORTRAIT
OF
BARRIE

by

CYNTHIA ASQUITH

GREENWOOD PRESS, PUBLISHERS
WESTPORT, CONNECTICUT

CONTENTS

I	FIRST IMPRESSIONS	1
II	MARY ROSE	31
III	A SECRETARIAL SIDELINE	39
IV	BARRIE'S HOUSEHOLD	46
V	FURTHER IMPRESSIONS	51
VI	COURAGE	66
VII	SPEECHES	73
VIII	BARRIE PRODUCING A PLAY	83
IX	FRIENDSHIPS	96
X	BARRIE AT STANWAY	132
XI	TEN AUGUSTS	149
XII	BACK TO SCOTLAND	184
XIII	LAST HOLIDAYS	196
XIV	THE BOY DAVID	201
XV	MOST INDIVIDUAL AND BEWILDERING GHOST	217
	INDEX	225

ILLUSTRATIONS

FRONTISPIECE: J. M. BARRIE

BARRIE WITH HIS MOTHER   *facing page*   16

BARRIE AT THE AGE OF SIX   32

BARRIE AT THE AGE OF SIXTY   32

BARRIE IN HIS ADELPHI TERRACE FLAT   48

RECTOR OF ST. ANDREWS   80

BARRIE PLAYING CROQUET WITH H. G. WELLS   144

BARRIE WITH ELIZABETH BERGNER   208

To Viola Meynell

CHAPTER I

FIRST IMPRESSIONS

(1)

WHAT was Barrie really like? I wonder how many times I, who for nearly twenty years was his secretary, have been asked that question. I could not attempt to sum up so complex a being; but I will try to give my day-to-day impressions of him and such snatches of characteristic speech as I can remember.

When Barrie asked me to become his secretary he said, 'It will be a confidential job. I shall want absolute discretion'. I cannot forget that injunction; nor his love of privacy. But there is much that I can tell—much indeed, which I feel I ought to tell; for not long before he died Barrie said that, as he knew his life would be written, he hoped I might be the one to write it. A biography was a task I did not feel able to undertake; a book that gives my own memories of him is a different matter.

As a secretary I could claim one outstanding, if negative, distinction. I was without training. I did not know shorthand. I could not even type.

How then, it may well be asked, did I come to be Barrie's secretary?

I owe my first meeting with him to the kindness of his and my friend, Pamela Lytton who, knowing that I needed paid work and cherished film ambition, thought he might be able to help me. She told him the circumstances, invited me to meet him at dinner, and placed us beside one another.

To me that first meeting seemed an utter failure. I at once

felt Barrie's immensely strong personality, but could find no crack in what seemed an impenetrable shell of sadness and preoccupation. Was this failure my fault, I wondered? Or *was* he inaccessible, this strange, sombre, dark little man with that hurt look in his eyes?

If so, would he always be like this, or did he just happen as it were to have his receiver off tonight? Whatever the reason, I felt completely baffled. It was like drawing a blank. I don't mean that I wasn't aware of Barrie. I was struck—almost painfully so—by the sad, sunken eyes, the huge domed forehead, the mournful, strangely deep—almost hoarse—voice. Even that shortness of stature which he himself minded so much— how much no professional psychologist could exaggerate—was somehow impressive. Did it perhaps make him more intensely, because so compressedly, himself—as it were, epitomise him, as well as focus attention on the large head that looked weighted with memories? In any event, his shortness seemed a positive rather than a negative quality. Many years later, I knew exactly what Bernard Shaw meant by his remark after Thomas Hardy's funeral, at which he himself had been the tallest and most obviously impressive figure. (The distinguished pall-bearers included Kipling, Galsworthy, A. E. Housman, Baldwin and Ramsay MacDonald.) 'I looked very well myself,' said Shaw, 'but Barrie, blast him! looked far the most effective. He made himself look specially small.'

Barrie was fifty-seven when I first saw him, but except for that deep hoarded sadness in his blue eyes—a sadness which might have come from aeons of secret experience, or from the death of innumerable dreams—he looked younger. His hair was still quite black. So it remained until the end of his life, which distressed him. He was afraid people might suppose he used dye!

Not long after this—as it seemed to me—abortive first meeting, at which films weren't even mentioned, I again—where I forget—sat beside Barrie at dinner. This time, things went better. He looked less sad, and now and again said something extremely 'droll'—no other word for it—usually wryly so. Objectively, I found myself deeply interested in this, surely not, as I'd been told, 'sentimental', but saturnine, personality. Still, there was no sense of intouchness. I wasn't at my ease.

To my amazement, a few weeks later I was offered the part of Margaret in Barrie's *Dear Brutus*.

Long afterwards I asked Barrie why this had been. The following snatch of dialogue comes back to me word for word: 'Whatever made you think I could play what is surely a particularly difficult part?' I asked.

'You happened to look very much as I imagined the girl!' answered Barrie. 'I wanted her to have a queer face, and your unprofessional voice would have been just right.'

'But you didn't even know if I could act at all,' I objected.

'Almost anyone', declared Barrie, 'can be made to act if they can be made to understand their part, know how to move, and haven't been taught stage tricks, and for this particular part I wanted someone who had never been seen on the professional stage before.'

Any previous year I would have leapt at such a chance, for I was still stage-struck, but, just then, I was not feeling well enough to have the nerve—or rather effrontery—to act with professionals. So I refused; but being anxious to earn some money, I told Barrie I thought I might venture on a film part.

The third time I sat beside Barrie was the first time we really 'met'. The occasion, some time in the summer of 1918, was a small dinner party given by Brenda Dufferin at the Berkeley Grill. Brenda—extremely pretty, vivacious, and light in hand —had a gift for diffusing ease around her. She had also discovered some very fine old brandy—or was it rum?—in the family wine-cellar at Clandeboye. Whether or not this dual influence had anything to do with what followed I do not know. It may have been just a change in Barrie's own climate, but, whatever the reason, the man whom at first sight I had set down in my diary as 'shy, sad, apparently morose little Barrie', was scarcely recognisable. For the first time I saw, not once, but repeatedly, that famous smile, which irradiating his face, made you feel you had 'rung the bell'. From that evening, the ambition to ring that bell was to remain with me for nearly twenty years.

I saw, too, that amusement and kindness—extraordinary kindness—as well as sadness, could look out of those seared, but strangely beautiful eyes. No longer did he remind me of a 'drear-nighted December'; no longer did I want to go and drown myself. Not only did he amuse me and put me on the best of terms with myself, he had become a fellow of infinite jest. How could I have labelled him '*shy*'! He held the table.

After dinner the party adjourned to the tiny mews where Brenda lived. Here, the atmosphere was even more comfortable. Barrie, now talking gaily and funnily, sat beside me on the sofa. Suddenly he said with that subtle Scottish burr which clung to his speech:

'I could easily put you into a film. One of my own things is going to be done. Only I don't really approve of film-acting for you. But, if you really want a job, why not come and help me?'

'Help you?' I mumbled. 'Er . . . Er . . . How?'

'My papers are getting into an awful mess,' he said. 'I must have someone to cope with them, but I don't want what agents call "professional efficiency".'

'But I can't type!'

'I could never stand the clatter of a typewriter,' said Barrie. 'Besides, there are very few people I can bear to have in the room with me for long.'

That was how, in one of those cross-road moments of life, I was asked to become what Barrie, not long afterwards, in an anonymous article to *The Times*, described as his 'Private, Private Secretary'.

At that time I was a V.A.D. in a hospital, doing work I didn't wish to give up, but the war was obviously nearing its end; a paid job was much to be desired—and, surely, for better, for worse, this could scarcely fail to be an interesting experience? Although, no doubt, I had already made up my mind to accept, I, of course, went through the usual farce of asking advice, thereby discovering widely divergent points of view. One or two friends recoiled from the plan, and expressed themselves forcibly. Others—fervent, devout Barrieites—looked at me as though the gates of Heaven had opened before me. They seemed to think it positively impious to hesitate. Naturally, I reacted from both extremes.

Here are some verdicts I happen to remember. I consulted Sir Walter Raleigh,[1] a friend whose opinion I greatly valued. Should I accept the offer?

'Of course!' he said, positive, but not in an off-putting way. 'Why ever not? After all, Jimmie is a genius, and it isn't every day you're invited to help a genius.'

'How would I be able to help him?'

Sir Walter did his excellent best to reassure me.

'But, take care,' he added, 'take care you don't kill the golden goose by curbing his sentimentality; not that it really is sentimentality. It's far more often—for he has a cruel side—satire that doesn't quite come off.'

The opinion of another man of letters, Charles Whibley, was characteristically emphatic. Declaring his great affection for the man as well as his admiration for the writer, he was vehemently in favour.

'But, Barrie's the greatest living master of stagecraft' he insisted, almost angry with me for hesitating. 'What's more, he's the only natural writer I've ever known—that enviable limpidity!'

I said it must be very nice for Barrie to be a 'natural writer', but how would that help me to write his letters or keep his accounts? And how, I added, remembering something Mrs Patrick Campbell, who had acted in one of his plays, had just told me, how would it prevent me from being weighed down by his depressions?

[1] Regius Professor of English Literature at Oxford

I hadn't asked Mrs Patrick Campbell's advice, but she had volunteered it.

'Of course,' she warbled in that unforgettable, deep-throated voice, 'of course you must accept! It's a marvellous idea. Jimmie's a magician. But remember, Cynthia, he's intermittent. Beware of his depressions.'

General Sir Ian Hamilton was lyrical in praise of Barrie.

'He writes like an angel,' he declared, urging me to accept. 'Besides, he has such charm.'

My father welcomed the prospect of increase of income for any member of his family; so, though much tickled by the idea, and obviously thinking 'poor Barrie' a lunatic to entertain it, urged—indeed, he almost commanded—immediate acceptance.

(2)

Barrie's parting words had been, 'Well, why not come to see me and discuss it?'

So, a few days later, I went up in the most dawdling lift in London to the top of the tall building at the river end of Robert Street, Adelphi, and had my first sight of that large, low, book-lined, tobacco-laden room, perched high above the Embankment. I looked out at the wonderful view. Through one window I saw down the river to St. Paul's, through another up the river to the Clock Tower of the Houses of Parliament. I admired the great cave of a fireplace with its high mound of silvery ashes, and its stage-property-like implements—a long steel prong for jabbing at the logs, and an immense pair of bellows. On the dais that raised this Homeric hearth some inches above the level of the room, stood the high-backed wooden settle I was soon to know as quite the most excruciating seat ever devised; opposite this, a short leather couch, little less uncomfortable. I saw the huge knee-hole writing-desk of unpolished wood, at which at this moment— thirty-three years later—I sit gnawing my pen in my Kensington flat. I noticed that the ceiling and walls were stained brown—dark brown—as though from years and years of mingled firewood and tobacco smoke. This was about all I took in at my first sight of that room, so unlike any other known to me.

My attention was too much engaged by its arresting occupant, who was looking very sad again—sad and ineffably weary, his face all dark shadows. Today, he might have had ink instead of blood in his veins. He was remote, too, and rather sombre. Nothing whatsoever to remind me of the gay being I'd seen the other night, and had, I suppose, hoped to meet again. I felt much the same sort of disappointment as when one finds a crackling fire gone out. And this didn't look at all an easy grate to rekindle. Nor had I, as yet, the remotest idea how to set about it.

I wondered, would knowing Barrie always be like 'Snakes and Ladders', that game in which after progressing quite a long way you have to go right back to the starting-point and begin all over again? A good sprint forward, then a long, long shunt. Disconcerting! But, if Barrie was remote, he wasn't morose. He was very civil, very kind.

As I mounted the dais I cracked—for the first of several hundred times—my head on the beam above the step. It was too low to allow for anyone much taller than Barrie himself. He made me pour out tea. I promptly spilled it all over him and the funny little leather couch on which he sat. A good omen? We 'conversed', but the talk didn't exactly bubble. I can't remember what we talked about except one great friend whom we shared—Bernard Freyberg. Were we, I wondered, both going to be too shy to broach the subject I was there to discuss? No, when Barrie had finished his tea, he started, pipe in hand—another, already loaded, lay on the table—to walk up and down the room. To and fro, to and fro, never had I seen anyone take so much exercise indoors! He might have been on the deck of a ship. As he walked, turned, and came back again, he told me—pretty vaguely—what he would want me to do as his secretary. I should have to open *hundreds* of letters, and answer nearly all without even showing them to him. Most of them, he added, didn't really deserve an answer. 'You wouldn't believe, for instance, how many idiots have written to ask *what* it is that "Every Woman Knows"!'

His letters seemed badly on his nerves. He said he looked forward to Sunday, because there was no post. Among other things, he told me, I should have to pester him to endorse the cheques he received—fancy anyone needing to be prompted to do that!—pay his bills, keep his receipts, and so forth.

Next, Barrie showed me what he called his 'best' and his 'worst' drawer. The 'best' was a welter—begrimed papers and perished elastic bands that looked like so many dead worms. With a scarcely perceptible change of gear, he then touched on the salary I should earn. After this, he talked of other things, and took me round that evidently memory-laden room. Pointing at its brown ceiling, he told me that the strips of ornamented bark, painted by South Sea Islanders, had been sent to him from Samoa by Robert Louis Stevenson. I noticed some cricket caps—Eton First, and Second, Eleven—that hung from nails in the wall by Barrie's writing-table, and wondered to whom they could have belonged. But Barrie did not mention them, and I didn't like to ask.

My feelings were tangled—shyness, interest, liking, concern, misgiving, conjecture. I don't know how long I stayed, but before I left I had promised Barrie to disengage myself from hospital work as soon as I could and then start coming to him.

Did I get up of my own volition, or had Barrie somehow intimated that my audience was ended? I don't know, but all of a sudden we are on the little landing, and he has pressed the button which summons up the lift. His right arm sweeps round to grasp my hand in good-bye with that queer characteristic action, described by his biographer Denis Mackail, as 'like the delivery of an old-fashioned bowler'. I see that smile I've heard so many try to describe, and for the first of many thousand times I make the drawling descent of that peculiarly dirty lift-shaft.

I went out into Adelphi Terrace, past the Savage Club, through the quietude of Adam Street into the roar of the Strand.

My own life reclaimed me. It gave me plenty to think about, but I continually found my thoughts reverting to that strange, ship-like room, and the yet stranger being therein who walked, smoked, coughed, and looked down onto the Thames far below—a poignant, haunting little figure. He obsessed me.

An 'escapist'? With a face like that—those harrowed, harrowing eyes! Whatever his intention may have been, he didn't look as if he'd succeeded in escaping.

(3)

About a month later, I went to the Adelphi for my first morning's work. My trepidation seemed to affect my bicycling. I collided with a taxi in Trafalgar Square.

'Why can't you go where you're looking?' shouted the driver.

Nothing being hurt except my feelings, I picked myself up, brushed the mud off, and arrived punctually at the appointed hour. I was soon to realise it didn't matter in the very least what time I arrived! I found Barrie pacing up and down, pipe in hand. He received me most kindly, but I felt very nervous. I told him of my misadventure with the taxi. He didn't smile. This time he looked something in between the two extremes I'd already met; neither sombre nor gay. Yet he seemed in a communicative mood, and instead of setting me to work. talked while he walked, walked, walked.

As I write the thirty-three intervening years slide away. . . . I am back in that, then strange room, which is to become so familiar—I'm to see it most days for nearly twenty years.

As Barrie paces up and down, I find myself watching him as intently as though I were about to draw him—he's curiously like a charcoal drawing. I'm surprised by the extreme blueness of his eyes in daylight. I notice for the first time how finely modelled his nose is, how much strength as well as sensitiveness there is in his face. Is he going to stop patrolling the room? No, with a swing he turns in his walk and sets off again. He doesn't gesticulate with his hands, but every now and again, as he talks, one black eyebrow shoots far up above the other, particularly when, clasping the great bowl of his bull-dog pipe, he relights and coaxes the tobacco. His words are frequently interrupted by smoker's spluttering, sometimes by collision with a cough. His voice, with that queer rumbling burr in it, is always deep, often rather hoarse; in his longer sentences a little sing-song.

As I listen, I notice a few more mementoes dotted about the room: a stuffed trout in a glass case—another trophy of the wearers of the Eton cricket caps?—a dagger, which I rightly guess to have been worn by the first Peter Pan; a portrait of a St. Bernard—not a good painting, but I have to look at it, for the great mournful dog wears that almost insufferable air of nobility common to his breed.

I'm specially struck by a queerly touching old-fashioned photograph of a little boy of about six with an old, old anxious face and an immense forehead. Obviously Barrie himself! Velveteen jacket and knickerbockers, heavily braided and be-frogged, with 'curly-cues' at the legs and wrists; button boots, diamond-check socks. My eyes keep straying back to this photograph.

Those cricket caps on the wall are no longer a mystery. Since my first visit someone has told me about the five boys Barrie had adopted eight years ago when their widowed mother died. He had known these boys since their earliest nursery days. In fact, so my informant had told me, it was through the games Barrie invented for them and the serial story told to them that Peter Pan had come into being. Barrie had been devoted to both their parents, who were Arthur Llewellyn Davies, a clever, good-looking barrister, and his beautiful wife Sylvia, a sister of Gerald Du Maurier. . . .

When Barrie has walked for some twenty minutes he places

me at his own writing-table and gives me an immense batch of unopened letters come by that morning's post. A typical assortment, as I am soon to know—'royalty' statements; invitations; requests that he should provide authors with prefaces for their books; offers to translate his own works into Chinese and other languages; a dozen or so pages from a daily correspondent—obviously a lunatic; quantities of begging letters; requests for autographs; an interminable letter from a would-be poet pleading for advice on what he described as 'the ascent of Parnassus'; appeals from actresses who, though 'resting' just now, might before long be persuaded to take a theatrical engagement in the West End (photographs and pitiful little Press notices from provincial papers are enclosed); about six manuscripts on which Barrie is asked to advise; a peremptory demand that he should 'push' in the Press the 'new sneezing cure for adenoids', and so forth.

Before I begin to write, Barrie says I must sign the letters I write for him by some other name than my own. I suggest 'Sylvia Strayte', the flowery pseudonym chosen for the film star I'd hoped to become, but he says it would be better to have something quite nondescript that wouldn't even disclose my sex. We decide upon the name 'C. Greene'.

That was how the 'mysterious and in a sense non-existent C. Greene'—Denis Mackail's description in *The Story of J.M.B.*—came into being.

How tired I was to grow of the joke 'the Sea-green Incorruptible' and—worse still—of its fellow: 'I never see you now, Cynthia, you are barried alive!'

When I'd written the letters we tore up some papers and peered into an appalling *oubliette*—a deep dark recess at the back of the huge writing-desk. I suggested tackling this, but Barrie shook his head violently and muttered, 'Oh no, that would take much too long.'

Did this mean my first day's work was finished? (Nothing had been said as to how long I should stay. Did Barrie want

me to go away at once?) No, he opens an exciting-looking iron
chest, like the locker in which James Hook might have kept
his doubloons and pieces of eight; but besides dust and cobwebs,
this discloses only a conglomeration of photographs, letters
and various odds and ends. It seems that Barrie, like his
secretary and others, finds it difficult to destroy any relic
of the past, however unidentifiable, for nothing is done. We
replace whatever papers have burst out, and then have great
difficulty in shutting the lid again. We both have to sit on it.
That's the end of C. Greene's first day's work.

Next morning, I was installed at a desk at the other side of
the room, and when Barrie had walked a mile or so he settled
down at his huge table and he, too, began to write. While I
dealt with his letters he asked me four questions, all of which,
by a fortunate fluke, I was able to answer—what was the
difference between a rector and a vicar; a debenture and an
ordinary share; were sponsors necessary at the baptism of an
adult, and what was the French for 'welcome'?

As I was answering a letter from George Robey, my eyebrows
began to twitch in unconscious mimicry of what, in *The Bing
Boys*, I had lately watched that great man do with his eyebrows
—that superb upshoot of mock rebuke. Barrie saw my feeble
imitation and grinned.

Robert Lorraine came in, and I was introduced as 'Miss
Greene'. This made me feel as though I were in a charade.
Lorraine, who was then in the R.A.F., asked Barrie to write a
play for his return to the stage. They talked of some of the
old plays. Barrie professed to forget them as soon as they'd
been produced, but spoke of one germinating in his mind on
the theme of three types of women—the Bird, the Cat and the
Cow.

When I'd finished writing the letters, I armed myself with
several dusters, dived into that daunting cupboard, and filled
seven waste-paper baskets. The question of what should be
kept, what destroyed, was left to my own indiscretion. Very
rash of Barrie, for at that time I wasn't able to judge. I knew

far too little about him, and his. What *did* I know? I had heard that he had come from a small Scottish town nearly five hundred miles from London, and that this town was the 'Thrums' of his books; that his father had been a weaver in the days of the hand-loom; and his mother the Margaret Ogilvie he had made world-famous by the book of that name. I'd been told, too, that some time in the early 'eighties he had come, penniless and unknown, to London to try to earn a living by his pen; and that, after two or three years' struggle as a free-lance journalist, he had begun to make a fortune by his books and his plays. Beyond that, I had heard nothing except rumours of an unhappy marriage, now broken up, and what I'd just been told about the five adopted boys.

In the confusion of papers, I came on several large bundles of letters in Barrie's own writing. He told me they were those he had written—one every day—to Michael, the youngest but one of the Llewellyn-Davies boys, when he first went away to Eton. Gradually I heard more and more about 'My Boys', as Barrie called them. The eldest, George, had been killed in the war. The second, Jack, was in the Navy. Peter, who to my delight turned out to have been my brother Yvo's greatest friend at Eton, was at the Front. Michael, to whom all those letters had been written, was about to go into the Scots Guards. Nicholas was still at Eton. Thus, when 'C. Greene' first came into being, all four were away, but once the war was over, I came to know them well and greatly to like them all.

Before long I was let loose on several chaotic drawers crammed with pages of manuscripts all mixed up together, and I took upon myself the task of trying to sort out thousands of fragments of plays. Their author, who did not yet realise the great value of his own handwriting, thought I was wasting my time. Had I known that a few years later I should see the MS. of a single one-act play fetch £2,300 at an auction, and that Barrie would be paid a thousand pounds to rewrite *one* missing page of *The Little Minister*—a task I had to drive him to—

I should have been more harassed by this self-appointed task. If my greatest salvage triumph was gradually piecing together the complete MS. of *Margaret Ogilvie*, my most sensational find was a bundle of uncashed cheques, which added together came to seventeen hundred pounds! In the then state of my finances the cool reception of this discovery was almost more than I could bear.

(4)

Not long after 'C. Greene' enriched Barrie with that seventeen hundred pounds' worth of unpresented cheques, Cynthia Asquith did him a still better turn by bringing back into his life Charles Whibley. The two writers had long ago been in close touch when both were working for W. E. Henley—Whibley was then assistant editor on *The National Observer*—but they hadn't met for years. One afternoon, Whibley called to see me at the flat. Barrie, delighted to meet his old friend again, invited him to luncheon next day, and we three had the first of many enjoyable meals together. At one time we used to lunch about once a week at the Café Royal, in the old Brasserie, then all crimson plush, mirrors and gilding. My diary describes one of these meetings.

Feb. 1919

Barrie blithe and expansive: not one second's glumness. Whibley has a kindling effect on him. They talked amusingly of their early journalistic days. Once, when Henley was ill, they had for some weeks run *The National Observer* at a considerable loss to the paper, but with immense enjoyment to themselves. Barrie wrote a slashing attack on himself in an anonymous article, upon which several of his admirers were so offended by this assault on their favourite writer that they wrote to protest. Some even went so far as to withdraw their subscriptions to the paper. Why—they complained—must Henley always quarrel with his friends!

The 're-uniteds' recalled old cricketing days, when Whibley played for Barrie's team, the *Allahakbarries.*

'No one,' said Barrie, 'no one threw in harder than you, Charles, unerringly in the wrong direction, but then Conan Doyle was the only exception to the depressing rule that the more successful were the members of my team as authors, the worse they played.'

'Anyway, I never let the blasted ball hit me!' boasted Whibley.

They exchanged reminiscences of that engaging fancy cricketer, Augustine Birrell, who, Barrie said, had required a little coaching in the finesse of the game—for instance, which was the side of the bat you hit with, and what to do when the umpire shouted 'Over'.

'D'you remember, Charles?' said Barrie, taking an extra long pull at his pipe and lolling back in his chair with one leg tucked under the other, as is his queer contortionary way when he feels most at ease, and is about to drop into his 'I always remember' vein.

'D'you remember when, at the very beginning of his innings, Birrell broke the bat kindly lent him by his captain, and, exultant at its having been struck by the ball, and quite un-grieving about my ruined bat, waved it towards the pavilion and shouted "Bring me some more bats!" '

Barrie, encouraged by Whibley's ready laugh, told several stories, two of which have stayed in my sieve. A London hostess wrote to a Russian ballet dancer to ask what her fee would be for dancing at an evening party. The dancer said she would come for a hundred pounds. The hostess, writing back to agree to this figure, added, 'I think, perhaps, I had better tell you now that I don't introduce the *artiste* to my guests.'

To this the dancer replied, 'In that case my fee will be only fifty pounds.'

The second story was about an engagingly uninterfering policeman. One dark night, while he was patrolling an unlit street, a busybody approached him and whispered officiously,

'I think I ought to tell you, Officer, that those two men at the corner of the street are talking German.'

'Well, perhaps it's the only language they know,' the policeman replied reasonably.

Was Barrie addicted to story-telling? Yes, he was—to the delight of many, if, no doubt, to the distaste of some. The happier his frame of mind, the more inclined was he to begin, 'I always remember'. But his stories were, of course, never of the 'have you heard this one?', variety. They were always incidental to the talk, and he told them so well, so *neatly*, with his unfailing economy, even parsimony, of words, with a welcome absence, too, of any challenging emphasis for the climax. He had above all the rare stop-short gift.

Barrie's spirits nearly always rose when Whibley was about. Another friend who had a tonic effect was H. G. Wells. He and Barrie had—and gave—great fun together. My diary tells how they disported themselves one evening when Barrie dined with my mother.

March 4th, 1919

Took Barrie to Cadogan Square. He was in high spirits; competitively and triumphantly funny. He and Wells bubbled into every kind of nonsense—physical as well as verbal. They even did tricks with tumblers, plates, corks and what not. When Barrie, who excels at these kinds of antics, had scored all along the line, he said mock pompously, 'Now I wish we could think of something Wells *can* do. Tell us about the Martians, Wells.'

The conversation turned on shyness, and we each gave examples of the kind of situation that demanded the self-assurance we lacked. 'Nothing,' declared Barrie, 'gives more impressive proof of self-assurance than to complain to the head-waiter at a tip-top restaurant.'

He gave a very funny imitation of the cool ease, the superb aplomb, with which he would do this himself, and then of the

Barrie with his mother

abject way—squeak and all—Wells would try to be equally daring. I asked him to show me how I would complain to the waiter. 'There are limits to the human imagination,' he said. Mamma, who had never before seen Barrie 'put an antic disposition on', was enchanted by him, And he was delighted with her, particularly—for I'd told him of her 'furniture manias'—when she started to trundle him about in his huge chair because, she explained, she couldn't 'see him where he was'. He said he would have her filmed emptying her drawing-room in record time and dancing the heaviest pieces off to appropriate music.

(5)

When I first became 'Mister C. Greene', I was writing long letters to my husband, who was still at the Front. He was, naturally, anxious to hear about my secretaryship; so my letters were full of early impressions of Barrie. Here they are—strung together.

Nov. 8th, 1918

So far as the actual clerical work goes, my job with Barrie isn't very difficult. I find I can answer nearly all the letters from strangers without even showing them to him. A few I have to coax him to attend to. One or two of these he must, he says, with a groan or a grunt, answer himself; others he tells me how to answer. Socially, my role is less simple. I don't know how much to talk, nor when it is time for me to leave; and as Barrie will speak and smoke simultaneously, I often find it difficult to hear what he says. (I envied Michael[1] the licence of his years when on his first visit here he said in crystal tones, 'Perhaps if you were to take that great pipe out of your mouth, I might be able to hear what you say.') Another difficulty is that it's almost impossible to read some of Barrie's exquisite, spidery handwriting; but as he often spends a large

---

[1] My son

part of the morning trying to decipher it himself with a magnifying glass, I needn't feel humiliated by my failure. He keeps note-books in which he jots down ideas for articles, and often asks me to help him to read the more illegible entries. Given time, I usually succeed. This morning I had great difficulty over one of his recent notes for themes, and when at last I made it out, was a little disquieted to find it was 'My secretary'!

One of my tasks is to keep account of the sums of money paid to Barrie in royalties. I get very flustered trying to convert dollars into sterling. Quite easy, had I the place to myself, but at any moment, while 'C. Greene' knits his brows, Barrie, prowling about the room, may address a remark to Cynthia Asquith, and then I feel myself painfully splitting into two. Some mornings he talks the whole time. Of course, in some ways it would be easier—if far duller—to be secretary to a red-tape business man who would clearly define my job. Here there's no vestige of any office equipment and I have to cut my own work out. We're a strange pair.

At times, I have an uneasy fear that now I'm about the place Barrie won't ever write again. Yesterday he looked rather wistfully at the comparatively tidy drawers in his writing-desk and said, 'I feel that perhaps I ought to die now that my things are in order. There seems nothing left for me to do.'

His things aren't in order yet—not by a very long way, but at least his writing-desk drawers are no longer stuffed too full to open and shut.

He's a queer mixture—an extraordinarily plural personality. For all that apparent haphazardness, there seems plenty of shrewdness, almost 'canniness'. As for the legend of his being himself 'The Boy Who Wouldn't Grow Up', I see no evidence whatsoever of this. On the contrary, he strikes me as more than old. In fact, I doubt whether he ever *was* a boy. But then, for the matter of that, Peter Pan isn't a boy, is he? He's a wish-fulfilment projection in fable form of the kind of mother—Barrie's an expert at her—who doesn't want

her son to grow up. Talking of sons and mothers, Barrie is an
immense admirer of D. H. Lawrence and speaks much of him.
I remember Lawrence telling me Barrie had been one of the
first people to write to him in praise of *Sons and Lovers*.

I find one important part of my job is to prevent Barrie
saying 'yes' to invitations, whose acceptance he would afterwards regret. He says he can never do any work at all with
an engagement hanging over him. Which invitations should
be accepted, which refused, I have to know by instinct, for
when the time comes and he finds himself confronted with a
blank evening—possibly one of several in succession—he may
well regret having refused. I suspect the truth is that he is
leading the cloistered, jealously-guarded life of a writer working,
as for so many years has been his habit, some eight hours a
day; whereas in point of fact he isn't at present, so far as I can
see, really writing at all. Were he in the grip of an inspiration,
surely he wouldn't spend so much time reading *The Times*?
Probably he courts solitude, but like quite a few others,
occasionally feels lonely when it's too successfully secured.
Long notice is what he hates. He likes some friend to ring up
and say 'Can I come to dinner tonight?' An invitation to
dinner three weeks off produces a nerve storm. Some hostesses
show remarkable persistence.

I love his burry voice, with its subtle Scottish lilt. He pro-
nounces certain words strangely. 'I had a haddock this
morning,' he declares now and again. At first, I thought he
meant he'd had fish for breakfast, and I didn't know how to
look suitably interested. Not until the third time, did it dawn
on me he was telling me he'd had a headache!

Last night I dined with him. He was in one of his garrulous
moods—in snatches even autobiographical, talking with some
pride of his early poverty, which I rather suspect he romanti-
cises. (I notice most people tend to exaggerate their own
poverty and other people's wealth.) He told me the greatest
shock of his childhood had been when he saw someone drop
a penny and not bother to pick it up. (I nearly told him the

greatest shock of my life had been finding someone hadn't bothered to cash seventeen hundred pounds worth of cheques!)

He declared that, while at Edinburgh University, he had subsisted almost entirely on potatoes which he kept in a sack in his bedroom, and that when he first came to London—a step taken on the strength of having had a few articles accepted by *The Pall Mall Gazette*—he ate very little except buns, and had often felt very lonely; also, that once when a tooth came out he hammered it into position again with the wooden back of his hair-brush.

When he confessed he'd never consulted an oculist, but had just adopted someone else's spectacles, I gave him no peace until he authorised me to make an appointment for him. I'd already forced him to go to an osteopath for what I'm sure is incipient writer's cramp, but he was very sceptical about this treatment. The aim is to make a certain bone in the patient's neck crack. So, to spare the osteopath disappointment, Barrie snaps his fingers from time to time. This hoax has taken in the osteopath so successfully that he has become intolerably complacent, and Barrie, having worked so hard to make things seem a success, now declines to undergo any further treatment.

Yesterday I plucked up courage to ask about that St. Bernard dog, whose soulful expression has been getting more and more on my nerves. It's a portrait of Barrie's dog Porthos, who came into *The Little White Bird*, and was, also, the inspiration for the character of Nana in *Peter Pan*. Barrie told me some children who had been to *Peter Pan* refused to go to sleep until their dignified nurse consented to bark at them. (I didn't, and I trust no one ever will, tell *him* that one child had been killed because, after seeing *Peter Pan*, he 'thought beautiful thoughts', and confident that these thoughts would enable him to fly, jumped out of the nursery window!)

Barrie said that, had it not been for Frohman, the great American impresario, to whom he owed so much, he didn't think any producer would ever have put on *Peter Pan*. Not only had Beerbohm Tree refused the play for Her Majesty's

Theatre, but after reading it, he had written a warning letter to Frohman to tell him that he was afraid 'poor Barrie had gone out of his mind!'

Besides the St. Bernard, almost the only painting in the flat is Charles Furse's portrait of W. E. Henley's adored only child, a lovely little girl who died when she was four. It was from her that Barrie took the name of Wendy, because she had always called him 'Fwend' or 'Fwendy'.

For the first time, Barrie spoke of some new ideas for plays, but he doesn't seem able to settle on any particular one. He looked pleased when I told him your father[1] had pronounced *The Twelve Pound Look* the 'best short play ever written', and the first act of *Dear Brutus*.the most ingenious. Barrie said that how to get his characters into the *Dear Brutus* wood had been a difficult problem, but that this act had been child's play to the third, which he wrote first because he knew it would be the most difficult.

Nevertheless, he finished—at least so he told me—the whole play in a fortnight. He said quite detachedly that he thought the first act of *What Every Woman Knows* good. He knew that he'd taken a considerable risk with that long silence when the curtain first rises—the longest in any play—and so was pleased when this succeded. He said the second act, even if good as a whole, was rather spoilt by the English ladies, but that the third act, though quite ingenious, was not 'dug out' of himself —but 'theatrical'. He spoke disparagingly of the play, *The Little Minister*, which he said he didn't intend to include in any future edition of his works. Ungrateful of him, for it earned him eighty thousand pounds in its first ten years!

*   *   *

This morning I packed Barrie off to France, where he goes as the guest of the American Army. The official invitation came to him through me. He accepted with alacrity, but soon began to jib at the prospect. However, he finally departed

[1] H. H. Asquith, afterwards Earl of Oxford and Asquith

quite meekly. I found him filling in his passport, rather rue-fully describing himself as 'very sallow', complaining of the heat—no wonder for his butler had wrapped him up like Tweddledum—and swallowing Mothersill in handfuls. I gathered—the kind of thing I have to telepathise—that he expected me to see him off at Victoria.

This room seems queerly empty without him. It is so per-meated by his amazingly strong personality.

'C. Greene' and Cynthia Asquith now have the place to themselves—a good opportunity to try to 'get straight'. By the way my neuter name has proved a great success. All replies come addressed to 'C. Greene, Esqre.,' and the other day Barrie had a letter beginning 'I.hear you have a secretary who is quite a human MAN'!

*   *   *

No pen could convey how widely Barrie varies. One day he looks so weary, sallow, lack-lustre, that had I to 'do' him, in our 'analogy' game I'd compare him to a full ash-tray and an empty ink bottle; the next day he may look positively tingling with health—alert, aglow. His aura corresponds with these physical changes, and of course such a strong—such an overpoweringly strong—personality has the most terrific effect on others. When he's grey ashes, he's devastatingly depressing. It's almost impossible to fight against the influence. On the other hand, on his good days, he's so alive, so full of charm—more than charm—a kind of benign wizardry, that it makes one feel well and happy. He can be so funny too—at times really funnier than anyone else!

I don't believe he has any idea how much he communicates his moods. I'm not sure that he's even aware of his own eclipses. What, I wonder, do they denote? Unproductive broodings? Withdrawal into some dark distant region of his own? Or—forgive bathos—just bad health; very likely nico-tine poisoning, for he's an insatiable smoker. He has an awful cough, at times really distressing. It seems callous to ignore such paroxysms, but I don't think comment would be welcome, for obviously it's a chronic cough, and comes from over-smoking. By the way, he declares that he hadn't begun to smoke when he wrote his great tribute to tobacco, *My Lady Nicotine!* Am I to take this as genuine autobiography, or as part of that novel?

My instinct, not to commiserate with Barrie on his cough until I knew him better, was right. When at last I did allude to it—one paroxysm was too alarming to ignore—he merely said, 'I'm quite taken aback when people remark on my cough. I suppose it's like Big Ben, so frequent that I've ceased to notice it.'

A guest, who came to luncheon one day, was less fortunate. 'Poor Sir James!' gushed this over-sympathetic lady, pressing a throat lozenge on him. 'Poor man! I'm afraid you've got a very troublesome cough.'

'It doesn't trouble *me*,' came the hoarse reply; after which the conversation, but not the cough, languished.

(6)

My surmise that, in 1918, Barrie wasn't 'really writing' was soon confirmed. Passages in my diary describe how he bewailed this fact.

Nov. 2nd, 1918

While Barrie was on his after-dinner prowl he began to tell me how desperately much he wished he could get started on some writing again. Though his head was buzzing with ideas for plays, he couldn't, he complained, settle on any particular one.

'Not long ago,' he said, 'I wrote—I don't know how many—one-act plays. I was simply slinging them off—I believe I wrote six in one week. But scarcely any of them seemed to be worth keeping. If only' (pause for prolonged tussle between smoking, cough and speech) 'if only I could exchange this spate for ONE engrossing idea!'

I asked couldn't he for a change write a book instead of a play, and quoted Whibley, who deplores his having become exclusively a dramatist, for, much as he admires his craftmanship as a playwright, he thinks it a thousand pities that such a pen—he's an immense admirer of Barrie's actual writing— should be limited to dialogue.

At this, Barrie left off walking, and after another absolute paroxysm of coughing, tapped out his pipe and refilled it while one eyebrow climbed, and the other descended, his forehead like two buckets in a well. Then, he settled himself on the couch with one leg tucked under the other, and talked about writing, and not writing.

'I'm glad you and Charles think I might have another book in me, and want me to get started, but at present I can't see one worth transcribing. I assure you it isn't because I don't go a-fishing for it, but I can't get hooked on to anything that seems worth playing. Besides, I now realise that I can't, as I used to, write books and plays alternately. I never catch myself asking, should this particular theme be used for a play or a book? If it seems to make for the one, it can't, not by me, possibly be made to serve the other purpose. And I'm sorry to say that for some time now all my ideas seem to seek the same outlet. Against my will they all form themselves into scenes and acts.'

'Do you think in dialogue?' I asked.

'Very often.'

I asked if he thought he would ever write a book again.

'Probably, as so often before,' he answered, 'I shall kick up another pebble again some day, and make more of it than anyone else could' (or *would* his tone implied). 'I'm almost a genius at the occasional pebble. I was once challenged to write an article about a scrap of paper that had been blown into the gutter, and I found it quite easy. The editor took it, too! Queer sort of writer to come out of Scotland.'

We talked of 'pebbles', his own and other writers'. He reverted to the misery of not being at work, declaring that at present he had to hang on to the memory of all the years and years in which he had revelled in being 'at it', and long before he wrote any books had been a legend in Fleet Street for 'the unrelenting doggedness of his output'.

He was interesting about his 'prentice days', telling me how at the age of twenty-two he left home in answer to an advertisement applying for a leader-writer for *The Nottingham Journal*. His only previous experience was that while a student at Edinburgh University, he had been given some book-reviewing to do, but only—so he told me—on the understanding that he never cut the leaves of the books! (Was I expected to take this as a literal truth? I don't think so.) Throughout all the seventeen months Barrie spent at Nottingham, his 'leader', he said, had averaged at least twelve hundred words a day. In addition to this, he had written all the book reviews and a couple of special weekly articles. (No wonder his writing became illegible!)

After his Nottingham apprenticeship, Barrie, encouraged by the editor of *The St. James's Gazette*, the great Greenwood's acceptance of some of the articles with which he had pelted him, decided to come to London. He wrote to ask Greenwood his advice on the proposed venture. He could, he assured the editor, keep himself in London on a £1 a week. At once, and most decidedly, Greenwood advised Barrie not to dream of taking so rash a step, at any rate not until a good deal more of his work had been accepted. Whereupon Barrie, refusing to be put off, promptly arrived at St. Pancras Station and set forth to find himself a lodging. He told me that for years after he had thus launched himself upon London with a 'penny bottle of ink to fling into its face', and twelve pounds in his pocket, he wrote as a free lance journalist at least two articles a day, many of which had, of course, been rejected. He said that he soon discovered that if he had no great mind of his own, he could 'enter for the space of a column or two into the

minds of other people'. So he wrote his experiences in multi-
tudinous adopted characters—as a 'medical man'; an M.P.; a
policeman; a blacksmith; a civil engineer in India; a professional beauty; a vagrant and so forth. 'I was even a bishop,'
he said, 'not to mention several deans. In fact, it is a wonder
gaiters didn't grow on my legs.'

Evidently, he looks back on those early journalistic days as
very happy, however hard. His boyhood's dread, he told me,
had been that he would have to become a clerk or a doctor
(queer bedside manner he would have had at times!) and it
had been such a 'glory and relief' to prove that he *could* live in
London by his pen. He said that to be able to keep himself
in London had been the one great literary ambition of his life,
and that he wouldn't have minded remaining 'quite unknown
in a corner, as long as it was a London corner'. He maintained
that he had never sought 'the popularity that was so largely
fluke', and whether or not this be true he certainly believed
it as he spoke.

'I've had so much more luck, than most other contemporary
writers,' he said, almost guiltily. 'I've a neat way of putting
things,' he added belittlingly, 'plenty of' (witheringly) 'fancy,
invention, contrivance and industry.'

Another evening, I remember Barrie reading to me one of
the very few recently 'slung-off' one-act plays he thought
worth keeping. This was *The Fight for Mr Lapraik*, a terrifying
drama about the struggle between the forces of Good and Evil
for the possession of one more or less average man. At first,
Barrie read dispassionately; then, suddenly kindling, dramatically, and in an utterly different voice for each character. The
effect was unforgettably eerie. It was the first time I realised
what an actor he might have been. I can't describe the disquieting tricks he played with face and voice, nor how both
visibly and audibly he split himself into the two Mr Lapraiks.

I don't think Barrie often remembered—if he did, he didn't
divulge—the starting points from which his plays had sprung,

but after curdling me by reading *The Fight for Mr Lapraik*, he did tell me that the theme of this singularly uncomfortable play had been suggested to him by a dream of his own—a dream dreamt more than once—in which some vaguely apprehended interloper, who was, and yet somehow was not, himself, kept on stealthily, persistently trying to push him off the couch on which he lay. This nightmare sense of some sinister, furtive being lurking about his flat, determined to oust and supplant him, remained with him after he awoke; and from this disquiet emanated the unhappy Mr Lapraik, who was afraid to go to sleep because of a recurrent dream—a dream from which 'the awakening was the worst part'.

Vague intimations of some such supplanter have troubled many others besides the unhappy Mr Lapraik, who could find no escape but death from that dread dream. 'Many men dream it more or less. Not the worst men.'

(7)

In *The Story of J.M.B.* Dennis Mackail generously gives to 'C. Greene' the credit for introducing into Barrie's life that lovable friend, and wonderful talker, Sir Walter Raleigh. This I can't claim, for, though they hadn't met for some time, the two had long known and liked one another. I was, however, the involuntary cause of a renewal of their friendship. One day 'The Professor', as all his friends called Sir Walter, wrote to say that he proposed to call on me in the Adelphi. I had qualms about the visit, for I was still quite a newcomer in the flat. I wrote to say I thought he had better not come, by which I brought on myself the retort:

'But Cynthia, J.M.B. is a very old friend of *mine*. I can't see why I should neglect him because I happen to have met his secretary!'

Thereupon I arranged for him to come, but, thinking it would be an excellent thing were he and Barrie to resume their friendship, I went out myself. The meeting was a great success.

'University life has failed to tie a single one of its cobweb
threads round him,' declared Barrie, and The Professor wrote:

I had a very good visit to my old friend. I believe we talked for quite
three hours. But isn't he sometimes rather lonely living all by himself in
that vast eyrie, year in, year out? It's mutton chops and ordinary people
that keep one cheerful, and they must be obtained for selfish reasons. Is he
selfish enough? I quite see that him being so lonely (even though he doesn't
know it) I mustn't call on you at Adelphi Terrace, but I shall go back to
see him. We talked amongst many other things about murders; also of a
projected dinner club to meet once a month and to consist of ourselves,
Maurice Baring, E. V. Lucas and perhaps a few others. But E. V. would
certainly introduce a whole scrum of actors and would be very angry if we
didn't adore them, for he is as tolerant as you, and man can say no more.

A week or so later, I was all but taken in by the following
joke-letter from The Professor, to whom I'd shown 'C. Greene's'
typewritten formula for putting off unknown applicants who
wrote to ask Barrie to read their unpublished works.

Lady Cynthia Asquith.
Dear Madam,
    I am informed that you are in a position to speak to Sir James Barrie.
I therefore venture to ask you to speak to him on my account. Some time
ago I sent him the first draft of my ten-act play as a sample of the work I
am doing, and offered to send him for his perusal and appreciation at leisure
the rest of my unpublished work, which I have here in four portmanteaux
and a barrel (padlocked) and which owing to this unfortunate delay, is
taking up room that in these hard times can ill be spared. I received from
a certain Mr C. Greene a very unsatisfactory reply to my letter. I am,
however, resolved that Sir James and none other, is to have the honour
and responsibility of being the first fellow-author to taste of my vintage.
Will you be so kind as to inform him of my determination? I will despatch
the goods tomorrow. It would perhaps save time and trouble if I were to
follow a week later to take stock of his impressions. If he should chance
unfortunately to have other work on hand, I can, at some inconvenience,
wait a week, but not more.

The Professor's fake letter was scarcely distinguishable from
many of the authentic appeals that poured in to the flat. At
first, I could hardly bear to rebuff an author. Bad as the book
might be, it had been written with heart's blood, and the writer

had perhaps spent his last fiver on having it typed; but I soon realised that, were Barrie to accede to half these appeals, he would have no time left to write his own books. Begging letters, too, reft my heart, but in nearly every case enquiries proved the writer to be a professional. Gradually, 'C. Greene's' skin grew thicker. It had to. And before long, I projected him into a personality separate from my own. I came even to have a clear picture of his appearance. I saw him as an undersized, scared-looking little man with rimless spectacles and a protrusive, mobile Adam's apple. I didn't see myself as 'Mister C. Greene' when I was with Barrie, but I always did while I wrote his letters or telephoned to strangers. Nor, to this day am I quite rid of the fellow! Whenever I have to end a letter 'Yours faithfully', I still tend, to the perplexity of my Bankers, and others, to relapse and sign myself 'C. Greene'.

The question of at what time I should leave each day soon resolved itself. It became understood that, unless I had some engagement of my own, I stayed on to luncheon. If more convenient to myself, I could come in the afternoon instead of in the morning, and stay to tea.

Before long I could deal with nearly all Barrie's letters without even showing them to him. Enquiries about the production of his plays were referred to his trusted dramatic agent, R. Golding Bright. All the rest were my affair. They gave me plenty of practice in the art of polite refusal. One of the requests I had most often to decline was that Barrie should sit for his portrait. 'I have long ceased to be on speaking terms with my face' he said, 'so, why have it painted?'

I am glad he made an exception in favour of his godson Peter Scott, whose painting of him was such a great success.

Another very frequent request was that Barrie should be godfather to some child about to be christened Peter or Wendy. His godchildren were legion. He couldn't possibly remember them all, but I had to buy Christmas presents for the more favoured, and from time to time he would write to

one of them. Here is an example from a letter to my niece
Sara Strickland, who had sent him some drawings:

> . . . I think the picture in your letter I liked best of all is the one of the
> 'very queer fish'. You have the art of making it look very queer indeed. It
> made me wonder whether baby scorpions have godfathers, and I think I
> should have felt a shudder if I had had to hold it up at the baptismal font.
> How proud you must have been to catch the 22 shrimps in your net. Of
> course, it is rather sad to think you eat them at tea-time, but I expect they
> know that is what they are for and took it all as a compliment as they went
> romping down.

CHAPTER II

MARY ROSE

WHEN I said that Barrie was not 'really writing' in 1918, I meant that he wasn't engaged on any work of importance. His pen always had occasional spurts of activity, and even these, however short, had an enlivening effect. Barrie invariably came alive the moment he began to write again. He would look kindled, brisk, alert, his very step become resolute —almost jaunty. This re-animation was specially evident when the lava bubbled up for the last time—but of *The Boy David*, hereafter. The first sign that Barrie had 'got going' again would be the appearance beside his bottle of ink—he never took to a fountain pen—of a pile of small sheets of paper closely covered with numbered notes. Soon after this a remarkably clean MS. would be sent to his typist, Miss Dickens, a descendant of Charles Dickens. When the typescript came back, he played about with it a great deal, or perhaps wrote quite another version.

My diary tells how once his pen was set off on a sprint he soon had cause to regret.

Feb. 20th, 1919

Very amusing evening at the flat. Barrie read—or rather, brilliantly acted—to me passages from a typescript just sent him by a publisher, and alleged to be the unaided work of a girl of nine. It's a story of 'High Life', in which King Edward appears at a levée 'rather sumshiously in a small but costly crown', and 'slips away to tuck into ices'. The hero, Mr Salteena, introduced as being 'really the sinister son of Queen

31

Victoria', grows 'jellus' of his successful rival Bernard Clark 'rather a presumshious man'.

Mr Salteena draws a most disarming picture of himself— 'I am fond of digging in the garden and I am parshal to ladies —I suppose it's my nature. I am not quite a gentleman but you would hardly notice and can't be helped anyhow.'

Barrie is so much amused by this book—certainly a remarkably sustained effort for a child—that he has consented to write a preface to it.

That was my introduction to *The Young Visiters*, which, published the following May and given a flying start by its preface, had a fabulous sale, and incidentally became a great, bother to Barrie (as to his secretary!) for not only did hordes of parents—American as well as English—send him their children's works, but there arose a widespread legend that he had invented Daisy Ashford and faked the book. It was impossible to kill this legend, and Barrie came, understandably, to resent people not accepting his denials.

Early in 1919 another sprint of Barrie's pen produced *The Truth about the Russian Dancers*, a ballet-fantasy, which, with music by Arnold Bax and *décor* by Paul Nash, provided an entrancing vehicle for the lovely Karsavina, who never spoke, but just danced her lines.

Most critics would have dismissed *The Truth about the Russian Dancers* as a 'charming trifle', but Barrie's votary, A. B. Walkley, gave it three-quarters of a column in *The Times* next day and a whole enthusiastic column on the day after that. Gossamer-light as *The Truth about the Russian Dancers* was, it had not by any means been 'knocked off'. That is to say that probably, as usual, the first draft was written in a day or two, then worked on, altered and polished with infinite care. Years later I found ten different typescript versions of this one little play!

But it was not until the late summer of 1919 that Barrie, for

Aged 6   Barrie   Aged 60

the first time since I had known him, became really 'engrossed'
—his own word—in writing. He embarked on a full-length
play—*Mary Rose*.

The pocket note-books in which he jotted down ideas as they
occurred to him reveal that the theme of *Mary Rose* had long
flitted in and out of his mind. One note-book dated as early
as 1905 contains the entry 'a sort of Rip Van Winkle', and in
a letter written in 1911 to Quiller-Couch, he referred to an
embryo play; 'I have often thought of it in three acts and see
the first two all right. The third seems to amount to this. No
one should ever come back however much they were loved.'

In 1912 Barrie rented a house called Amhuinnsuidh in the
Outer Hebrides, where there still lingered a Kilmeny-like
legend of a girl taken and returned by the fairies. The phrase,
'The sea likes to be visited', in the future play 'The *island* that
likes to be visited' appears in Barrie's current note-book; and
writing of Amhuinnsuidh later, he referred to it as the 'place
where we caught Mary Rose'. But if Barrie didn't 'catch'
Mary Rose until 1912 the motive that compelled her to haunt
the home of her childhood had been clearly set forth in *The
Little White Bird*, published in 1902, 'The only ghosts, I believe,
who creep into this world, are dead young mothers, returned
to see how their children fare. There is no other inducement
great enough to bring the dead back.'

It is now thirty-two years since *Mary Rose* was produced, so
not very many theatre-goers can remember the spell this
strange play cast throughout its very long first run.

Here is what Denis Mackail wrote of its immediate effect:

Once more a Barrie play was packing the Haymarket from floor to roof.
Again there were the inveterate victims in front, who wept, who came
staggering out, and instantly tottered back towards the box-office. . . . It
was revived at the same theatre five years later, and again three years
after that. It has been played all over the world in any number of languages,
and has mystified and enchanted millions of human beings wherever curtains rise and fall. There has of course never been anything in the least
like it. And there never can be now.

It was *Mary Rose* that A. B. Walkley, the distinguished critic of *The Times*, had in mind when, addressing Barrie at the Critic's Circle, he said,

'I'm not thinking of your lighter moods when "Queen Mab hath been with you". You have given us glimpses into the mysteries of life and death and time that have sent us away strangely taken, almost beside ourselves.'

There were, of course, some dissentients about *Mary Rose*—there was always a minority who couldn't like Barrie—but a remarkably wide cross-section of the public wept, rhapsodised, went again and again. For the author's secretary—possibly partly because she was there when it was written and produced—it is the most moving of all his plays; steeped in what, for want of a less over-worked word, must be called 'magic', and, technically, a masterpiece of compression; 'Never' wrote Desmond MacCarthy, 'never have tricks with time been played with such dexterity.'

Mary Rose, as the author was the first to acknowledge, was greatly enhanced by Norman O'Neil's haunting music. And how wonderfully fortunate Barrie was in Fay Compton's creation of his heroine! Both in appearance and in aura, this enchanting actress with her lovely gradual smile—a delayed smile, like stage lights 'rising on resistance', was exactly right for Mary Rose. Her voice, too, with its remarkable power of investing words with more than their surface meaning, was invaluable where so much—so very much—was left to the imagination. One moment Mary Rose's voice and manner would be quite everyday—almost homely: the next, some quick, subtle inflexion made it shiversomely eerie, and whatever she said was charged with mysterious significance.

It was a wonderful cast. Mary Jerrold and Norman Forbes were perfect as the father and mother; Jean Cadell unforgettable as the terrifyingly terrified caretaker; Ernest Thesiger admirable as the erudite but superstitious ghillie.

The First Night of *Mary Rose* is one of my most vivid theatre-memories. Barrie, white as paper, for well he knew he'd condemned his company to walk a tightrope, was hidden at the back of a box. I visited him in between the acts, but watched the play from the front, where I sat beside Desmond MacCarthy, who the moment the last curtain fell had to telephone a criticism to *The Manchester Guardian.*

I can't remember how many times I saw *Mary Rose.* I loved to take other people to it and see it afresh through their eyes. My diary gives the impressions of two writers.

Oct. 1920

Went to *Mary Rose* with Maurice Baring. He said he thought the scene in Act 3 where Mary Rose comes back the most moving thing he'd ever seen on the stage. 'What a genius he is!' he exclaimed, 'Though his foot does sometimes slip.'

Nov. 1920

Took 'The Professor' to *Mary Rose.* He raved about it, particularly the part in the last act which Maurice Baring admired so much, and also the island scene—especially the dialogue just before Mary Rose disappears. He loved even the butter-dish incident, the dialogue of which some of my more squeamish friends find so embarrassing.

I overheard many strange comments on *Mary Rose,* as the audience, blinking and bemused, came out of the Haymarket Theatre into the light of common day. My favourite was a woman saying briskly to her companion, 'I don't know what *you* think, but I must say the plot strikes me as highly improbable.'

Naturally, many people clamoured for some more definite explanation of the play than was ever vouchsafed, and Barrie grew wearied of the hundreds of letters that came asking what *Mary Rose* 'really meant'.

'I wish *you* could tell me what it means,' he said to me one day, 'and settle the matter once for all.'

I couldn't. Neither did I want the matter settled. I pre-

ferred the play left unexplained, but as full of mysterious intimations as Fay Compton's voice—and eyes.

Many wrote offering the weirdest solutions of *Mary Rose*;
some even declaring it to be empire-building propaganda—
Australia being the 'island that liked to be visited'.

A stranger, professing himself an ardent admirer of the play,
wrote to ask if I would let him come to my house to study the
manuscript, which Barrie had given me. He said he knew
Mary Rose held some message of immense importance to
humanity and felt it to be his mission to interpret this message
to the world. He must have had a remarkable gift for reading
between the lines. After weeks of study he arrived at the
startling conclusion that *Mary Rose* was 'a widely and deeply
obscene work'! Perhaps I should add that a few weeks later
the poor man wrote to me from a mental hospital.

What did Barrie think of his own play? I remember his
saying, 'When one is at work on a theme one gets so lost in it,
dwells on it so much that to oneself it becomes so real, so living;
and then one is chillily disillusioned when it is finished and one
reads it in cold blood. You and some others find in this play
things I tried to put into it, but so feebly that to most people
they're probably not there at all. . . . I'm told an American
critic has said that what my work fails in is robustness. I've
never heard it put exactly like that before, but I fancy he is
right. I seem too often to be trying to catch the wind with a
net.'

Another time, I remember Barrie's telling me he was sure
that, if *Mary Rose* had been anyone's first play, no one would
have put it on.

Barrie never seemed to me much interested in the reviews
of his plays—at all events he subscribed to no press-cutting
agency. He said that when he first started to write, he had
deferentially read all criticisms in the hope of guidance, but
could never find any constructive advice. He was, however,
I think, very grateful for all the encouragement given him by

A. B. Walkley, who had early declared him to have 'transfigured our drama'. I remember Barrie saying that Walkley's review of *The Admirable Crichton* had given him more pleasure than anything else written about his plays. I am not surprised, for Walkley had rhapsodised over 'the subtlety and complexity of the ideas underlying *The Admirable Crichton*'s entertainment value. In form, a brilliant extravaganza, in substance a piece of hard logic, of close-packed thought, this play of Mr Barrie's is something Voltaire could never have succeeded in writing . . . disquieting by the reach of its intellectual suggestion . . . brimful of ideas, and quite apart from the sheer amusement of the thing, you welcome it for its ideas, for what the English stage most surely needs is ideas, and the advent of a dramatist who like Mr Barrie can *play* with ideas is a rare piece of luck.'

I remember, too, Barrie's being quite touched because, when *The Admirable Crichton* was revived, Walkley wrote to him to implore him to 'keep his hands off it'.

'But,' said Barrie, 'I'm apparently so constituted that I can't possibly sit out a month's rehearsals without meddling and tinkering with the script.'

No one will be surprised to hear that Barrie hated to be called 'whimsical'. I remember his delight when some London critic wrote of his 'sneer', and pronounced him 'cruel as well as sinister'. Apart from this, I don't think I ever heard him comment on any criticism of his writing, except once when he said laughingly, 'In the days when Bernard Shaw was a critic he began an article on a play of mine with the words "This is worse than Shakespeare". I admit that this rankled!'

I am sure, however, that Barrie remembered the penetration with which R. L. Stevenson had long ago written to Henry James, 'Barrie's a beauty . . . but he must see not to try to be too funny. Genius in him, but there's a journalist at his elbow —there's the risk!'

Except for the unfinished *Shall We Join the Ladies?* the

brilliant first act of which was performed by a dazzling galaxy of stars at the opening of the new R.A.D.A. Theatre, and *The Boy David, Mary Rose* was the last play Barrie wrote. I have often wondered to what extent my being on the premises was responsible for this. How many plays, I ask myself, did I involuntarily nip in the bud? Barrie fell into the way of telling me of any newly-conceived idea. And alas, no light responsibility was laid upon the listener, to whom Barrie, speaking through clouds of smoke, felt prompted to impart the first stirrings of an inspiration. Delicate, nebulous fantasies, prematurely released from incubation behind that domed brow, and too soon exposed to unconditioned air, shrivelled and perished. Even as Barrie spoke, I would see the light go out in the saddening eyes; and, with a pang, not wholly free from self-reproach, I would realise that yet another embryo play was lost—its gossamer filaments as irretrievably dispersed as the smoke from his laid-down pipe. It was rather like a bird deserting its eggs because they've been looked at. This discontinuance may have been a purely subjective process; but if, as Barrie sketched out some moonlit fantasy, you showed signs of bewilderment—and you could scarcely be blamed if you did, for the weavings of his mind weren't easy to follow— then so sensitive a man, so self-distrustful a writer was only too likely to be fatally put off.

Yes, by failing to look responsive I may well have murdered hundreds of plays—done Barrie out of several small fortunes. At all events I came to be so much afraid of these stillbirths that the moment he started to tell me of a germinating play I would rush, fingers to my ears, from the room. Thus, despite consuming curiosity, I refused to let him talk about *The Boy David* until the play was well advanced.

CHAPTER III

A SECRETARIAL SIDELINE

My 'job' soon expanded in various directions. Sometimes the work was 'C. Greene's' affair; sometimes Cynthia Asquith's. As time passed more and more devolved on Cynthia Asquith; but though 'Mister Greene' slipped farther and farther into the background his co-operation always remained essential.

Not long after I came, Barrie amused himself by playing a trick on *The Times*, and in so doing found a tactful way of telling his secretary, still new to her far from humdrum job, what he expected of her. At that time I was contributing, under the heading of 'The Woman's Point of View', a series of anonymous articles to *The Times*.

One morning Barrie gave me an article he had just written himself called 'The Private, Private Secretary', and told me to send it in as though it were mine. The real authorship of this unsigned article was not suspected, and the fact that Barrie had recently refused a record sum to write a signed article made him all the more pleased with his hoax.

I remember being slightly piqued to discover that his article hadn't had a single word cut. Mine always had.

This was how Barrie's article 'The Private, Private Secretary' ended:

'The post is thus not merely confidential, it calls for an understanding of the man who is employing you, particularly an intimate understanding of his weaknesses, out of which you may well get some private entertainment. You must know by instinct that he does not want to lunch on Tuesday week with Lady A., but that, if the answer is left to him, he will weakly say Yes, and then when Tuesday comes scowl at you for not having improvised an ingenious No. You must also know that if it had been Mrs B., and he had shouted at you (while in the grip of an inspiration) to tell her to go and drown herself, what he really means is that by Tuesday he will want to attend that luncheon. If you are the right sort of person you will soon be worth more than your salary, and you will also have the satisfaction of knowing, as he does, that you are using your brains intelligently.'

Thanks to one of Barrie's Lob-like moods, soon after this article appeared, his 'Private, Private Secretary' found herself engaged in what Denis Mackail described as a 'distinctly odd secretarial side-line'. Dressed as a parlourmaid, I twice waited through dinner at the flat. The first time on a very small party—merely two Elder Statesmen, my father-in-law H. H. Asquith, Augustine Birrell and their host. Disguised by a black fringe, frowsy side-curls, and spectacles, my appearance was not prepossessing; but my 'colleague', Brenda Dufferin, who, being unknown to the company, hadn't needed to dis-figure herself, looked so pretty that both guests' eyes widened at the sight of her.

Brown, the butler, chuckling with delight, drilled us in our duties; Barrie collaborated, his first act being deftly to remove the spoon from the vegetable-dish with the pleasing result that Birrell helped himself to mashed potatoes with his fingers.

'I'm afraid The Premier has recognised you, My Lady', hissed Brown into my ear after the second course. (My father-in-law had some time ago ceased to be Prime Minister, but Brown preferred still to call him The Premier.)

I thought I'd seen a gleam in my father-in-law's eyes, and, sure enough, when I handed him the savoury he said, 'Thank you, my dear,' with a loud benevolent sniff.

Determined to make Barrie a victim of his own joke, I whisked the brandy out of his reach before he'd had time to help himself. I tried to do the same with the cigars, but after a prolonged tussle, he wrested one from me.

Brenda and I enjoyed finishing up, in the pantry, what came out of the dining-room, and Brown, revelling in what he called the 'prank', was excellent company, but his tender heart was wrung by his beloved master being done out of his glass of brandy.

In the dining-room conversation wasn't nearly as lively as in the pantry. It just meandered on from President Wilson and General Pershing, to casualties and Spanish Influenza. But it's only fair to remember that both Mr Asquith and his host were preoccupied by the waitresses. At all events, if the three wise men hadn't much to say, their massive heads were an impressive sight.

Barrie led the men out of the dining-room, then slipped back to confer with his parlourmaids about the 'Curtain' of his farce. He was still under the impression that both his guests were quite unsuspicious, but I afterwards learnt that, as his host left the room, my father-in-law whispered to Birrell, 'Have you noticed those two young females waiting on us? I have a shrewd suspicion that one of them is my daughter-in-law.'

The 'parlourmaids' carried in the whisky tray. I emptied a box of cigars onto Birrell's lap. We plumped ourselves into armchairs. Brenda was then formally introduced. Birrell declared he'd had 'no inkling', but thought he had noticed something unusual about, what he called, my 'tenue'.

My father-in-law said he wouldn't have recognised me had I not tried to disguise myself by wearing spectacles. They had made him look at me.

Each parlourmaid was given for her services seven shillings and sixpence, at that time the recognised fee.

It wasn't long before Barrie and I encored our own joke, but on a far larger scale. Evan Charteris, A. E. Mason, Fred Oliver, Professor Tonks, General Freyberg and Charles Whibley were all invited to dinner on purpose to be waited upon by me and my cousin, Olivia Wyndham. This time I didn't disfigure myself, but took the precaution of keeping out of the dining-room until the first course was well under way.

By then I hoped, tongues and knives and forks would be busy, eyes no longer straying. The three guests who knew me well, Charles Whibley, Professor Tonks and my uncle Evan Charteris—General Freyberg was an accomplice—were all designedly placed with their backs to the sideboard. Despite these precautions, Evan Charteris's quick eye soon recognised his niece. Having heard of the previous parlourmaid prank he was probably not wholly unprepared for a revival, but, he gave no sign of his discovery, and became an active accessory. As I handed vegetables to his neighbour, Tonks, he deliberately wrenched the conversation on to me. 'Have you seen my niece, Cynthia, lately?' asked my uncle. Tonks promptly began to expatiate on what he called the 'singularity' of my 'head'. This, of course, made it quite impossible for me to move out of earshot. Long after Tonks had helped himself to potatoes, I stood stock still, holding out a shaking dish.

'A face it would be impossible to disguise,' declared Tonks, with this positive freak of a face only three inches off his eyes.

Whibley, characteristically, was much too engrossed in talk, food and drink to look up. No fear of recognition from him! Had I been a kangaroo in cap and apron he wouldn't have noticed me.

This time the talk was extremely lively and entertaining. Those who knew who we were, were made to pay for seeing through our joke. Evan Charteris helped himself to two glasses of brandy. Both were promptly whisked away. Though Tonks saw this atrocity, and took a long look at its perpetrator, he still failed to recognise her 'unmistakable' face. Clutching his own glass of brandy he muttered, 'That tall maid is like an intervening goddess of Temperance!' When he saw me remove Barrie's and Whibley's brandy, he thought—so he told me afterwards—that I was a drunkard filching the liquor for my own consumption.

Save for their deliberate tricks the amateur parlourmaids waited as efficiently as they possibly could. In fact, ceasing to be either 'C. Greene' or Cynthia Asquith, I forgot all former

selves in my new role, and—as though my livelihood depended
on how I acquitted myself as a waitress—shook with anxiety
to impress Brown with my efficiency.

Observing the company from this new angle I found myself
awarding good or bad marks for manners towards the dishes
I handed. Whibley I could have rapped over the head with
a tablespoon, because too busy talking, either to help himself
or to refuse the food, he invariably kept the waiter waiting.
From the pantry point of view, Fred Oliver had the best
manners. He never failed promptly and civilly to say either
'Thank you' or 'No, thank you'. But as dinner proceeded he
began to look frostily disapproving. Intercepting winks
between uncle and niece, he had reluctantly come to the conclusion that Evan Charteris was carrying on a vulgar flirtation
with, what he afterwards described as 'that very flighty-looking
parlourmaid'.

My uncle, driven desperate by the sight of the others sipping
liqueur brandy, made a sally behind the screen and helped
himself to another glass. As a punishment his coffee was made
undrinkable by the addition of six lumps of sugar. Despite
Brown's whimpering protests, Barrie had his coffee spoilt too.
So did Freyberg.

The dénouement of this one-act Barrie play was crude.
Five minutes after the now well-mellowed diners had left the
dinner table, Olivia and I slipped noiselessly into the room
where President Wilson was being vehemently discussed.
Syphon in hand, I crept up behind Whibley, who, sputtering
with vituperation, was foretelling with remarkable prescience
exactly what would befall the League of Nations. Taking
careful aim at the back of his neck, I squirted him with soda
water. He leapt from his chair almost up to the ceiling, but
showed remarkable restraint, for though a man of so many
words, he used none stronger than 'Damn!' 'I know who that
is!' he shouted, and seized the syphon for reprisals.

'Curtain! Curtain!' called the playwright.

*　　*　　*

Not long after Barrie acquired his 'Private, Private Secretary' she took to writing for publication. Any other way of bread-winning would, I felt, have been in better taste. This occasioned too much 'shop'—discussions of publishers, terms, bindings and so forth. But Barrie couldn't have been more kind and helpful. He, also, derived considerable amusement from seeing his secretary in the throes of authorship.

My first book was about the upbringing of children. Having to spend so much time on the theory of motherhood left me, of course, much less to give to its practice, a plight made fun of by Barrie in a pretence-letter, supposed to be written to him by my then four-year-old son, Simon, but really written by Barrie himself.

> i am very unhappy and neglected and sow is Michael. U. R. the only one we have to look to now. Mother is writing a book about children and she takes notes of all the things we say. Daddie is writing a book too and he is putting us into it and he squeezes us to make us say literary things. Mother crawls about the nursery stairs listening with the same objec. They have fights which is to get the study to write in. For a test, Michael ran down and called out 'I've flung Simon out of the nursery window same as Punch does the baby'. and all Mother said was 'I'll see to it at one o'clock,' and all Daddie said was 'All right—I'll put that in'.

Besides writing, I took to editing books, Children's Christmas Annuals, and collections of new stories for grown-up readers. This affected Barrie far more than my own writing, for the publishers stipulated that the collections must include a contribution from him. My job being largely to protect him from other people's demands, I felt like a watch-dog biting his master, or a policeman turned burglar. But, as he was always so much happier and so much better in health when writing, I soon came to feel that I had really done him a good turn. If I had killed a number of plays, I had at least induced some stories.

The osteopath, to whom I had driven Barrie, failed to cure his 'writer's cramp'. So he was obliged to take to writing with his left hand. I remember his announcing this change quite formally, as though in dismissing his right hand he were giving notice to a servant of many years faithful service.

'I'm going to take to writing with my left hand. It shouldn't be as difficult for me as for others for I have really been ambidexterous all my life. In fact, I was naturally left-handed, but was compelled to use my right at school. Hence perhaps what Stevenson called "the besotted ambiguity of my writing". I still *kick* with my left foot', he added wistfully.

This change-over immeasurably lightened his secretary's labours, for Barrie's writing now became, relatively speaking, legible. He always maintained that once he began to use his left hand his writings took a definitely sinister turn. 'Anything curious or uncomfortable about *Mary Rose* and *Shall We Join The Ladies?* came', he declared, 'from their being products of my left hand'.

He enlarged upon this theme in a letter to Whibley. 'My dear Charles', he wrote, 'You see I am still left-handed and likely to remain so. It isn't so difficult as you might fancy to write with the left hand, but it's the dickens to think down the left side. It doesn't even know the names of my works. Also, it seems to have a darker and more sinister outlook on life, and is at present trying to egg me on to making a woman knife her son.'

CHAPTER IV

BARRIE'S HOUSEHOLD

HARRY BROWN the butler, under whose direction I played the parlourmaid, had been with Barrie since 1908. Not much taller than his master, he was a beaming North-countryman with an engagingly ugly, humorous face. Brisk, constitutionally cheerful, and sufficiently robust to stand up to the 'atmospheric disturbances' that from time to time permeated the flat, he was yet sensitive enough always to understand and sympathise with 'The Master'—his own name—whom he loved and guarded with unstinted care. Efficient in every way, Brown excelled as a front-door watch-dog—one of his most important functions. He had the knack of making every expected guest feel specially welcome, yet knew how to turn away the unwanted without offence.

I'm told Brown was an excellent mimic of many to whom he opened the door—shrieks of merriment came from his precincts—but this was an entertainment I never had the privilege to enjoy. Nor did he object to being made a butt of himself. To my shame, he discovered one day that he had 'waited' through luncheon with a well-placed fox's brush dangling from the inside of his coat to which it was pinned! Seldom can such a liberty have been taken with a butler, but he at once joined in the laughter and shouted 'Tally Ho!'

Mrs—to give her brevet rank—Stanley, the cook-housekeeper, one of the best women I've had the good fortune to know, had been with Barrie for some years before I appeared on the scene, and stayed, an inseparable part of the unique atmosphere of the flat, until the very end. She was as untiringly devoted and dependable as Brown.

Mrs Stanley, like many other gentle souls, could be very obstinate. Armed with a dustpan, she was difficult to deflect; and from time to time her determination to clear away, or at least to lower, the great mound of ashes which Barrie liked left for ever undisturbed on the hearth, collided with another strong will. At times, altercations arose.

'Mrs Stanley has destroyed my fire again,' I can hear Barrie growl; 'but,' he added darkly, 'she hasn't yet dared to do what she most wants to do—get at the ceiling of my study.'

Poor Mrs Stanley! She would dearly have liked to whiten that smoke-blackened ceiling.

Barrie never ordered his meals. The choice of food was left entirely to Mrs Stanley. It never occurred to him to complain to her, but he did to others. 'If I say I don't want *always* to have sausages for breakfast, they never appear again. Worse, if I praise some particular dish, it's set before me every single day until, rather than have to see it once more, I'm forced to leave London!'

Barrie's taste in food was simple. He liked nearly everything, reputedly indigestible—stone-hard boiled eggs, and cold plum pudding. 'Butcher's meat', having been such a rarity in his youth, he rather relished slabs of it, cold.

It can't be said that Mrs Stanley was an artist. Her everyday food—nursery fare, plain 'roast' and milky rice puddings—was adequate. Her attempts to rise to special occasions were disastrous. In her opinion anything worthy to be called a 'dinner-party' demanded oysters, but her idea of serving these delicacies was not to send into the dining-room dozens of them lying in state on a mattress of ice in their opened shells, but to place beside each napkin a small raft of toast on which reposed a dreadful little object—one single oyster, stark naked! In fact, precisely the same horror which in a patty made an American soldier cry out, 'Gee! I guess something's died on my bun!'

As time went on I did take it upon myself to advise on the bill of fare when Barrie entertained. For this, Mrs Stanley appeared grateful, but only, I think, because I artfully pretended I was advising her of individual fads. She deplored the queer coincidence that so many guests should happen to share my own failure to appreciate her *specialité de la maison*—that solitary corpse on a 'bun'.

It was a great blow when in 1922 the serious illness of Brown's wife obliged him to leave. How could such a treasure be replaced? By a wonderfully fortunate coincidence, the very day Barrie told me of his impending bereavement I had a letter from a friend asking if I knew of anyone in need of a paragon manservant. I interviewed the Frank Thurston about whom I'd read pages of praise, and at once engaged this truly remarkable man, who though he had spent all his life, except for an interlude in the trenches, in domestic service, turned out to be not only admirable at his job but widely and deeply cultivated. Dictionaries and various learned tomes soon cluttered up the pantry, where I would constantly find him reading Latin or Greek while he polished the silver. For a change I one day discovered him poring over a Spanish book.

'Is that a difficult language, Thurston?' I asked respectfully.

'No, My Lady, it presents little difficulty if one has a fair knowledge of Latin and French.'

Thurston had an astonishing memory for other things besides living and dead languages. He could supply any forgotten date or quotation. One day, Barrie remarked that the only line in any Oxford prize poem that had survived was, 'A rose-red city half as old as Time'. Though we all knew this line, not one of us could remember the name of the poet.

'By the way,' asked Barrie, 'what was he called, that young prize-winner?'

When, but not until, the company had had ample time vainly to search their memories, a quiet voice came from the sideboard where Thurston was carving the lamb—'John William Burgon, Sir.'

Barrie in his Adelphi Terrace flat

My husband then confessed that he had forgotten the name of the 'rose-red city'. No one at the table could tell him.

Thurston: (Now passing round the meat.) 'Was it not Petra, Sir?'

Thurston's erudition was an unceasing delight to his employer, who loved to compare him with certain Etonians and Oxonians and to contrast his choice of books with the addiction to light literature shared by most distinguished authors. Barrie would counsel guests that if they must take a 'thriller' to bed, they had better 'hide it in between a Pliny and the latest theory of Ethics', or they might feel abashed when Thurston came to draw their curtains in the morning.

Barrie delighted, too, in his attendant's choice of words.

'You are becoming inimical to your apparel, Sir,' said Thurston in mild rebuke when Barrie took to burning large holes in his clothes by dropping tobacco sparks. Barrie was, indeed, 'inimical to his clothing'. His 'gentleman's gentleman', who, I think, chose his suits for him, saw to it that they came from good tailors, but they were soon spoilt by his unbreakable habit of carrying in his pockets too many of his few personal possessions. He was unhappy in evening dress.

Occasionally, Barrie would pretend to be awed by his butler's universal culture. 'I still haven't found out,' he said one day, 'what it is that Thurston doesn't know, but I don't give up hope. There surely must be something?' And from Italy he wrote to me, 'The beauty of Venice is almost appalling, and so was Thurston's knowledge of it as we entered it.'

Neither Thurston nor Mrs Stanley 'lived in'—Barrie preferred to have the place to himself at night—but at times, when his master was ill, Thurston would 'oblige' and burn the midnight oil in the flat instead of his own abode, about which none of us knew anything.

Thurston, uncommunicative, inscrutable, puma-footed—no one ever heard him enter or leave the room—was so unusual, indeed, so mysterious a being that he might almost have been written by his master. Some people questioned whether he had any separate existence of his own. That, I never doubted. I wondered, at times, was he perhaps engaged in writing some book more important than any yet published by those he waited upon, but I am inclined to think his was a scholar's rather than a creative mind. How critical that mind might be, he never betrayed. Whatever his inner life, he was an unforgettable figure; a man who inspired not only instantaneous respect, but—for his heart was as good as his head—growing affection.

It was to this incomparable servant, by that time a friend of fifteen years standing, that Barrie wrote his last letter from the Nursing Home in which he died.

June 1937

I have been quite comfortable here though it would be better of course to die in one's own home. No one could have done more for me than you and Mrs Stanley and I bless your names. I want you besides the monetary bequest to pick for yourself a hundred of my books. Few persons who have entered that loved flat have done more honour to books.

CHAPTER V

FURTHER IMPRESSIONS

As time went on I was often asked whether any of my first impressions of Barrie had been discarded or modified. Had I, for instance, come to subscribe to the theory that he himself had been the inspiration of his own myth of The Boy Who Wouldn't Grow Up? Never, for one moment! His face continued to impress me as the most adult, the most experienced, I had ever seen, and each glance at the photograph of that six-years-old boy in braided and frogged velveteens, noticed on my first visit to the Adelphi flat, confirmed my suspicion that the creator of Peter Pan had been a case, not of arrested, but of precipitated development. The precocious concern on that shockingly thoughtful countenance made it pitiably plain that the little boy, at whom life had too early bared its teeth, had never enjoyed his share of that irresponsibility which, for a few years at least, should be every child's birthright.

That photograph told the truth. In that tiny Kirriemuir cottage where Barrie was born, it had been, by a strange inversion of the laws of nature, not the mother, but the infant son, who had ceaselessly strained, plotted, contrived, to make and keep, the other happy.

That Barrie had escaped one particular kind of lop-sided growing up is true. He had never, as could be seen at a glance, been to a boarding-school to be taught to 'keep a stiff upper lip'—in other words, to conceal, if not to suppress his feelings. On the contrary, from earliest infancy he had been constrained to play on his emotions, to exploit them in efforts, as tireless as they were ingenious, to distract, console and amuse the mother, who never for one moment allowed him to forget her grief for her adored elder son.

'Jamie', as at home Barrie was always called, was only six years old when his elder brother, David, a remarkably promising boy, was killed by a fall on the ice. From that age, 'Jamie' took charge of his weeping mother. This premature strain, of which Barrie never spoke, but which for the rest of his life his eyes betrayed, was, I'm sure, the reason why the very thoughtlessness—heartlessness, if you will—of happy childhood appealed to him so strongly.

His determination that the children he liked should enjoy to the full what he had missed made him tend to exaggerate the joys, privileges—above all the *immunities*—of their age. The 'Boy Who Wouldn't Grow up' was the conception of a man who had had to grow up much too soon.

What gave rise to the fallacy that Barrie had never emerged from his own boyhood? His amazing power of entering into the heart and mind of a child? But after all, this was only one manifestation of his extraordinary insight. In *Sentimental Tommy* he wrote of himself; 'The most conspicuous of his traits was the faculty of stepping into other people's shoes and remaining in them until he became someone else.'

It would, I'm sure, have been just as easy for Barrie to enter, at any time in his life, into the feelings of the very old as of the very young. In the jargon of our time he has, no doubt, been diagnosed as a case of 'infantile regression'. I contend that at twenty he might just as deservedly have been diagnosed as a case of 'senile precipitation'.

Barrie, like all those whose power of enjoyment lies at the mercy of their nervous systems, tended to invest the past with delights which, if they ever existed, he had at all events failed to appreciate at the time. In an address delivered in Edinburgh where as an undergraduate he must often have been very lonely and unhappy, he spoke of 'the walls we love when we have done with them'.

Childhood being the phase of our life whose walls we have

most completely done with is the phase most easily glorified. And glorify it Barrie undoubtedly did. But not, as I see it, in a deluded way. Nor with Wordsworthian sublimation. 'Thou best philosopher', 'Thou eye among the blind' was not in the least his approach to a small boy. Neither did he believe—still less wish him—to come 'trailing clouds of glory'. On the contrary, it was precisely the earthiness, the impudence, the very ingratitude of happy boyhood that delighted him.

Besides Barrie's genius for collaborating with children in endless games of make-believe, what else is there to support the theory that he himself never grew up? Admittedly, he never tired of any pastime in which a ball is either hit or thrown, but, in this country, that surely is no evidence of infantilism? It must be remembered, too, that when he adopted an orphan family it became an important part of his undertaking, as well as a pleasure, to play with children. Five lively boys gave him many years of practice in teaching cricket as well as in telling stories. A natural gift was developed into an art.

It is true that a note-book, dated 1922, contains the entry: 'It is as if long after writing *Peter Pan* its true meaning comes to me. Desperate attempts to grow up, but can't.'

But private note-books, in which one entry contradicts the next, are not intended to be read—still less to be quoted. They record passing thoughts, antics of fancy and conjecture. Any inference could—no inference should—be drawn from such fragments of soliloquy, in which a writer may well pick up and lay down theories much as a woman tries on hats.

When I said that Barrie had been deprived of childhood, I did not, of course, mean that he had enjoyed no fun as a lively and, in many ways, quite normal little boy. He had happy memories, not only of the entrancing serial games of make-believe inspired by himself but also of every variety of Scottish game played, with marbles—'spyo, smuggle bools, kickbonnety, peeries, the preems and pilly'. He had revelled, too, in fishing, and in prodigiously long walks, feats for which he was famed. But all these delights were enjoyed against a background of anxious solicitude. Seldom, if ever, was he free from a sense of responsibility. The cares of the day had weighed far too heavily on his small shoulders. Too early, he had begun to take thought for the morrow.

'In many ways a perfectly normal little boy,' I wrote. Not, of course, in all ways. It was assuredly no ordinary little boy whom others used to pay to write for them their letters of condolence, a task the willing scribe, with the tears running down his cheeks, discharged to the satisfaction of all.

I distrust and deprecate verdicts on the character of a writer based on inferences drawn from his fiction, but it is not possible to deny that *Sentimental Tommy* contains some admirable self-portraiture.

'You—you ain't like any other cove I knows!' says the little cockney Shovel to the Scottish boy, to which Tommy replies:

'I'm so queer, Shovel, that when I thinks about myself I'm sometimes near feared.'

And 'he has a devouring desire to try on other folks' feelings, as if they were so many suits of clothes.' 'He never forgot to have an impulse to do that.' 'There are no questions so offensive to the artistic nature as those that demand a "yes" or "no" for answer.'

Most self-revealing of all—'it was characteristic of Tommy that he soon had Elspeth happy by arguments, not one of which he believed himself.'

One of my first written comments on Barrie was: 'No pen could convey how much he varies.' Was this a lasting impression? Or did Barrie happen, when we first met, to be passing through an April of the spirit? No, I was always to remain intensely aware of his 'weather'—often it must be confessed, to be very much under that weather. Yet, I sometimes asked myself—I still ask myself—did Barrie in actual fact vary so very much more than other people, or was it, rather, that his extraordinarily strong personality—his very clothes seemed to absorb the character of their wearer—made others exceptionally aware of his moods? It must be admitted that he made little effort to conceal his moods. At times, indeed, I think he was scarcely aware of them, but—like Ophelia, incapable of his own distress—had no idea of the gloom he was diffusing around him.

How often is it said: 'So-and-So is always the same'—in many cases scarcely a recommendation! No one could have accused Barrie of sameness. He was much too natural—too undisciplined, if you like—for continuous geniality. Unless really amused he couldn't laugh. If he could never conscript a laugh, he could usually, if absolutely necessary, contrive a smile. But this wrung-out smile could be rather like the drawing of a cork. 'A ghastly grimace' was his own description of it.

New acquaintances who, happening first to meet Barrie in a forthcoming mood, had been enchanted, were often dashed next time they saw him to find him scarcely recognisable. Because today's welcome was so much less bright, they would question the sincerity of yesterday's. They might just as well have doubted the reality of the sun because a cloud can obscure it. The sombre and irradiated Barrie were equally genuine.

Nor was it only acquaintances who suffered from this intermittent quality in Barrie. Even friends, tried friends—tried in every sense of the word—would not seldom be disappointed to discover that, though they'd found Barrie bodily in his flat, he was yet not in any satisfactory sense 'at home'. At their last meeting he had been dazzlingly communicative, had seemed to give them the very freedom of his soul. Today he was bafflingly remote. The drawbridge was up. They would leave saddened by a sense of friendship in eclipse. But next time, as likely as not, everything would be just as good as before.

> So sinks the day-star in the ocean bed,
> And yet anon repairs his drooping head,
> And tricks his beams.

Barrie was remarkably good at 'tricking his beams'.

Friends who knew Barrie well could await the passing of a dark mood as confidently as one waits for the weather to clear. The truth was that, though he naturally liked a large number of his fellow-creatures—liked them to like him too—he didn't always feel that today—or, indeed, perhaps any definite day— was the right time to see even those he was fond of. 'It seems a law of my nature,' I can hear him say, almost regretfully, 'that I must be a good deal by myself.'

Often, too, though he would be delighted to find a friend actually on his doorstep, and joyfully invite him to come in, he might nonetheless be strongly averse from making any un-immediate engagement, particularly in answer to an invitation received through that pistol-to-the-head, the telephone.

As I have said, Barrie detested long notice. Not so much because—the least self-observant of men—he was particularly conscious of being intermittent. Far more, I am sure, because having for so many years been in the habit of writing nearly the whole of every day he never quite lost the hope that at any moment some sudden inspiration might plunge him back into that utter absorption which was happiness. This die-hard hope made him hate mortgages on his time, particularly social engagements that might compel him to lay down a racing pen.

If Barrie's occasional failure to respond could disappoint— even hurt—his friends, he was richly endowed with that almost unfair gift of being so easily able to put everything right again. This he could do with just a few words and a smile. Or by the briefest exercise of literary craft. Many of his most charming letters were, indeed, acts of atonement. Conscience would tell him that he hadn't been nice enough to some friend. In a spasm of contrition he would rush to his writing-table and pick up his pen—a pen that could heal any hurt. At times this gift proved a curse, for in these fits of remorse he often went too far, and involved himself in future trouble.

Similarly, like a child who gathers flowers his hands are too full to carry, he was apt to make himself much too charming to casually-met strangers, thus raising hopes of a lasting intimacy—hopes he had no time to satisfy. Again and again, I would see him caught in a web of his own weaving.

Another danger was that in his relief, when at last some visitor rose to go, an almost passionate gratitude might make him, as he speeded the parting guest into the lift, so overact the charming host as to encourage the question, 'And when can I come again?' whereupon the smile on his face might well change into a scowl before the lift had carried the gratified guest far enough down the shaft.

I used to call this dangerous last-minute burst of bonhommie his 'Putting-into-the-Lift-Manner'. ' 'Ware lift' came to be an accepted code warning between us. Whenever I saw certain symptoms I would whisper those two words, even though the good-bye wasn't being said anywhere near a lift.

I soon had ample opportunity to become acclimatised to Barrie's changes of weather and to recognise his 'Putting-into-the-Lift-Manner'. For many years in succession, my husband and I had to let our London house for May, June and July, and during these months we used to stay with Barrie in his Adelphi flat.

Barrie's London routine was, then, pretty regular. Breakfast, at about half-past nine, was followed by a long session with *The Times* and letter-writing. Peter and Nicholas Davies often, other guests occasionally, came to luncheon, for which Barrie very seldom and reluctantly consented to go out. But, directly after that meal, he invariably set off, a countryman's stick in his hand, for a short walk. When he came back, he would lie down for half an hour or so and ring for tea as soon as he got up. Usually, he dined at home, sometimes with a guest, more often alone; but he never went to bed until very late. He was a bad sleeper. Fortunately his eyes remained strong until the very end of his life, so he could read for hours and hours at night. One of his great solaces was Anthony Trollope, whom, like many others, he rediscovered after the First World War. 'I feel,' he once wrote to me when I was abroad, 'I feel that Anthony Trollope and I are living in my flat together, for I seem to spend so much of my time with him, especially in the long hours after midnight. We then wander about Barsetshire in a heavyish carriage drawn by two slow horses with long tails and the motors whizz by us, but with Anthony on the box we do reach our destination which they perhaps don't.' How fortunate for Barrie that, unlike his beloved Emily Brontë, Anthony Trollope was so prolific a writer!

At whatever hour I might return from a dance, I would find Barrie still up, either reading in his great cavern by the fire, or prowling round his uncurtained room gazing out at that glittering night view of the Thames of which he never tired.

I had been told that Barrie was an expert cook and, on my first visit to the flat, I noticed a small gas stove in the living-room. This was a legend. The stove must, I think, have been a passing whim. At all events, it soon disappeared. Barrie did, however, excel at one kind of invalid cooking; he could make Benger's Food to perfection, a rare accomplishment on which he rather prided himself. It soon became a ritual that, before going to bed, I must partake of a cup of this invaluable but rather insipid beverage. At times I was very glad of it, but if I came back replete from a generous supper it was difficult to swallow.

Now and again Mrs Stanley would be thrown into a twitter by the announcement that there was to be a dinner party of eight, ten, or twelve guests. My job would then be to avert social disaster by tactfully preventing the reappearance of those single oysters apiece which she thought the occasion deserved.

Barrie liked to go out to dine at a restaurant fairly often, usually to the conveniently-nearby Savoy, sometimes to the Ritz, Berkeley or Claridges. This seemed the one expensive luxury that never quite palled, even after he had for many years been able to indulge it. I don't believe he ever ceased to find a certain satisfaction in the consciousness that he could now go wheresoever he chose and order whatsoever he fancied. I doubt whether he ever strode into one of the great restaurants to be greeted by his name by a smiling, bowing commissionaire or head waiter, without remembering the lean young Scot, launched on London with no resource but his pen, who must so often have wondered from where his next meal of kippers and buns would come.

Except for meals at good restaurants and his many secret acts of startling bounty, nearly all manifestations of wealth were, it seemed to me, distasteful to Barrie. For instance, on the rare occasions when he hired a car, he preferred it to look as unostentatious as possible, and had, I felt, almost to restrain an impulse to jump out before his destination was reached rather than be seen arriving in, what he thought, plutocratic style. I am inclined to think that being rich gave him a sense of severance from—almost of disloyalty towards—his own youth and kindred.

On evenings spent in the flat, we would very often read aloud. Barrie so much liked this gentle, now outmoded pastime that it actually stopped him walking about the room. He would sit silent and intent. Often, he would ask for Dickens, particularly the *Nicholas Nickleby* chapters about the Vincent Crummleses, whom he thought the best comic characters in all fiction; but usually he wanted poetry—the same favourites over and over again. *The Scholar Gipsy* I must have read thousands of times. Certain passages in Shakespeare were often demanded, especially the description, in *Henry V*, of Falstaff's death. Other frequent encores were *Comus*, Tennyson's *Ulysses*, certain poems by William Barnes, Blake, Christina Rossetti, Emily Brontë and Hardy; and—year in, year out—over and over again we read the whole of *The Shropshire Lad*.

Charles Whibley, knowing of Barrie's intense admiration for A. E. Housman, arranged that they should meet at a dinner in Cambridge. Alas, each writer came up against the other at his most silent. For all the communication between them, they might have been two hermit crabs burrowing into the sand.

'What was it like?' I asked Barrie when he came back from Cambridge.

I can still hear his mournful reply. 'We growled amiably at one another.'

(No witness of this meeting described the 'growling' as 'amiable'!)

The subject was dropped, but a few minutes later Barrie rather wistfully asked me to read 'Be still, my soul, be still.'

A few days later Barrie described, in a letter, this eagerly awaited meeting: 'I went to meet Housman, but, alas, it was one of those dire dinners of dons and wine. I knew I should be appallingly silent and dull, and I was. The awful feeling that you will never be able to speak or think again!'

After this sad encounter the following letters were exchanged:

Adelphi Terrace House,
1922.

Dear Professor Houseman,

I am sorry about last night, when I sat next to you and did not say a word. You must have thought I was a very rude man: I am really a very shy man.

Sincerely yours,

J. M. Barrie.

Dear Sir James Barrie,

I am sorry about last night, when I sat next to you and did not say a word. You must have thought I was a very rude man: I am really a very shy man.

Sincerely yours,

A. E. Housman.

P.S. And now you've made it worse for you have spelt my name wrong.

I wondered why Housman hadn't retaliated by spelling Barrie's name with a 'y'—Barry, as was my own way for quite a time after I became his secretary!

Sometimes—rarely—Barrie read to me, instead of I to him; once or twice Burns in their native tongue.

But on one memorable evening in the flat, the reader was neither Barrie nor myself. This was when Mrs Patrick Campbell invited herself to dinner and, bursting with grievance, stayed until half-past two in the morning reading her *Memoirs* to us and inveighing against the laws of copyright. Her grievance was that Bernard Shaw wouldn't allow her to include in her book all the letters he had written to her. This brilliant woman was constitutionally incapable of understanding why, if the actual letters were her property to keep—or if she wished, to sell—she yet could not publish them without the consent of their writer.

'What an unteachable devil you are!' wrote Shaw. 'Can't you understand that the copyright of my letters belongs to *me*, and the sheets of paper on which they are written to *you*?'

My husband, in his dual capacity as a barrister and literary adviser to a publisher, did his best to try to make 'Mrs Pat' understand this distinction. No good! She remained invincibly 'unteachable', but overwhelmingly articulate. Barrie, still more ambitious than my husband, endeavoured to make his guest see that, even leaving aside the question of the law, the wishes of the letter-writer ought to be respected. His well-chosen words were wasted. Hour after hour the discussion raged while Barrie and Mrs Pat went on smoking cigars at one another until I could no longer see them for smoke. Before midnight such spurious sprightliness as Barrie had mustered for this emergency had petered out. By one o'clock his courtesy was beginning to creak. At half-past two, he looked so near to death that invoking the 'C. Greene' half of myself, I telephoned for a taxi, and escorted to, and down, the lift the frustrated memoirist.

An exhausting session; all the more so, because the great actress's diatribes were interspersed with brilliantly witty irrelevancies that left me weak with laughter; while every now and then—launching a sudden attack on our sympathy—she made me weep by bewailing her lost beauty.

'My face is like a burst paper bag!' keened this mistress of the comic-tragic, the strange music of her voice turning even these words to poetry. And, as she spoke, the beauty that she mourned would revisit her face. For a gleam or two she would look just as I remembered her when, casting her spell over my childhood, she had melted me as Mélisande, frozen me as Electra.

Occasionally, Barrie was persuaded to leave his flat to go to a Saturday-to-Monday country-house party. As a rule he accepted reluctantly, set off despondently, and, then, passed in rotation through several familiar phases. Saturday evening he wondered why on earth he had come; much of Sunday was spent in counting how many hours must still be lived through before Monday morning brought release; by Sunday evening, as likely as not, he was sorry so few hours were left.

A letter he wrote while staying with some Americans who had taken a large country house gives a characteristically embroidered description of his sufferings as a guest:

There have already been sixteen hours of morning and it's still an age till lunch. I don't have the spirit to say that I must go tonight, nor the nerve to cut and run. Occasionally I listen at my door to make sure that all is quiet in the well of the house and then I steal out for a walk. I walk miles and the clock says I have been gone ten minutes when I steal back. I have nothing to read but an Oppenheim I bought at Waterloo and find I read a week ago.

1.0. Thought I heard the lunch gong and by a mighty effort went down to face the function. Find lunch not till 1.30 and stole back to room less able to face function.

Everyone is very kind and there are evidently lots of nice people about but I don't know any of them even by name except —— and he's no refuge in a storm. The new American ambassador is attractive and I cling to him until he bolts. . . .

I went for a long walk with a lady who talked about the New Rich. I am not going to walk with her again.

1.30. Now is the time when I would accept a challenge to play golf. How delightful to be sitting for my portrait. I would receive with rapture an announcement from Frank that a deputation is at the door wanting to chat with me about my opening a branch of the Ladies Debating Society in Upper Tooting.

1.40. They are all so much alike and yet they can sort themselves out. This gives me the loneliest feeling.

1.45. Lunch looms. I have made one plucky resolution, not in any circumstances to sit beside the New Rich lady. But how to know which she is?

1.50. I descend. Several more arrivals. I find a pretty lady and sit beside her far from New Rich.

3 p.m. I decide New Rich is best one. I steal off alone and go to look at the shrubbery, which I have been going to see repeatedly since arrival last summer.

5.0. Tea. Sat beside New Rich. Have decided never to leave her.

5.30 to 8. Locked self in bedroom.

Dinner shouldn't be so bad, and later I can have several looks at the shrubbery. Tomorrow early! But at last I miss a car, as many of the fellow guests will be in my train! . . . It is very cold and I have garments quite unfitted to cope therewith. This all sounds churlish for I have host and hostess who are both kind and attentive. Just serves me right for venturing out of my natural way of life. . . .

I would love anyone who would burst into my room with a warm pair of socks. Oh for a sweater, or a dog to converse with! I'll never go anywhere again without a dog. And yet they are all quite nice. But who are they? And why am I?

Monday morning. Arrived London safely. Sunday evening much better than expected, and evidently I was the one at fault.

It must not be inferred that Barrie enjoyed no country-house visits. There were some people with whom he delighted to stay, for instance his great friends the Lewises, the parents of the writer Eiluned Lewis, in their home in Wales; the F. Olivers at Jedburgh; the Lyttons at Knebworth, and the Horners at Mells.

Now and again, Barrie liked to stay for a few days in an hotel. Sometimes my husband and I went with him to the Royal Albion at Brighton, where Harry Preston, hailing him as 'My Lord and Master'—that inimitable hotel-keeper conferred a different courtesy title on each of his many famous guests—would welcome him with offerings of champagne and cigars.

Barrie, who used to enjoy winning all the games of skill on the Palace Pier, generally treated Brighton as a holiday place, but once I remember his going to the Royal Albion for an intensive bout of writing. That was in 1931, when his thoughts, turning back to the past, set his pen off on a tale of the scenes of his boyhood and the strange legends that haunted their snow-bound glens. *Farewell Miss Julie Logan*, eventually a long-short story of twenty thousand words, was, I think, originally intended to be a full-length novel, but compression had become a habit —almost a compulsion.

If the Royal Albion seemed an incongruous environment in which to write so strange a story—the last story Barrie ever wrote—it served its purpose: Barrie returned to London exhilarated by more than the sea breezes.

Granville-Barker, writing of *The Boy David*, pointed out that, before this play, 'Barrie had written nothing of importance for twelve years'—'nothing of importance for the *theatre*', he added. 'But if faultless taste, unerring skill, and that apparent ease which is the reward of much winnowing labour of mind and pen, make for importance in literature, then *The Greenwood Hat* and *Farewell, Miss Julie Logan* are important enough.' And it was one of these two late works—which of them I forget—that made George Moore, in a rare moment of enthusiasm, describe Barrie as 'one of the most beautiful writers of the English language that ever lived'.

For all the delights of the Palace Pier and the coming of Miss Julie Logan, the scene of my happiest seaside memories of Barrie is not Brighton but Kingsgate in the Isle of Thanet. Here, year after year, while their London home was let, my two sons spent the summer months. My husband and I joined them, each week-end, at this paradise for children with its rocks, pools and mysterious caves. Barrie often came with us. I can see him now—small and dark against the yellow sands and white cliffs of that lovely seaweed-strewn bay—one of a happy 'Seaside Troupe' forever printed on my sight: two red-headed, freckled little boys burned terra-cotta by the sun, who wear green oilskin paddlers, carry buckets, spades, long glistening banners of seaweed; their smiling Nannie, her hands and lap filled with sea treasures, shells, live crabs, dead star-fish, a washed-up boot; a gracefully-swirling, plume-tailed golden retriever; a biscuit-coloured Cairn terrier with dark, beseeching eyes.

Barrie loved those two dogs. He never tired of watching the golden retriever's unending game of chasing sea-gulls on the wing—a game in which the birds seemed to join; and a strong fellow-feeling existed between him and the short-legged terrier, on whom the size and stride of the swift retriever had obviously inflicted an acute inferiority complex that made him bark and snap.

I see that 'Seaside Troupe' enjoying, in that little bay, the discomforts of tea on the shore. The cloth, anchored by large flat pebbles, is spread with shrimps, jam sandwiches, 'Playmate' biscuits.

When sufficient shrimps have been eaten, a long slow pipe is smoked, a story told. Then, Barrie, never able to resist a stretch of grass or sand, improvises a wicket, rolls up his sleeves and patiently, persistently bowls, not at the wicket, but at the unspliced bats of the boys. The game goes on too long. The dogs grow bored. Surely the time for throwing sticks has come? The terrier begins to bark and snap at the legs of the cricketers. The retriever flashes into the midst of the game, picks up the ball, as though it were a wounded bird, and gallops away with it. . . .

Those two dogs are long dead; those two boys long since men. But I have only to think of Kingsgate, and in my mind's eye, they are again just as they were in those far-off summer days when Barrie watched them play.

CHAPTER VI

COURAGE

IN 1919 Barrie was invited to stand for the Rectorship of St. Andrews University, and at the election in November he polled more than twice as many votes as the rival candidate, Lord Bute.

This meant that he must some time during his three years of office deliver a Rectorial Address, and though for various reasons this was postponed until 1922, the obligation, I think, lay heavy on his mind all through the long delay. The notoriously 'elusive' dramatist and novelist was troubled by the thought that this time, instead of hiding behind the characters he invented, he must speak from, and for, himself. That was why in a spasm of his hide-and-seek instinct, Barrie now invented 'McConnachie', whom he defined as 'the unruly half of himself: the "writing half".'

Barrie soon came to regret his creation (and, with good cause, so did his secretary!) for 'McConnachie', once raised, was impossible to lay. For the rest of his life Barrie was expected to smile whenever a joke about 'McConnachie' was made.

As the time to deliver his Address approached, Barrie was not only nervous; he was oppressed by a heavy sense of responsibility. He understood that the Rector of a university was expected to try to say something which might conceivably help the students. This meant that he would have to be serious. *Could* he be serious for three quarters of an hour on end? Moreover, having been a student himself, he remembered only too well how easily on these occasions a body of students

66

can turn into a mob—how often indeed, they make it impossible for themselves to hear a single word spoken by the Rector of their own choice. Stage fright? Far worse than before any First Night! This time, instead of hiding behind the curtains of a private box, he must go into the arena himself—be the performance as well as the author.

True, he had long ago distinguished himself as an after-dinner speaker. I remember my father-in-law, Lord Oxford, declaring that one of his after-dinner speeches, of which unfortunately no record exists, was the best he had ever heard. But Barrie hadn't spoken at all for fourteen years: besides, what an utterly different audience he would have to face this time! Not contemporaries, mellowed by wine, soothed by tobacco; but critical, callow representatives of the notoriously 'difficult' younger generation, none of them placated by drink or smoke; many of them just out for fun. For all he knew they might have chosen him as likely to provide the most amusing kind of butt. Worst of all, he wouldn't be able to smoke! No stage 'business'—making play with a cigar.

Barrie, as his ordeal neared, had plentifully to draw on the virtue chosen for his theme—courage. He took infinite trouble over his Address. Draft after draft was written—and scrapped. The supposedly final version was finished a fortnight before the date of delivery. This, though he knew it by heart, I copied out in very large handwriting, so that, should memory fail, he would be able to read it without having to put on his loathed spectacles. But on the very eve of our journey to Scotland so many alterations and additions were made that, greatly enjoying myself on lashings of black coffee—I had to sit up till four in the morning to copy out again the whole thing—eight thousand words!

One of the Rector's duties had been to submit a list of names of those who, as part of the Installation Ceremony, were to have honorary degrees conferred upon them by the Chancellor of the University, Earl Haig. Barrie's team was Thomas Hardy, Robert Nichols, Sidney Colvin (unfortunately none of these three was able to attend the ceremony), Sir Squire Bancroft, General Freyberg, V.C., John Galsworthy, E. V. Lucas, Charles Whibley and Ellen Terry. A. E. Housman had been asked, but characteristically wrote to say that he never accepted any 'Honour'.

Barrie, E. V. Lucas and I went to Edinburgh by the night train on May 1st. My diary tells of the next four crowded days.

Tuesday, May 2nd, 1922

After late breakfast Barrie conducted us round Edinburgh. Nerves not too bad; only one brief flare of irascibility because not one citizen of the capital of Scotland could direct us to R. L. Stevenson's house. Up to St. Andrews in the afternoon. Met at station by throng of singing, cheering students, who looked as if they might prove formidable raggers. Barrie carried off to stay with Principal Irvine and his wife. The rest of us went to hotels.

Barrie had to make the first speech of his campaign at an academic dinner. Later, we all attended an evening party at the Principal's house. Lovely torchlight procession. I was told Barrie's speech had been a great success.

Wednesday, May 3rd

Bitter, bitter cold. To chapel where Haig unveiled War Memorial. Except for Ellen Terry—a solitary flower in a vegetable garden—the LL.D.'s in their hoods looked like so many conspirators or dubious monks. I had a few minutes' talk with Barrie. Suffering from reaction after last night's success, he was now convinced that his Address would be a fiasco, and to my alarm—it had already been given to the Press—he was marking it for huge cuts.

I was in the hall some time before the ceremony began. The uproar terrifying—yells, paper streamers—even *boots*—flying about. Pandemonium! I despaired of anyone being able to quieten the students and, despite the respect which I'm told they really feel for Haig, he entirely failed. It was impossible to hear one word he said.

Never have I felt such vicarious terror as when Barrie, chalk-white, visibly quivering with nerves and looking even smaller than usual, came forward to address this shouting, stamping mob. To think that I had feared he might disregard R. L. Stevenson's warning and be 'too funny'! He began almost inaudibly, and, though the uproar had died down, it was all too clearly touch-and-go whether he would be able to 'get', and hold, the students. A heaven-sent, funny little incident saved the situation. Fumbling in his nervousness, he had picked up a large paper-knife that lay on the table beside him, and with this he was comically sawing the air when suddenly, from the back of the hall, a young voice shouted, 'Put it down, Jamie, or you'll cut your throat!'

This friendly, if cheeky, admonition pulled Barrie together. He dropped the paper-knife. He smiled. He took a deep breath. His voice became firm and clear. There was no further sign of nervousness. He didn't cut a single word but, Ancient Mariner-like, held the whole assembly enthralled for an hour and twenty-seven minutes. From the moment he dropped that paper-knife he was able to do exactly what he liked with the students. He made them cheer and laugh as he celebrated Ellen Terry and Freyberg. He hushed them into awed silence when, exhorting Youth to demand its fair share in the building up of the future, he tolled out, 'The spring of the year lies buried in the fields of France. By the time the next eruption comes it may be you who are responsible for it and your sons who are in the lava. All because this year you let things slide. We are a nice and kindly people, but it is already evident that we are seeking cushions for our old bones rather than attempting to build up a fairer future. That is what we mean when we say the country is settling down. . . . Look around and see how much share Youth has now that the war is over. You got a handsome share of it while it lasted.'

The students were visibly moved when Barrie reminded them of their predecessors at St. Andrews, killed in the war.

'Are you,' he asked, in a voice like a broken bell, 'who stepped into their heritage only yesterday, whose books are scarcely cold to their hands, you who still hear their cries blown across the links, are you already relegating them to the shades?'

I think the most tense silence fell when Barrie read, in example of courage, passages from the last letter written to him by Captain Scott of The Antarctic. 'We are in a desperate state—feet frozen, no fuel and a long way from food, but it would do your heart good to be in our tent, to hear our songs. . . . We are very near the end. . . . We did intend to finish ourselves when things proved like this, but we have decided to die naturally.'

From first to last, Barrie gave a marvellous performance—every inflection of his voice exactly right. I'd been nervous about the very end of his Address, for the last words 'Fight on you, for the old red gown till the whistle blows', had struck me, when I copied them out, as an anticlimax, not to say bathos; but even this passage came off, because written—as, of course, the whole thing was—to be heard, not read, it was so well delivered, in fact *acted*, that it really did sound spontaneous.

When Barrie sat down there was a second's silence; then came peal after peal of thunderous applause. A real triumph. What a relief! . . .

Attended University Banquet. Barrie, now in marvellous form—every tap of charm turned full on—made game of Haig in a brilliant bantering speech. Dignity and Impudence? Haig did look like a noble, mournful dog by Landseer.

After this effort, Barrie looked so ghastly ill that I feared he would collapse; nevertheless, though his two Nannies—Freyberg and myself—had both, obeying instructions, told the authorities that any further effort would be quite impossible that night, he Jack-in-the-boxed up again to make a dramatically unexpected appearance at *Gaudeamus*, where he was given a terrific reception, and addressed both the men's and the women's Students' Unions.

Thursday, May 4th

Bitter cold again. Barrie put over a pretty stiff course. Freedom of the City conferred upon him in the Town Hall. This, of course, involved a speech, and then he had to make another long one at a huge male luncheon. Meanwhile the Provost's wife entertained the women. Among them Ellen Terry—frail, perplexed, un-remembering, all but blind, poor darling, yet still streaming out enchantment! 'There was a star danced, and under that star was I born!' The mere sight of her made those words ring in my ears. What a strange disguise of old age she must now wear, but how defiantly that undying youth at the very core of her being still stares out of her dimmed, bewildered eyes!

Enormous garden party at three o'clock—always poor Barrie's zero hour. Both he and Freyberg given a tremendous ovation. The 'Rector' obliged to shake hundreds of hands. To my relief, he did contrive to wring out a semblance of a smile each time his poor little arm was pumped up and down, but after this protracted ordeal he looked so ill that, becoming alarmed, I arranged for him to have his dinner in bed. Principal Irvine and his wife both charming. He couldn't possibly be in better hands. I dined with them. Dinner followed by a big evening party for which Barrie resurrected and, still staunchly smiling, played up marvellously. All the newly-capped LL.D.'s told me that they'd thought his Address the most effective they had ever heard. I talked to that oldest veteran of the stage, Sir Squire Bancroft. He told me he'd been some dozen times to *Mary Rose*—that he 'just couldn't keep away from it'.

Friday, May 5th

Copied out Barrie's luncheon speech for him. To Dundee for ceremonies at its College, which is part of St. Andrews University. Drove with Barrie to the opening of the sports ground, where he literally started the ball rolling by bowling at Principal Irvine. Haig made a solemn speech; Barrie a very flippant one, mostly about cricket. Then, Haig batted in full uniform! Freyberg was bowling to him, but Barrie very soon snatched the ball and got Haig out with a googly.

Luncheon of about two hundred and fifty people, and, so it seemed, almost as many speeches, but I could hear only two of the speakers—Barrie and Duke-Elder,[1] the President of the Students' Union, who, Principal Irvine says, is his 'most brilliant undergraduate'.

Garden 'fête'—an eternity of handshaking and hauled-up smiles from poor Barrie, who once 'off stage' subsided into such dejection that our dinner—he, Whibley, Freyberg and Self— was no lively affair. But he rallied to burst into a last blaze of bonhomie on the station platform. The students had all assembled to see him off, and the band of the Hood Battalion appeared to play to Freyberg—very moving. Some students all but pulled our arms off after we got into our carriage. It was a relief when the train at last moved off and slowly chugged out of the station. Once we were safely out of sight, Barrie put up no further resistance. Appalling reaction set in. He guttered right out (I was reminded of his recent complaint that one of his photographs made him look like a tallow candle in distressed circumstances!). It felt as though such a weight of depression must retard the train. *I* wept from fatigue. Even Whibley was subdued.

The black reaction described in my diary was mercifully brief. Barrie, two days afterwards, was none the worse; but for weeks C. Greene's desk was snowed under by an avalanche of letters; many of them, to my rising irritation, addressed to McConnachie, c/o Sir James Barrie.

[1] Now Sir Stewart Duke-Elder, F.R.C.S.

CHAPTER VII

SPEECHES

COURAGE was acclaimed in the Press—I remember only one dissentient—with the result that for the rest of his life Barrie was besieged by requests to speak at every possible kind of ceremony. Certain speeches could scarcely be evaded; for instance, when he was presented with the Freedom of a town; but many of the invitations he did accept—invitations to preside at Public Dinners; appeal for funds; address institutions; unveil memorials and so forth—could without offence have been declined.

'Barrie's letters of excuse,' wrote Viola Meynell in her introduction to *The Letters of J. M. Barrie*, 'would in themselves fill a volume called "Please Excuse Me". In one's dotage one might teach the children lisping at one's knee that the word barrier derived from the inaccessible playwright. His attitude to personal publicity was too constant not to have its set formula; it was always "Please Excuse Me". To invent a new phrase each time would have been like saying good morning in different words every day.'

Perfectly true! How came it, then, that after St. Andrews Barrie so frequently refrained from using his 'set formula'? From one who had so long professed to detest all public functions, a succession of conspicuous speeches seemed a rather extreme way of submitting to, if not courting, publicity. What was the reason for the apparent inconsistency? Sense of obligation to causes he thought deserving? Fear of being called a curmudgeon? Subconscious hankering after a different kind of self-fulfilment? I really don't know. His loud groans as the

73

time approached for him to fulfil the next engagement to speak repeatedly gave me my cue to say, 'Why, then, do you *do* it?' but I never did ask that question; had I done so, I don't think that he would have known the answer.

Whatever the motive or motives that actuated Barrie, the decade that followed his Rectorial Address might well be called his oratorical period. All through those years—years in which he wrote very little—whatever speech he made was front page headline news, and reported in full length in *The Times*.

As one triumph followed another it seemed to me that, while beforehand Barrie suffered less from nerves, the after-effects became worse. It was like an illness of which the incubation is shorter, the quarantine longer. And his black reaction was akin to shame. I remember how dashed I was by his reply when I congratulated him on a very successful speech, which at the time he had seemed to enjoy almost as much as his audience. 'Looking back on my effusion, it makes me rather ill,' he croaked.

Sometimes, his face, even while he was delivering his speech, wore a perceptible look of faint disgust, almost as though he felt himself to be performing a rather shabby trick. He must have known that he did possess the art of the after-dinner speech, but I'm sure he thought it the lowest of arts—little more than a mere knack—and considered its exercise rather a degradation.

'He was an actor,' wrote Hugh Walpole, 'he knew that his accent although honest was bewitching. He knew just when to pause, when to be sad, when to be gay. And although he meant all that he said, he meant also a great deal more than he said.'

Even if each speech were a performance—a studied performance—the speaker often moved himself as well as his audience, and surprised himself, too; for, however much trouble he had taken beforehand, something quite unprepared, felicitously born of the occasion and unmistakably characteristic, invariably slipped into his speech.

Barrie's delivery was remarkably good, except on one occasion—the 1922 Annual Dinner of the Newspaper Press Fund—when for some reason he wouldn't raise his voice or keep his pipe out of his mouth and so was inaudible.

He specially excelled at a typically short, neat sentence with an adroit twist to its tail—for instance 'the first time I saw Warner bat, he made one. The next time he was not so successful.' And, speaking of a young couple crossed in love, 'I can tell you, however, that it all ended happily, and that not many years later they were married—though not to each other.'

One more example: in his speech as chairman at the Royal Literary Society Dinner, Barrie spoke of his early days in London, of Rudyard Kipling already at his high noon, of Galsworthy just beginning to come into fame, of H. G. Wells and other blazing or ascendant literary stars. . . . 'And about this time, a new comet flamed; a young Irishman. He could do everything. . . . He could write plays scintillating with wit; he was a dramatic critic, an art critic, a music critic. He made speeches. He wrote about Karl Marx. There was nothing he did not adorn . . . (pause for removal of cigar). I have often wondered what became of him.'

Needless to say Bernard Shaw, by this time at *his* high noon, was seated at the top table.

Most of Barrie's speeches were compounded of the same skilfully-blended ingredients; banter-homage adroitly paid to the guest of honour, playfulness, fantasy, mock reminiscence, and a brief emotional appeal, deeply moving to most, if embarrassing to a few.

Those who never heard Barrie speak must find it difficult to believe how much he made his audience laugh. That was where the actor in him scored. Economy of facial expression, as well as of words, made every flicker of his face tell, as well as every inflection of his voice.

Reading his speeches can give no more idea of the spell he

cast than a photograph can convey a skilfully painted picture. So much of the enchantment was in the beautiful hoarse voice, and the poignancy of the tiny mournful figure with the weary, wrung face, majestic brow and large cigar. It must be remembered, too, that his speeches were carefully written to sound impromptu, and to be *acted*.

If most of Barrie's listeners were entranced and a few embarrassed, many must have been more than a little perplexed by their inability to know how far this strange being was telling them the truth. Were they listening to autobiography or to fiction? . . .

It was, of course, impossible for Barrie to tell of his own past without drawing on his imagination as well as on his memory, and where one collaborator left off and the other began, no one—least of all the narrator himself—could tell. In talk, as well as in public speaking, he tended to wander in some entrancing borderland between fantasy and fact. For him the frontier between these two realms was never very clearly marked. Once, when he had just told me some ostensibly autobiographical anecdote, a genuinely puzzled, even worried, expression came into his face. 'I can't remember, now, whether the actual incident ever really took place,' he said wistfully.

He never invented, or even embroidered, deliberately to deceive, but the art of weaving fantasy with fact, always natural to him—the art which had made his fortune—had come to be his master as well as his servant.

Although in a sense Barrie talked more about himself in his speeches than is usual, he revealed himself less than do more ostensibly objective speakers. He told innumerable anecdotes about himself; he spoke of his boyhood; he romanticised his early poverty; he recounted how he had wooed and won his early editors, and so forth. But, though he told of many things that had happened to him, of what he really thought, of what he really was, he gave scarcely a clue.

What, I wonder, could a professional psychologist deduce

from a careful study of Barrie's speeches? How much genuine self-betrayal filtered through the dense smoke-screen—figurative as well as literal—behind which he invariably spoke? It seemed to me that one note was several times rather suspiciously over-stressed—his almost over-hearty welcome to the younger generation of writers knocking at the door. (Who was it said 'the worst of it is the younger generation never *do* knock at the door'?) Was Barrie a little on the defensive when he struck this particular note? Did that determined cordiality camouflage an awareness of the debunking process already begun? I have known no writer who less resented—more genuinely welcomed—the success of others; and in his attitude towards minds and epochs different from his own there was real and deep humility. Nonetheless, he may have felt that some of his youngers—perhaps writers with doctrines, rather than, like himself, with fantasies to sell—did not realise that what is easy to read is very difficult to write; nor that what is 'light' is not necessarily 'slight'.

Hugh Walpole wrote: 'Barrie never boasted, but he must secretly have known that in one thing at least he was superior to any living man—the technique of the theatre.'

The tendency to judge authors more by their opinions than by their mastery of a craft was rapidly growing, and if Hugh Walpole were right, the dramatist may well have thought that some of his detractors did not know very much about the technical difficulties of writing a play. Here, from a speech, made in 1928 to the Incorporated Society of Authors, Playwrights and Composers, is one example of the kind of passage I have in mind.

'Before sitting down, just a word of warm greeting to those with whom the future lies. Your motto, I suppose, is "whatever was is wrong", and, though it is possibly wanting in perfection, I am sure it is better than the one that I now see did for me, "whatever is, is right".'

Surely a little 'forced'? Never for one single moment can Barrie have thought that whatever was was right! He was speaking out of character.

Here, again, in his speech to the Rhodes Scholars. 'If to despise us helps you in your enthusiasms, then, gentlemen, continue. Far worse than your scorning us beyond reason would be your not having a cheery belief that you can do better. If in firing at some of our performances you feel that the straightest line is through our bodies, still fire.'

One more example: 'They have a short way with the old hands, but in our pride in them we forgive them for that. Perhaps they sometimes go a little to excess, treating even God as if He were, shall we say, the greatest of the Victorians.'

Certain passages in Barrie's speeches, I think, bear witness, too, that however much he jested at being called 'sentimental' and 'whimsical', these oft-levied charges did, nevertheless, make him wince. Speaking of his fellow countrymen, he said, 'We are undoubtedly a sentimental people, and it sometimes plays queer games with that other celebrated sense of ours, the practical. The wild dances these two have as partners, making everybody dizzy but themselves. I say this with genuine feeling.'

To my mind this passage betrays unease as to his repute as a writer, rather than any genuine awareness of a split in his psychology. Isn't it an attempt to disarm criticism by forestalling the laugh against himself, as though to say 'I know what you think of me. I can laugh at myself with the youngest of you!'

I think the time Barrie spoke most from the very core of his being was at his Installation as Chancellor of the University of Edinburgh. This was, of course, a solemn and important occasion. Perhaps, too, he was sobered by the weight of his gorgeous robes in which, no doubt, Bernard Shaw would have said he made himself look 'specially small'.

'Och! Does he no' look tremendously wee!' tearfully exclaimed one of his country-women.

If the new Chancellor did not speak the whole truth he spoke at all events nothing but the truth when he pronounced the 'entrancing life' to be 'an infinite love of taking pains'; and he was drawing on his memory, not his imagination, when he said, in favour of modern times, 'Unions and hostels such as, alas, were not in my time, now give students that social atmosphere which seemed in the old days to be the one thing lacking; the absence of this maimed some of us for life.'

He spoke, too, for himself—for many others as well—when pulling out a still deeper stop in his hoarsening voice, he said, 'Are we not all conscious, fitfully, of a white light that hovers for a moment before our lives? It comes back for us to the very last gasp of our days—comes back for us—to take us where?'

Apart from the St. Andrews and Edinburgh University Addresses, of those I heard the most effective, best delivered and most enthusiastically received of Barrie's speeches was the one made on behalf,' so to speak, of Mary, Queen of Scots, when he opened a bazaar to raise funds to keep up the house in Jedburgh, presented to the town by Mr F. S. Oliver, which that ill-fated Queen had occupied in 1556. Whimsey? Yes, undeniably, but, as an American among the audience exclaimed, 'Some whimsey!'

This speech was the 'mixture as before'—but blended with even greater effrontery than usual—courtesy, mockery, fantasy and a flight of imagined reminiscence in which he described himself as in the presence of 'Scotia's proud-fated, starry mistress'.

'I dared to flash my lantern and almost immediately a lamp shone for a moment in a turret window. Without a sound the celebrated door opened softly and I found myself in the presence of Mary of Scots. She was but a moving part of the night, but a mother will forget her child and rivers flow uphill before a Scotsman is unable to recognise that face and form. . . . She clapped her hands and exclaimed, "Whoever buys at my bazaar, I will always have a leaning to him!" "*Him*", she said, though I had told her most of the work was done by ladies.'

The least successful speech I heard Barrie make was to The Royal Literary Fund, when, in 1930 he presided over its 140th Anniversary Dinner. Possibly, he was oppressed by the personal occasion, his seventieth birthday; perhaps—indeed, doubtless—he was embarrassed by the Order of Merit suspended round his neck. He couldn't but be aware that among so large a gathering of the distinguished, there could scarcely fail to be some who did not approve of his being in the Chair, or of his having been awarded the Order of Merit. Whatever the reasons, he wasn't always audible. The 'business' with his cigar was overdone, and some of the things he said struck me as rather forced, almost—though I hate to say it—arch. 'Not for years have I written anything, and it is rather sad to know that nobody seemed to have noticed this except myself. . . . The characters we think, we "create". That is surely the most comic word in an author's vocabulary. The heroine of course is the worst one. Very obedient until she gets into your book, but you are a lucky writer if, a week after, you know her by sight.'

On this occasion Barrie, it seemed to me, was too obviously on the defensive. He even protested that he couldn't abide children!

I wish I had heard his *Captain Hook at Eton*. This brilliant extravaganza reads so well, and I remember Charles Whibley and other fastidious critics saying what a 'masterly' piece of writing it was. *Captain Hook at Eton* had been evoked by my asking Barrie to contribute to a book I was editing for children, something about Captain Hook's boyhood.

As this speech was delivered to 'First Hundred' at Eton, Barrie had the advantage of addressing a more homogenous audience than usual, and the theme was one in which he could give free rein to his imagination—be as extravagant as he chose—without fear of collision with objective facts. No one could challenge anything he cared to invent about his own creation. Captain Hook is described as a 'one-armed apparition, cadaverous, black-avised and wan', revisiting after death

Rector of St. Andrews

the school he has dishonoured, because he has a deed of awful renunciation to do—to destroy the evidence that he had ever been a member of 'what is probably the most exalted assemblage in the world, the Eton Society, or Pop'.

'First Hundred' listened spell-bound as Barrie told them how this spectre, 'with Eton written all over him—there was something even more than that, as if (may I venture) he were two Etonians rolled by the magnanimous Gods into one'—obtained access to the sacred precincts—once the old meeting-place of Pop. 'It was a difficult room to enter quietly for as soon as you open the door there are several flights of steps down, and it is therefore a sought-after habitation by boys who await visits from their relatives. He must have come and gone as soft as snow.'

Barrie added to his own myth a curious record of Jas. Hook's boyhood. When he was hurt on the football field he 'bled yellow', an idiosyncrasy which saved him from many beatings from the head of the house who 'though Keeper of the Fives, fainted at first sight of it'.

I like the description of Hook's hair. 'He was dressed in modern fashion in the incomparable garb of Pop, and wore a silk hat, from which his long curls dripped like black candles about to melt.'

From what I hear, the most rapturously received of Barrie's speeches were those made to the Australian Cricketers. These were certainly the ones he best enjoyed making. In addressing cricketers he was bowling on the most favourable wicket. There was a natural sympathy between him and his audience. He could do exactly what he liked with them—make them shout with laughter; then suddenly strike them solemn, and leave them moved. According to the Press reports, the speech, made in 1926 to the Eleven captained by the great Collins, though short, was punctuated by thirty-six 'outbursts of laughter'; and before long each cricketer was happily grinning over some jest made at his expense, yet to his glory—for instance, 'Mr Gregory is now joined in the slips by Mr Hendry and Mr Mailey. Three to one! I don't know what they think they look like with their arms stretched out imploringly, but to me they look as if they were proposing simultaneously to the same lady.' . . . 'Then there is Ponsford, who, I'm told, has only been out twice in the last five years.'

The Australians were convulsed when Barrie declared himself to be the only man in the room who knew who were to be in the next English Eleven. 'Our fast bowler—I mention this in confidence—is W. K. Thunder, who has never been known to smile except when he hears Mr Gregory referred to as a "fast bowler". Of our batsmen, I shall merely indicate their quality by saying that Hobbs is to be twelfth man!'

After this sally, Barrie, passing with the minimum perceptible change of gear from the humorous to the emotional, spoke of 'the cradle of cricket'—English village greens. 'The Tests', he said, 'are but the fevers of the game. As the years roll on they become of small account, something else soon takes their place, the very word may be forgotten; but long, long afterwards, I think, your far-off progeny will still of summer afternoons hear the crack of the bat, and the local champion calling for his ale on the same old bumpy wickets. It has been said of the unseen army of the dead, on their everlasting march, that when they are passing a village cricket ground the Englishman falls out of the ranks for a moment to look over the gate and smile.'

CHAPTER VIII

BARRIE PRODUCING A PLAY

SOMETIMES—not very often—I went to a theatre with Barrie. On these occasions, I found him rather a disturbing companion. He could so seldom suspend his critical faculty and enjoy a play just as an entertainment. Technicalities, faults of construction that left me comfortably unconcerned jarred on his nerves, and unless the play was in blank verse he couldn't tolerate even the shortest soliloquy. 'Who are you talking to?' I remember his muttering when an actress had to explain in long monologue, a situation he would have deftly revealed in brief dialogue. Another annoyance was the use on the stage of the telephone, an instrument which, when he learnt his craft, hadn't yet been invented. I suppose the objection was that this new means of communication too easily resolved so many of a playwright's difficulties—cut knots, in the untying of which he had found an enjoyable challenge to his ingenuity.

One evening, however, I remember Barrie sitting through a whole play in rapt silence, so deeply moved that he quite forgot to cough or even to wish that he could smoke. This was when I took him to *Journey's End*, a play I had already seen seven times.

To accompany Barrie when—rare occurrence—he went to one of his own plays after it had been on for some time, tended to be a nerve-racking experience. Staleness, giggles, overacting, 'improvements' of the text, were not well received. I can imagine few ordeals more dire than to sit beside him through a present-day production of *Peter Pan*.

Though, after *Mary Rose*, no new full-length Barrie play was produced until 1936, there were frequent revivals of his earlier

83

plays—at one time no fewer than five running in London at once. As these gave me plenty of opportunity, gladly seized, to attend rehearsals, I came to know how amazingly Barrie was able to make his silent presence felt all over the theatre. Had that small bowler-hatted figure in the fourth row of the sheeted stalls been a ticking bomb one could scarcely have felt more aware of its presence. I learned, too, how deftly he could build up confidence when encouragement was needed; how surreptitiously undermine over-complacency. He could be very funny, too, at a rehearsal—particularly of a play by someone else. Granville-Barker once petrified a young actor by telling him to try to look as if he'd read Shelley in his youth. Barrie instantly capped this injunction with: 'And now try to look as if you had a younger brother in Shropshire.'

I can still see Barrie, white from exhaustion and indigestion, eating biscuits and cheese out of an envelope, at impossible hours in an ice-cold theatre, while everything seemed to be going wrong. But, however tired and disheartened he might be, some piece of acting would suddenly delight him; or some absurdity make him laugh, as at a chaotic rehearsal of *Peter Pan*, when, dissatisfied with one scene, he called for the whole exhausted company—just dismissed for the night—to come back upon the stage, whereupon the producer's nerves snapped:

'Impossible!' he yelled.

'Why?' asked Barrie.

'Crocodile under fourteen—gone home,' replied the producer without a flicker of a smile.

Rehearsals made me realise that the finished article of a play owed almost as much to Barrie the producer as to Barrie the author. There was no part he couldn't act—or, at least, show how it should be acted. I knew, too, that for him the writing of a play was never finished. New ideas continually sprouted. To the dismay of the producer not even the dress rehearsal was thought to be too late for some major alteration or addition.

From long experience I knew how much Barrie put into rehearsals, and how much they took out of him. But I never saw him so entirely focussed on one purpose, so determined—at times almost direfully determined—to wring the very best out of his company, as when I watched him produce, at my father's home, Stanway, a play he had written for the eight grandchildren of the house.

This children's play *Where Was Simon?* was acted at the Christmas of 1926—quite the most exhausting 'holiday' I ever enjoyed.

As I was either mother or aunt to each of the young performers, I was held responsible for the health, behaviour and —heaven help me!—the *punctual* attendance of the entire company. I was also the more or less official safety-valve for the nerves, at times highly-tried, of the author. Besides all this, in conjunction with my—fortunately—dazzlingly efficient sister-in-law, Letty, I was Assistant Stage and Property Manager, and also 'Costumes' and 'Noises Off'.

Prompting was a thankless, nerve-racking job. I couldn't see the actors; so had to judge by ear whether, or not, a prolonged silence was deliberate. Dilemma. If I broke in on a 'dramatic pause'—furious indignation. If I didn't prompt a child, who'd really, as they say, 'dried up'—haunting reproach. The eldest of our company was thirteen, the youngest, who gave a memorable performance as 'Battling Hugo', only four years old.

The eight young actors were, of course, pleased—not to say puffed-up—at having parts specially written for them by a famous dramatist. They gloried in the thrill of a 'real' stage, professional lighting, printed programmes, a large audience, and the necessity to stay up long after bedtime. But they soon realised that to have all that fantasy and will-power focussed upon their small selves was no light privilege. They weren't, as occasionally the author must have wished them, marionettes, but children. And it was their holidays. Exciting as rehearsals might be, they were hard work, and, as the weeks passed, the children did at times remember that life offered, and Stanway provided, other kinds of fun besides acting. It wasn't always easy to enforce their punctual attendance or their undivided attention. Nor was it easy to tell Barrie, who was accustomed to the zeal of professionals, that some frivolous counter-engagement—a meet of hounds or a tennis tournament—was being offered in excuse for failure to turn up at a rehearsal.

While things went well, Barrie, in rapturous appreciation of some childish performance, would declare that no one over fourteen should ever be allowed to act. At less propitious moments he might, understandably, wish his company more subject to professional discipline.

As a rule the rehearsals did go remarkably well. At times there was considerable tension—times when all our solar plexuses suffered. It was only when Barrie was too tired to be quite rational that he would fail to make allowances. He would then temporarily become unable to understand why children should ever want to do anything except rehearse. But on the whole he showed wonderful patience, as well as determination, and skill—not to say cunning.

His gift for teaching children to act was almost magical. Give him a boy with imagination, and Barrie, croaking at him through clouds of pipe-smoke, would expound his part so inspiringly that the child would deliver his words with intense feeling and with precisely the right inflexions. Everyone would declare him a 'born actor'. The more promise a young actor showed, the more would be piled on to his part. One boy of six was soon appearing in eight different impersonations. With material less impressionable Barrie worked differently. On a child who couldn't be inspired to act from its own emotions—from within outwards, so to speak—he would graft technique, his method in such a case being to show by example what should be done with face, hands and voice, and to galvanise his pupil into copying him. And what a master of acting he was!

Our play was never finished. No matter how advanced the rehearsals might be, it was still a growing thing, continually breaking into new bud—sometimes, to our ill-concealed consternation, even shooting an additional branch. The little drama, a masterpiece of ingenuity, grew more and more complicated, its action finally taking place, not only in front of the spectators, but also behind them—amongst them too. No change was necessarily permanent. In a burst of delight at how admirably a well-coached or wisely-let-alone child will acquit himself on the stage—'act' is hardly the word—Barrie would suffer a violent reaction against some recent elaboration of his own. 'Isn't it the very "simplicity" of this kind of thing that sets it so far above anything on the professional stage?' he would indignantly ask. The latest addition would be ruthlessly cut.

An imaginative child tends to identify himself with his part so completely that an alteration may be terribly disturbing—like having his very personality tampered with. More than one crisis arose from these impulsive, revolutionary changes. Sometimes, indeed, the very latest weaving of the author's fantasy had to be relinquished almost as soon as propounded. As a rule, Barrie recognised this necessity; but once it was my painful task to make him see the impracticability of some fresh 'improvement'. This change would have compelled a small child to learn several hundred more words on the very eve of the first public performance.

Much as I'd heard about Barrie's 'stage-craft', never until I myself took part in the production of a play by him did I fully appreciate his possession of that mysterious faculty.

'Barrie', Henry Irving had long ago declared, 'has such a *kind* way of bringing his characters "off" and "on" that actors will always like to play them.' I heard many actors elaborate this praise: one, a member of the cast of *What Every Woman Knows*, in words to this effect. The difference between Barrie and other dramatists is that at no point in a play of his does any character ever feel left out. That is to say, each actor, no matter how subordinate his part, knows precisely what at each given moment he is supposed to convey to the audience. He is always involved in the action of the play: never a mere fielder with no ball to field. Unless he has something definite to contribute to the general effect he is not on the stage, and there's always some perfectly plausible reason both for his coming on and going off.

Another point agreed upon by actors expatiating on Barrie's infallible sense of the stage was that, however many times you might act in one of his plays, the impression its 'stage effects' made on you never wore off. 'I acted the Australian soldier throughout scores of performances of *Mary Rose*,' said Francis Lister, 'yet every single time that door into the empty room opened from the inside my stomach turned to water.'

Our rehearsals at Stanway showed how deserved these tributes were. No performer could ever plead in self-defence that he didn't know what he was *supposed* to be expressing—a great help to the producer, particularly with an amateur company. As for the 'stage effects' each ambush—and there were many—in *Where Was Simon?* startled me as much on the last performance as at the first rehearsal.

Our stage had been set up in quite the draughtiest hall in England, so I lived in dread of the performers being disfigured and hoarsened by colds in their heads. I was terrified, too, of accidents, and not without reason, for *Where Was Simon?*—a play chockful of action—gave the young actors ample scope to inflict grievous bodily harm one upon the other. The exacting part of Cocksure, the detective, repeatedly placed my younger son, Simon, in extreme jeopardy. On the awful occasion when he failed to come out of his ambush—he was concealed inside the loose cover of an armchair—my ill-divining soul leapt to the conclusion that he'd been suffocated.

One niece decided to turn her foolish aunt's nerves to profit. Setting up her own tariff, this young blackmailer extorted a shilling, cash down, each single time she returned my son undamaged to the wings—and no actor ever had more exits.

The weather played a very large part in our drama. On the

day before the 'first night', a serious atmospheric crisis arose. In the middle of a tense rehearsal the butler approached Barrie:

'If you please, Sir,' he said, fully aware of the gravity of the news he bore, 'if you please, Sir, The Wind has not come from London. The car has been to the station to meet the train, but The Wind was not on it.'

Without wind—plenty of howling, lamenting wind—this most atmospheric play couldn't possibly be performed; so, for want of the expected machine, one of the latest theatrical gadgets, my sister-in-law and I had somehow—how I quite forget—to improvise the sound of wind.

'Noises Off' was no light job. Few plays can have introduced a greater variety of sounds. To this day I never hear horses' hooves but I see the two halves of the empty coconut I had to work—clip, clop, clipperty-clapperty, clopperty-clop. Nor can I hear falling snow or rain without remembering how much better we did these things by slithering sago up and down a tilted drawer. As for thunder, Nature's efforts have seemed paltry since I mastered the technique of the tin tray.

My worst moment in all the weeks of rehearsal was on one of the last evenings. The exhausted author had just dismissed his company several hours after their bedtime with the command, 'Ten o'clock tomorrow morning', and I found myself faced with the job of telling him that his leading lady had made another plan for the appointed hour. How break to him the shocking news that instead of rehearsing she intended to go hunting? HUNTING! I couldn't screw up my courage to tell him over night. Providentially before morning a severe frost saved the situation. The meet was off.

Where Was Simon? had been specially written for eight children, but it provided, too, a very important part for the grandfather of those children—a complication. To have to answer for the punctual attendance of my father, elaborately but unconvincingly disguised as a clergyman, was a tricky business; and to be responsible for his exemplary behaviour, too! My father was good at acting, and very fond of it, but he had definitely arrived at the reclining age. He liked to go to bed at hours of his own choosing and was addicted to an afternoon siesta. Furthermore, he was even less—far less—accustomed to discipline than were his grandchildren. Once or twice, leaving the stage in dudgeon, he stumped upstairs to snatch a siesta; but, on the whole, he was wonderfully tractable —no small testimony to the power of that wizard's wand which Barrie could wave over nearly anyone whom he liked enough to want to please.

Spiritedly as my father played his part, he couldn't of course forget, as his descendants did, that he was only acting, and identify himself with the clergyman he represented. So, when the action of the play involved his standing for some moments with his back to the audience, he gladly availed himself of this opportunity to relax, and gave his facial muscles a well-earned rest. Unfortunately this respite coincided with a dramatic moment for other characters in the play, and at the dress rehearsal, a wildly excited grandson, quite carried away by his own part, was shocked to see no expression on the clergyman's face. The child—aghast—felt the whole play was being let down. He tugged at the impassive clergyman's surplice. 'Act, Grandpapa, ACT!' he hissed in loudest stage whisper. I can still hear that impassioned appeal. It seemed to give utterance to my own lurking fear that at the eleventh hour the eldest of the company might prove the most childish of the lot and throw up his part! Maybe, at moments the thought of desertion did cross my father's mind. Indeed, such craven questions as '*Is* it too difficult? Would it be wiser to give it up?' may have flitted through younger heads than his. But, one glance at the author, where he stood in the wings, his face working with emotion, banished any thought of betrayal. Who could have the heart to inflict such disappointment—dare to frustrate the latest fantasy released from the incubator behind that domed brow? Barrie's strange creation, 'Lob', came into my mind—his exclamation:

'It is the thing I wanted, and it isn't good for me not to get what I want!'

It's good to remember how triumphantly on this occasion 'Lob' *did* get the thing he wanted.

At the last rehearsal the brink of despair was reached, as it always is. It was the eve of the first public performance. Half the company was being poulticed for bronchial colds; one actress had a boil on her pretty face, and that night I and other unskilled stage-hands were battling until two in the morning with recalcitrant lights.

Nor did the actual performance go without hitches. There was a bad moment when the curtain stuck; several bad moments when one actor failed to make his entrance because he couldn't find his totally unnecessary hat. This left two of the children—Martin Charteris and Michael Asquith stranded on the stage with nothing whatever to do but gag, and very well they acquitted themselves, making hideous faces at one another throughout a seemingly interminable pause, while, demented, I chased the hat-hunter from room to room. Then there was my shocking lapse of memory. My youngest son, Simon, distrustful of my discretion, was afraid I might prompt him when he didn't need it. So, we arranged a signal. If he wanted help he would stamp his foot. Otherwise I mustn't prompt him. Harassed out of my wits, I forgot our signal. At a critical moment Simon did forget his words. Stamp, stamp, stamp, went the little boy, right across the echoing boards—just as though he were trying to kill black beetles. Panicking, I assumed a wasp had got inside his sock, and quite forgetting I was prompter, hysterically relapsed into sheer motherhood!

My anxieties weren't confined to one side of the curtain. Immediately before it rose I caught, through its chinks, distracting glimpses of my mother, who, characteristically, had invited a far larger audience than could be seated. She was performing the most astounding feats in the way of shifting chairs. Unfortunately, this access of 'furniture mania' reached

its noisiest climax just as my father was introducing the play in
a short, very pointful speech. Some natural huffiness had to
be soothed and the children's giggles stifled.

My mother, besides being concerned at the inadequate
seating accommodation, was justifiably worried by the hurricane draughts that swept the auditorium. To this day a picture
often flashes on my inward eye. I see her battling with my
feebly-struggling father-in-law, Lord Oxford, who is vainly
trying to unravel himself from the festoons of Shetland shawl
in which she is swathing his large statesmanlike head and
roseate face. His urbane protests at being made into a cocoon
become audible, whereupon one of the younger members of
the company shouts out, 'Silence, Oxford!'

The applause at the end of the play was so prolonged that
Barrie acceded to the calls of 'Author! Author!' For, I believe,
only the second time in the whole of his career he appeared in
front of the curtain. Characteristically determined if he did a
thing at all to do it thoroughly, he was led onto the stage, in
handcuffs, by the six years old Cocksure. So effectively had the
diminutive detective snapped on the 'bracelets' that, when the
manacled author wanted to light his pipe, he couldn't free his
hands. His exasperation at finding himself veritably a prisoner
led to an extra thrill for the little actor, who was already flown
with triumph and his first taste of port wine. It was an almost
awful thrill. He heard his godfather use a mild expletive.

The whole company went to bed justifiably self-satisfied.
They felt, too, that they had 'been through something'. This
feeling was delightfully expressed by their youngest member,
the four-years-old 'Battling Hugo', who, told to say his prayers,
said, 'I don't think I need say my prayers tonight. I'm sure
God knows I've been acting.'

After this successful First Night, at which the actors had
enchanted the audience almost as much as themselves, *Where
Was Simon?* was repeated to large 'houses' no fewer than three
times and revived for the Easter holidays. This encouraged

the writing of a second play for the same children and their grandpapa. *The Wheel*, produced in the Easter holidays of 1927, was even more elaborate than *Where Was Simon?*

ACT I

Bachelor Days

ACT II

Scene 1. Through the Wheel
Scene 2. Falters between the Forest of Arden and
a wood near Athens
Scene 3. A balcony in Verona
Scene 4. A quiet evening at Glamis

ACT III

The Return

Characters in order of their disappearance:

Ann Charteris
David Charteris
Laura Charteris
Michael Asquith
Martin Charteris
Simon Asquith
Mary Rose Charteris
Grandpapa Wemyss
Hugo Charteris

The Wheel, though perhaps the most irrepressibly original play Barrie ever wrote, was, as its programme shows, to some extent a collaboration with a greater dramatist. It had also something in common with *Dear Brutus*, inasmuch that the characters, by passing through a wheel, instead of through a door, enter a world of magic. Yet, since this play was specially written for the Stanway children, all of whom had for a long time unconsciously sat for their portraits, each character, though called Macbeth, Romeo, Rosalind or Juliet, was yet, in a fanciful moonlit sort of way, the performer's real self. This meant that the point, humour and pathos of the play could be fully appreciated only by those with inside knowledge of the actors and actresses. To those possessing no latchkey to their personalities, certain subleties—above all, certain ironies—couldn't 'get across'. I was reminded of how Ellen Terry had said of a part created for her by Barrie, 'I feel as if I'd had a lovely dress made for me, but that in some places it fits too tightly.'

There were times when it struck me that some of the seams in the eight lovely dresses specially made for us by Barrie were being strained almost to bursting point.

Yet, this strange play had, besides masterly stage-craft, many moments that were hauntingly touching; others that were deliciously funny. One of the loudest laughs was when Mary Rose, a delicious dumpling of six years old, who had somehow turned into Lady Macbeth, was exhorted to bring forth men children only:

'Bring forth men children only,' finely declaimed Macbeth.

'I have,' piped Mary Rose with her sweetest smile.

Later, the little girl, having herself murdered Macbeth off stage, re-entered looking just like a kitten who had been at the cream, and gleefully rubbing her dimpled hands, lisped,

'Who would have thought my old man had tho much blood in him?'

The entire company did their surprisingly good best, and the audience was loudly appreciative.

Again, there had been no little tension both behind the scenes and in front of the house. At times the author—alas, this winter noticeably more than twelve months older than the previous year—now exalted, now in blackest depths, was more than once very near the end of his own, as well as everyone else's, tether. Prompting was just as harassing; 'Noises Off' as numerous; and, in addition to our previous responsibilities, my sister-in-law and I had got mixed up in Shakespeare, and each had to act the part of a witch in Macbeth. Besides the extra strain on voice and nerves, our attire and make-up as the 'weird sisters' made it no easier for us to command the respect and obedience of our children.

My mother's rampant hospitality also added much to the strain of the last days. She had asked so many too many, people to stay in the house that one never knew whom one might find sharing one's bedroom.

Counter-attractions were even stronger. Perhaps the most effective red herring was Maurice Baring, who if he wished was a veritable Pied Piper to children. One afternoon when a critical rehearsal was to be held, he lured the entire cast to play truant, and organised a game of Hare and Hounds, from which he, the ringleader, returned the most purple and panting of all the hounds.

CHAPTER IX

FRIENDSHIPS

(1)

It soon struck me that for a reputed recluse Barrie had an astonishing number of devoted friends. The most diverse people, attracted in the first place by his personality, had come to rely on him for sympathy and for advice. He was, I should say, the most widely-consulted man I have known. Friendship often cost him much, for his imaginative insight could expose him to almost shattering vicarious suffering, but it gave him, too, the far rarer capacity to share in other people's happiness —and to rejoice in their success; for he was born incapable of envy, a quality he once described as the 'most corroding of all the vices, and also one of the greatest powers in the land'. Another safeguard of friendships was that he infallibly followed his own advice, given in *Courage*, 'Never ascribe to others motives meaner than your own.'

My impressions of a few of Barrie's friends—by no means necessarily his greatest, but those whom I happen to associate with the Adelphi Terrace flat—may help to give some idea of his versatility in friendship.

I hadn't long been 'Mister C. Greene' before I was introduced to T. L. Gilmour (the 'Gilray' of *My Lady Nicotine*), a very early friend of Barrie's, who acted as his Business Man, and in this dual capacity was much at the flat. Gilmour, in size, as in other respects, a contrast to Barrie, was a burly, simple, warm-hearted, lovable man. He reminded me of a large affectionate dog permanently 'On Trust'.

The two friends had first met in the offices of the *Nottingham*

Journal. This was the paper on which Barrie, at the age of twenty-two, started his career as leader-writer at £12 a month. Gilmour had then just relinquished his job on the paper to become a student of Edinburgh University. Some newspaper articles he wrote while at Edinburgh attracted Lord Rosebery's notice, with the result that the young Scotsman became, only for a short time, but to his lifelong glee, that statesman's private secretary. Gilmour was thus the first of the two young Scotsmen to reach the Mecca of both their ambitious— London. But Barrie wasn't long behind. When in 1884 he, too, launched himself upon Fleet Street, the two friends usually shared lodgings until Gilmour's marriage three years later. From that first meeting in Nottingham until their death, within only a few months of one another, fifty years later, Gilmour remained Barrie's dazzled, not seldom bewildered, but ever staunchly-devoted friend and admirer.

My most vivid memories of the trusty Gilmour centre round biennial pitched battles over the demands of the Inland Revenue, for—bold man—he had made himself responsible for Barrie's Income Tax Returns. For several days at a time the great writing-desk in that book-lined room above the Thames would be strewn with 'royalty' statements, and the air— denser even than usual from pipe smoke—filled with the rumble of Gilmour's voice doggedly expounding the inexplicable, and with Barrie's moans of bewilderment.

'But what *is* Schedule D?' I can still hear Barrie cry, a purely rhetorical question, yet what a tap it turned on! A soliloquy quite half an hour long—patient, detailed exposition, droning on and on but elucidating nothing, mingled with snarls from Barrie—snarls that gradually grew fainter and fainter.

These sessions devoted to the payment of his successful friend's Income Tax were the Red Letter Days in Gilmour's year. He took such immense vicarious pride in the largeness of the sums involved; positively gloating, growing visibly bigger, as he wrote out the figures. I recall no mention of anything so petty as an 'Expense Claim'. No, Gilmour wasn't interested in small sums of money; nor indeed would a 'Rebate'—any reduction of the impressive total—have been welcome.

After some hours' colloquy Gilmour withdrew, sleeves rolled up, wet towel round his forehead, to make his final computations in solitude. An hour or so later he came back flushed and beaming.

'Just as I thought,' he declared exultantly. 'Quite a large miscalculation!'

Barrie merely gave a non-committal grunt. His secretary, seated at her desk, idly wondered how much less was owed than had been expected, for naturally I took Gilmour's evident satisfaction—he looked as if he'd been left a small fortune—to denote cause for congratulation.

'Yes, Jimmie,' burbled Gilmour, rubbing his hands with glee. 'I greatly underestimated matters. You have several hundreds more to pay!'

No wonder Barrie had shown no exultation, for apparently much the same thing happened each year, and when at last the final adjustment in the Inland Revenue's favour had been made Gilmour would go off as swollen with genial self-importance as though on his way personally to present the Chancellor of the Exchequer with a very handsome sum earned by the sweat of his own broad brow.

The financial association between these two friends had started in a fantastic arrangement through which Barrie used Gilmour as his Bank. Nothing will make me believe there was ever a time when Barrie's innocence was such that he went about inconveniently short of cash, though his pockets were stuffed with cheques—nor to do his veracity justice did Barrie ever ask me to believe that Fleet Street legend—but it is true that he didn't open a Banking Account for several years after he had begun to earn a large income.

Denis Mackail has described the extraordinary system by which Gilmour acted as a living Bank.

Barrie's only method with the cheques he received had been to cash them when they were open and to put them in his pocket-book when they were crossed. But Gilmour wasn't that kind of a Scotsman—if indeed, there has ever been another one—and an early glimpse of Barrie's pocket-book made him take action at once. The crossed cheques were paid into his own account, and he wrote out an open cheque for the total. . . . If an individual cheque was unduly large, then Gilmour must exchange it for a batch of more convenient size. If Barrie wanted to pay anybody by cheque, then Gilmour must write it.

These crazy transactions were often complicated by Barrie's preference for a 'round figure' prompting him to ask for a larger or a smaller sum than had been handed over. Passages in Barrie's letters make one wonder how either friend kept his sanity—for instance—

1885. Can you exchange cheques again? If you have as much as £15 lying idle, I would be glad if you would let me have it. I enclose cheque. Take off your £10 and let me have the remainder.

I enclose a *Dispatch* cheque. Let me have four small ones. . . .

I enclose cheque. Let me have it in tens. . . .

Let me have two cheques for this one—one for £100.

From certain not very Scottish passages in Barrie's letters to Gilmour, it appears that, in his youth, gold exercised no little fascination over him.

Let me have the cheque as soon as you possibly can. I want to see how it looks in gold and chuck it away.

You might send me the money in gold in a registered envelope. The odd shillings can wait.

Incredible though it seems, this went on until 1890, when Gilmour firmly took the now thirty-year-old Barrie, all his pockets bulging with cheques, to the Pall Mall branch of Barclay's Bank, and showed him how to open an account of his own.

Barrie has told in *The Greenwood Hat* why this decision was reached, and how it was carried out:

It was, if I remember aright, a hole in my waistcoat pocket, that finally decided me to begin the practical proceedings. My friend had got me sovereigns galore in exchange for some cheques, and they had gnawed a hole in my waistcoat pocket, through which they forced a way into the lining and ran round me like mice in a wall. To get at them I had to tilt myself this way and that, or instead of paying my creditors promptly, I had to invite them to listen while I gave myself a jerk. From this dilemma I proposed to extricate myself by following the now familiar arrangement of selling more cheques to my friend, but though I had worried him successfully for so long by appeals to his finer feelings, he finally rebelled, and said that as far as he was concerned I must open negotiations with a Bank or starve. Of course he had me in his power, and I yielded, though with misgivings, for I have ever liked to go on in the old bad ways. . . .

We now approach Step Two in opening a Cash Account. I feared Step Two would mean a great deal of anguish for me, such as going to houses where I should meet the Directors. This made me anxious, for my appearance is against me. I pointed this out to Gilray, but he replied that he had more sense than to let the Directors meet me before they were too compromised to draw back. In short, Step Two had already been taken without my cognizance. . . .

Have you ever been in a Bank? I had only time to glance furtively around when we were shown into a small room. The door was quickly closed, and we were alone with the Bankers. My first reflection was that the window could not be more than five feet from the ground. Then I saw that Gilray was introducing me to the Bankers. Bankers are of medium height, slightly but firmly built, forty or forty-one years of age, and stand in an easy attitude, with nothing about them to suggest their vocation save that they keep their hands in their trouser-pockets. They have pleasant voices, but you do not catch what they say, and all that is expected of you is to bow when they have completed a sentence. You also hand over your cheques and sign your name twice on different pieces of paper, so as to give them some sort of a pull over you, and then after a last look at you which is rather trying, they hand you your cheque-book. Cheque-books are in blue covers and of a shape which makes them wobble in the hand like a trout.

A letter from Barrie to Gilmour shows that some bewilderment attended this tardy opening of a Bank Account.

My dear G, I meant to consult you about this last night. The fiends of the Income Tax are on me for what I am liable for. Do I pay it to them therefore from the year when I had a Banking Account (beyond that I don't know what my income was, and don't want to know), or is there a limit of years beyond which they can't claim arrears? And what is this about taking the average for three years? Should each year be calculated in this way, and if so, how if the years before I had a Banking Account come into the calculations? Then how should I calculate '90, which was the year I began to bank?

Gilmour was not only Barrie's Income Tax accountant; he acted also as his investment adviser. Whether in this capacity he was unwise, unfortunate, or both, I can't say, but whatever the reason it must be admitted that many investments turned out badly. Seldom indeed, can one man conspicuous for his honesty have relieved a friend of more money. But I don't think any resentment was felt; certainly none was expressed; and, after all, mere monetary loss was a small price, and one Barrie could well afford for so many years of devotion and good companionship, not to mention the saving in time of having all these troublous matters taken off his hands. Moreover, the genial Gilmour's blunders, if blunders they were, tickled Barrie, who loved to be able to laugh at, as well as with, his friends. Gilmour, besides his sterling qualities, had just that endearing touch of involuntary funniness which was such an added recommendation. Barrie was a good mimic and his imitation of his old friend speaking reverently of Rosebery was one of his best. 'Gilmour in great form' frequently occurs in Barrie's letters, a bulletin which one can be sure didn't mean Gilmour had been particularly witty or particularly wise. It just meant that he had been especially like himself, and a willingly consenting butt.

(2)

I've heard it said that Barrie preferred so-called Men-of-Action to Men-of-Letters—a meaningless generalisation. To put human beings into categories would never have occurred to him, and, in any event, several of the niches in his private Pantheon had been filled by literary heroes. It is true, though, that physical courage and enterprise did appeal to him, especially when united, as they so often are, with unself-consciousness and a certain simplicity, and that he greatly preferred the company of people more concerned with what they had to do—with some goal outside themselves—than with introspection.

It often struck me that Barrie got on specially well with men whose attack on life had been made with weapons quite different from any in his own armoury.

'I like well to be in the company of explorers,' he declared in his Rectorial Address.

This was true and had been so ever since, in very early boyhood, he had been thrilled to meet the African explorer Joseph Thompson. I can't help thinking that the friendship which sprang up between them must later on have been strained by the four weeks' Continental walking tour they once took together. Still, it did survive even this test, and Joseph Thompson might well be regarded as a kind of forerunner of Captain Scott of the Antarctic, whose life and death cast so strong a spell over Barrie's imagination. If Barrie liked well to be in the company of explorers, *they* felt a natural sympathy, almost a kinship, with him. The trust placed in him by the men whose prowess he admired, and the fondness they felt for him was put into words by the most famous of them—words startling in their simplicity and modesty. A letter written to him by Captain Scott, just before the end, was found long afterwards in the tent with his body:

As a dying man, my dear friend, be good to my wife and child. Give the boy a chance in life, if the State won't do it. . . . I never met a man in my life whom I admired and loved more than you, but I could never show how much your friendship meant to me; you had so much to give, and I had nothing.

It struck me that soldiers as well as explorers were instinctively drawn to Barrie. He seemed to have an intuitive understanding of what he had never experienced, the different aspects of battle—the hell of it and the compensatory gleams glimpsed from that hell. I remember my husband paying him a remarkable tribute. 'I would sooner talk about the war to Barrie', he said, 'than to any other non-combatant.'

Just before I came on to the scene a new soldier friend had swum into Barrie's life; a young soldier, the very personification of physical courage and enterprise. This was the war hero, Bernard Freyberg, V.C., D.S.O. with two bars, and gold wound-stripes all the way up his sleeve.

Barrie celebrated in his Rectorial Address at St. Andrews one of Freyberg's most famous exploits. Citing him as an example of that light-hearted courage which he loved, he told how the young New Zealander, then an officer in the Naval Division, had been the first of our army to land at Gallipoli:

He was dropped overboard to light decoys on the shore so as to deceive the Turks as to where the landing was to be. He pushed a raft containing the decoys in front of him. It was a frosty night, and he was naked and painted black. Firing from the ships was going on all around. It was a two hours' swim in pitch darkness. He did it, crawled through the scrub to listen to the talk of the enemy, who were so near that he could have shaken hands with them; lit his decoys and swam back. He seems to look on this as a gay affair.

The admiration and liking that sprang up between Barrie and Freyberg at their first meeting lasted until the end of Barrie's life. Understanding bridged the gulf of thirty years; each enjoyed the other's company; each felt a protective responsibility for the other.

Now and again, one of Freyberg's nine wounds would break out and send his temperature soaring, upon which Barrie, self-appointing himself 'next of kin', would firmly take charge, confer with the doctors, and—an office he specially loved to perform—keep off other would-be visitors. Freyberg too, when his turn came, was an excellent nurse, displaying skill, tact and sympathy and also—for it must be admitted that Barrie's illnesses were no light business for others—commendable patience. I remember how Freyberg once slept at the flat with a string tied round his wrist for the patient to pull. This was during the illness in which Barrie was given heroin, then a newly-discovered drug prescribed to make the patient sleep. The doctor was disappointed. Barrie, blissfully exhilarated by his injection, defiantly sat straight up in bed all night. Sleep! What was sleep? This new sensation was far too good an experience to lose by unconsciousness. 'I feel all silver!' he exclaimed ecstatically, 'entirely silver!'

I wish I had seen Barrie in his silver beatitude—I'm told he talked as one inspired—but unfortunately I wasn't on the premises. No, I only came in for the reaction on the following day. That my pen couldn't attempt to describe. Nor is it a memory on which I care to dwell.

Barrie loved to hear Freyberg, for whom the war had been not only an arena, but also a Pentecost, talk of his experiences. He often told me how much impressed he was by the eloquence which at times visited the young soldier, particularly when speaking of the men who had served under him. When the Armistice came, Freyberg's friends could not but wonder how this Happy Warrior, who had never known an England not at war, would readjust himself to so-called peace. Might it be a case of 'Othello's occupation's gone'? No such misgivings need have been felt. I remember Barrie's amused pride when Freyberg showed how well he could wield a pen in place of the sword he had been compelled to sheathe. Barrie wrote:

Freyberg was in last night. The first I'd heard of him for a week. The fury of writing for which he has a great natural gift, is the cause. I have seldom seen anyone so struck down by the malady. He already looks the pale student of the midnight oil. He may talk vaguely of mundane affairs but all the time words like 'no adjectives', or 'by style I mean' keep falling off his lips where they gather unbeknown; and every hour of the day, so to speak, he is going over the top, waving manuscripts and reading them to prisoners.

(3)

The three chief literary heroes of Barrie's life were R. L. Stevenson, George Meredith and Thomas Hardy. Of these, the first two were dead many years before I knew their votary, but to my delight the third—a god of my own idolatry—came to stay at the flat shortly after I began to work there.

I had heard it said that Hardy—'that quietest figure in literature,' as Barrie described him—looked like a shrewd country solicitor or the provincial architect and surveyor he had, in fact, been. But at first sight he struck me as far more like a wary, weather-wise farmer. I could picture him in leather gaiters at an Agricultural Show, either leading round, by the ring in its nose, a red-rosetted prize bull, or delivering in the luncheon tent a quiet, sagacious, pithy speech. Superficially there was certainly little in Hardy's appearance to remind one of the popular conception of a poet. One could scarcely imagine those steady eyes 'in a fine frenzy rolling'; nor would one have expected their calm gaze either to conjure up the beauty of Tess, or to see into the mind of Napoleon. Yet in the very inconspicuousness of Hardy's appearance there was something unobtrusively impressive, and as you watched him this impression deepened. The high, broad forehead was very fine, the resigned eyes—they looked as if nothing could ever surprise them again—unforgettable.

Hardy, besides being so unstriking in appearance, was the most unassuming, the least pretentious of talkers. Apparently, without any ambition either to impress or to amuse, his talk seemed no more than a mild inclination uncontentiously to exchange ideas in the simplest possible words.

While Thomas Hardy was staying at the flat he attended the rehearsals of *Mary Rose*. I sat beside him in the empty stalls and watched his alert interest in everything, particularly in certain technicalities of production. Like so many others who have excelled in one branch of literature, he, who had excelled in two, had set his heart on writing a successful play, an ambition never realised, for though, mercifully, he was never, like Charles Lamb, given the opportunity—that opportunity so gamely seized—to join in the hissing of his own play, all his dramatisations of his own books proved disappointments. He spoke with wistful respect of that mysterious 'sixth sense' of Barrie's—the sense of the stage which he said he was sure he did not himself possess.

The wordless singing of the 'Island Voices' in *Mary Rose* fascinated Hardy, and he was greatly interested to learn that the eerie effect of this music was largely produced by a concealed musician playing on an instrument seldom included in an orchestra—a carpenter's saw! He said he thought this might be effective in the production of the *Dynasts*, a word which I noticed he pronounced with a short 'y'.

After these rehearsals, Hardy wrote and enclosed in his 'Collins' to Barrie the following verses:

> If any day a promised play
> Should be in preparation,
> You never see friend J.M.B.
> Depressed or in elation.
>
> But with a stick, rough, crook'd and thick
> You may sometimes discern him,
> Standing as though a mummery show
> Did not at all concern him.

I can't say that Barrie ever gave his secretary the impression that the 'mummery show did not at all concern him'.

To my great delight, Thomas Hardy, not long after his London visit, invited me to come with Barrie to stay at Max Gate, his house near Dorchester. On our long journey down to Dorsetshire, Barrie talked much of Hardy. There was about him, he maintained, 'something more attractive than in almost any other man'. 'He has,' he said, 'a simplicity that merits the word "divine"; I could conceive some of the disciples having been like him.'

Next, he spoke of Hardy's perception.

'That man,' he declared through a particularly long drawn-out tussle with pipe and cough, 'that man couldn't look out of a window without seeing something that had never been seen before.'

If I have said or implied that Barrie was capable of hero-worship, it mustn't be supposed that this propensity could ever suspend his sense of humour. On the contrary, the bigger the man, the more delightfully funny he found his foibles. The admiration he felt for Hardy—veneration, it might well be called—did not stop Barrie smiling at him. He was especially tickled by Hardy's preoccupation with plans for his own burial—plans, continuously changed. 'One day Hardy took me', Barrie told me in the train, 'to see the place where he's to be buried, and the next day he took me to see the place where he would like next best to be buried. Usually he says he is to be buried between his wives; but sometimes, so many inches nearer the first; sometimes, so many inches nearer to the second.'

Barrie spoke, too, of Hardy's posthumous idealisation of his first wife, who from all accounts had made his life a misery because, being connected by birth with some bishop or rural dean, she considered herself socially her husband's superior, a fact she was for ever rubbing into poor Hardy, telling him he wasn't 'County'.

Though Barrie had emphatically warned me to expect neither a beautiful nor a picturesque dwelling, I must admit that the almost startling commonplaceness of the house Hardy had designed for himself came as a shock. I suppose I had cherished a lurking hope that this Wessex home would have about it something to remind me, however faintly, of shepherds, dairymaids—the Greenwood Tree. I had expected that its appearance and atmosphere would at least be what its owner would call 'rustic'; instead of which it might have been a residence in some suburb of, what he would call, the 'Metropolis'. Moreover, it was very closely and densely surrounded by the dreariest shrubberies.

Entering the house through a gloomy little porch, we arrived at about four o'clock and were given very strong tea in the small, dark, rather overcrowded 'parlour', of which my memory holds only a jumbled impression of blue Bristol glassware, bowls of potpourri and—sole characteristic item—a collection of large hour-glasses. If I remember rightly, a door out of this room opened into a curiously dismal little conservatory.

My diary tells of that evening at Max Gate, now over thirty years ago:

After tea at half-past four we sat talking till seven without being shown our rooms. Barrie began to look as pale and wan as I felt.

The household is dominated by the most despotic dog I've ever suffered under. To which, if any, breed 'Wessex' is supposed to belong is impossible to discern through the wild tousel of his unbrushed coat. He has, I gather, quite the longest biting-list of any domestic pet—Hardy told us with some pride that the thrice-bitten postman had refused to deliver any more letters at the house!

Wessex very uninhibited throughout dinner, which he spent not under, but on, the table, walking about quite unchecked, and contesting with me every forkful of food on its way from plate to mouth. Undistracted by the snarling and scrunching of his dog, Hardy, who exerts himself much more as a host than as a guest, talked more than I had yet heard him. The only thing he seems to take the least pride in is his descent from the Trafalgar Hardy, and he much resents the attempt to convert Nelson's last words from 'Kiss me, Hardy,' into 'Kismet, Hardy.'

At times Hardy was quietly caustic, particularly about a certain, what he called, 'Well-known Society Lady', who, though he has never met her, has just sent him a complete set of his works with the request that he should inscribe each volume 'To So-and-So from her friend Thomas Hardy!'

The question was asked which, if any, living author would be known in five hundred years from now; 'Someone whose name we have never heard,' quickly answered Hardy.

While Hardy and Barrie sat on in the dining-room, I had some talk with Mrs Hardy. 'Florence' is no prettier than the house, but extremely nice. She obviously adores her husband, and seems very good at what can't be—she looks very strained —an easy job. She naturally feels responsible for Hardy's health, and his refusal to see a doctor makes things difficult. I had supposed Barrie to be exaggerating when he talked in the train of Hardy's posthumous canonisation of his first wife, but Florence told me a little wearily, if unresentfully, that only the other day her husband had made her walk six miles to show her a seat on which he used to sit with her predecessor during his courtship of her! Poor Florence! I wondered, but didn't like to ask, whether Hardy keeps her up-to-date as to the shifting relative adjacency to him after death of his two wives.

Later in the evening Hardy read us some poems by Charlotte Mew—heart-rending name for a poet!—for whom he has a great admiration. The reading had a temporarily repressive effect on Wessex. He flopped on to the floor, and subsided into silence, until conversation was resumed, when he again took the centre of the stage. We sat up till close on midnight—a delightful evening.

On arrival, the commonplaceness of the house had struck me as strange, but how utterly unimportant this soon seemed! Perhaps immediate surroundings don't much matter to those who have 'vision'.

Hardy's indifference to the visible comes, no doubt, from his being so grandly independent of reality; vide a passage I've just re-read in *Tess of the Durbervilles*. 'Trees became attached to fantastic scenes *outside Reality*, and the occasional heave of the wind became a sigh of some immense sad-souled Being conterminous with the Universe in Space, and with History in Time.'

I've found Hardy much more impressive than I did in London. His eyes are so unflinching and the expression in them, however sad—and it is very sad—suggests that he has arrived at a certain serenity. Yes, it looks as if the President of the Immortals had finished his sport with Thomas Hardy. . .

Next morning Hardy came down very spry—positively garrulous—to breakfast, after which he took us upstairs to see the small 'study' where he writes. This, bare, simple, workmanlike and pleasantly shabby, was the only room in the house that had any character at all. I can't remember many details. The well-faded walls were distempered an unusual shade of coral-pink. Several tin deed-boxes, piled one on top of the other, stood under the very plain, exceedingly neat writing-table in the middle of the room; a framed 'wage-sheet' —Hardy's father's or grandfather's, I forget which—on the shelf over the fireplace. I can't remember a single photograph, nor I think were there any pictures, but Hardy's old violin hung on the wall above the book-shelves which faced the window.

Soon after breakfast, Hardy took Barrie and me for a long walk. At over eighty he still had the stride and the figure of a young man—we could scarcely keep up with him—and when he came to a hill he quickened his pace. We went to see the churchyard where the Dorsetshire poet Barnes is buried, and then to Hardy's native village, Higher Bockhampton. He pointed out the cottage in which he had been born, a genuine cottage, but compared with that, with 'but and ben', in which Barrie was born twenty years after, a commodious dwelling. The cottage was locked. This led to an incident for ever graven on my mind. Barrie, refusing to be thwarted in his intention to enter the hallowed precincts, made me hold together two decayed ladders while, treading on my fingers, he precariously clambered up to the window and contrived to open it. He scrambled through, and shortly afterwards, with a bow, opened the door to Hardy, who, returning the bow, re-entered the home in which, eighty-one years ago, he had first cried because—to quote words so much after his own heart —he had 'come to this great stage of fools'.

The 'famous dog Wessex', as his doting master described him on his tombstone, accompanied us on our walk. Wessex, like most dogs, had a habit of pelting on ahead and turning round at intervals as though in sudden misgiving, to look back at his master with an anxious, wistful, questioning expression.

Hardy spoke at the time of that enquiring, almost apprehensive look in a dog's eyes, and a few years later wrote of it in some verses he gave me to publish in *The Flying Carpet*, a book I edited for children—verses with their touch of deliberate uncouthness—peculiarly his own:

> I live here: 'Wessex' is my name,
> I am a dog known rather well:
> I guard the house; but how that came
> To be my lot I cannot tell.
>
> With a leap and a heart elate I go,
> At the end of an hour's expectancy,
> To take a walk of a mile or so,
> With the folk who share the house with me.
>
> Along the path, amid the grass
> I sniff, and find out rarest smells
> For rolling over as I pass
> The open fields towards the dells.
>
> No doubt I shall always cross this sill
> And turn the corner, and stand steady,
> Gazing back for my master till
> He reaches where I have run already,
>
> And that this meadow with its brook,
> And bulrush, just as it appears
> As I plunge past with hasty look
> Will stay the same a thousand years.
>
> Thus 'Wessex'. Yet a dubious ray
> At times informs his steadfast eye
> Just for a trice, as though to say:
> 'Will these things, after all, go by?'

(4)

If Hardy did not wear his Muse upon his sleeve, scarcely anyone could have failed to guess Sir Douglas Shields' vocation. Alert, compelling, steely-eyed, with those square tips to his fingers and that look of being aseptic, he was the very stage convention of a surgeon. I always picture him in his white linen coat—almost in his 'theatre mask'. Barrie and Sir Douglas didn't appear to have many shared interests, but they were great friends and suited one another remarkably well. Shields seemed to have a bracing effect on Barrie—to set him up like strong air. In matters of health, Barrie, without attempting to understand Shields' theories and dissertations, had so much confidence in his judgment that he several times consented to go for treatment into Shields' Nursing Home, 17 Park Lane. He was even once persuaded to go to Cannes, where Shields was building a hospital, but despite the sunshine, and all the luxury and attention lavished upon him, such was Barrie's longing to return to London that his stay on the Riviera proved one of the several experiences he was able to enjoy only in retrospect, in the golden haze of which many dark ordeals became bright memories.

(5)

Of Barrie's women friends, Elizabeth Lucas—E. V.'s wife— plays far the leading part in my memories of the flat, but 'Mister C. Greene' was quite an old hand at his job before I met her, for she was away in France, where, for some time after the Armistice, she stayed on in charge of the children's hospital set up and financed by Barrie, in the Chateau de Bettancourt on the Marne. This was the hospital Barrie described in *The Princess Elizabeth Gift Book*, edited by Eileen Bigland and me, to raise funds for another hospital, the Princess Elizabeth of York's Hospital for Children. Barrie's contribution was a letter addressed to our present Queen, then nine years old:

Our hospital started with eight beds, but in a few months there were nearly a hundred, though I daresay the inhabitants of your hospital would not have called them beds. . . . The procedure, you see, was to begin constructing another bed, woodwork and all, when another stretcher was seen coming down the avenue. . . . It was a hospital for French children wounded

by bombs, and many of them had lost a leg or an arm. . . . They invented
games of their own in which to have a limb missing was a help rather than
a hindrance, and I taught them cricket with rules never conceived by the
M.C.C. in which the bat was a crutch and the ball was made out of lint
purloined from the medical stores.

I took an instant liking to Elizabeth Lucas when, one evening
shortly after her return from her work in France, we both
dined with Barrie at the flat, and she soon became one of my
greatest friends. Subtle, sympathetic, quick-minded, she could
be, as occasion needed, delightfully ribald or delicately ironic.
I remember Charles Whibley saying she was one of the only
three women he knew who was equipped with a sense of irony.
He, and several other men, remarked too on her possession of
another faculty then also rare in women. Besides her quick,
sure taste in furniture and decoration—at one time profession-
ally exercised—and her skill in gardening and in cooking, she
had, they acknowledged with surprise, a palate, and a very
well-trained palate, for wine.

As well as being such good company Elizabeth Lucas was
a great help to me in many ways. She had been a close friend
of Barrie's for many years, so to talk to her about him was like
meeting someone who had read the first volume of a book I had
been obliged to begin in the second volume. She could supply
so many missing clues. Knowing all the *Dramatis Personae* of
Barrie's life, she understood everyone's crochets, quirks, kinks,
and foibles, and thus was an invaluable ally whenever Barrie
was troubled in mind, body or estate; or if either he, or someone
near to him, was being 'difficult'. As she was devoted to Barrie,
I could, without any sense of disloyalty or fear of misinterpretation, freely discuss him and his affairs with her. Indeed, when
a crisis arose, he would often encourage us to hold a consulta-
tion, like two doctors or family solicitors. If Elizabeth was
about I could always be sure—inestimable blessing—of a kindly
twinkling eye to catch, an eye sympathetic, however much
amused; amused, however much distressed. She was devotedly,
yet discerningly, fond of Barrie—to me a great recommendation

—for, as I think I've already said, I suffered from his tendency to inspire either utterly blind infatuation or purblind prejudice. Moreover, however sad Elizabeth might be, and her life was full of sadness, she was a great exponent of an art which never failed to stir Barrie's admiration—the art of being able to appear bright when she couldn't possibly be feeling it.

(6)

Sister Thomlinson was another friend and ally in the flat whom I remember with great gratitude. A wonderfully skilled nurse, she had inexhaustible patience, and so remarkable a capacity to give out strength that people instinctively leant on her. She was also great fun. Sister Thomlinson first came into my life when she nursed my husband through a long and very serious illness. After this, whenever Barrie fell ill, I would rush to the telephone to try to secure her. Kind but bracing, neither severe nor 'soppy', Sister Thomlinson gave equally wide berth to both the extremes to which many admirable members of her profession are prone. She addressed her patient neither as if he were a malefactor nor as if he were a backward child. She did not confer nicknames on portions of the body. She never used the editorial 'We'—'Have we had a good night?' 'Are we going to make a good dinner?' Nor was it—and this is unusual —a disappointment to see her for the first time in mufti instead of in uniform. Barrie took to this rare nurse at once. Sensitive to his moods, but never 'downed' by them, 'Mildred', as she soon became, suited him admirably and he came greatly to rely on her. The only trait he didn't wholly approve was her sharing my addiction to 'cross-purposes'—as in wilful ignorance he miscalled crosswords—in which he thought we became at times too much absorbed to give sufficient attention to our patient.

Often as Sister Thomlinson benefited Barrie, I don't think she ever did him more good than when, while he was con-valescing at Margate, she fell ill herself with tonsilitis, where-

upon the patient resurrected and looked after his nurse; a
reversal of roles which completely cured him and also put a
feather in his cap—'I have a wonderful professional nurse,' he
wrote, 'who hies to me when I am low, and the last time she
got bowled over far more than myself, and I rose to nurse her
and felt gloriously happy at being of some use again.'

(7)

The member of Barrie's family whom I knew best and liked
most was his delightful niece, Lilian, the shrewd sterling
daughter of his elder brother, Alexander Barrie, the very able
school-inspector, who had helped him so much over his education. Lilian, a redoubtable mathematician, had adopted her
father's profession of teaching with great success. I remember
how struck I was at first sight by the almost shining commonsense in Lilian Barrie's humorous eyes, and by a certain in-
domitable look as if nothing on earth could daunt or tire her.

Lilian, who often came to stay in the Adelphi flat, had twice
provided her uncle—to whose writer's mill all was grist—with
excellent 'copy'. Her first birthday had inspired the first
chapter of *My Lady Nicotine*, and when in 1924 she prevailed
upon him to address the pupils of Wallasey High School for
Girls, of which she was then headmistress, she had to pay for
this favour by being made the subject of the bantering passages
in her uncle's speech.

However gratifying the occasion, it can't have been easy
for a headmistress to know what expression to wear while her
uncle spoke of her in the following vein to her doubtless gog-
gling pupils:

'I can recall her when she was much smaller than any of you,
and it is with a queer mixture of emotion and awe that I see
her now sitting there, as cool as you like, the head of a great
school, and with an air of never having been anything else. We
could get a moral for you by pretending that she had from the
earliest years been this majestic spectacle. But no, I remember

particularly one day when she was about a year old, and wearing one of those white bonnets then so fashionable. The scene was a pleasant Scottish town, and a great man was passing at the end of our road. So I whipped up our heroine in my arms and ran with her to the gate that she might be able to say in after years that she had once seen Thomas Carlyle. . . . I hoped he would bless your Miss Barrie that day, and perhaps he did, but it didn't sound like that. In any case it is interesting to know that they once met. When Miss Barrie's biography comes to be written by one of you girls, don't forget to say that this was one of the turning-points of her life, and that from this moment she put away frivolous things, and plucked triangles instead of daisies. I expect Carlyle had pointed with his staff at Wallasey.'

Before Lilian had had time to compose her crimsoned face, Barrie announced that he would like to set the girls an examination paper on their headmistress. His first question was: 'Is her intimacy with the Differential Calculus quite seemly?'

It wasn't until, after Barrie's death, I was in Kirriemuir with Lilian that I ever had much opportunity to enjoy talking to her alone, or realised the depth and discernment of her affection for her uncle. A few days after his funeral she sent me some lines she had written in the place of his birth and his burial.

J. M. B.

With loving care we bear you to your hill,
Grieving we lay you with your own loved dead.
But now—behold once more your mocking power!
Against your standing stone I see you lean
Fondling your pipe;
You smile your slow sardonic smile;
Your eyebrow lifts, without a word
You fill my heart,
And by the grave
I laugh with you.

(8)

When Barrie went to St. Andrews to deliver his Rectorial Address an instant liking sprang into being between him and his host, Sir James Irvine, the shrewd, kindly Principal of the University. This liking deepened into a lasting friendship, and from time to time when business brought the much occupied Principal to London he would stay at Adelphi Terrace. Among my most vivid memories of the flat is a Conversation Piece picture of the two Scottish Sir James's happily locked in talk. The guest, an ardent talker, is perched on the world's most uncomfortable seat—that narrow wooden settle; the host, contentedly smoking, curled up on the world's second most uncomfortable seat—that small leather couch.

If Sir James Irvine, who positively glowed with charm, sympathy and eagerness, was more immediately forthcoming than is usual with his countrymen, he was yet somehow as Scottish as peat. Of his many lovable traits perhaps the most endearing to his London host was that passionate delight in hard work that never failed to enchant Barrie. To the best of my belief, Barrie took little or no interest in his friend's subject, which was Chemistry. No matter! Whatsoever excited it, he loved keenness.

In *Courage*, Barrie described their Principal to the students of St. Andrews as 'one happy in that, like Carlyle, all his life he was grinding at the job he revelled in'. True. Yet 'grind' as Sir James Irvine might at his 'job', no fervour of specialisation could ever narrow his interests and sympathies. To the end of a dedicated life he remained the most responsive, the most companionable of men.

(9)

Barrie's relationship to a very different kind of Scotsman, the Kirriemuir ironmonger, James Robb, was a good example of that rarely successful thing—a resuscitated friendship based on shared memories. It was in 1928, when the funeral of Barrie's sister-in-law took him up to Kirriemuir, that after a very long interval, the two men met again where as boys they had been playfellows. Over sixty years ago they had acted together in the little 'Washhouse' now known as 'Barrie's First Theatre'; they had walked over the hills; they had fished in the river; they had played at Red Indians in the woods, and Robb still bore on his rugged face the scar inflicted when Barrie had cut his upper lip open with a spade. The two old Kirriemuirians, one of whom, on a road of his own making, had travelled so far from his native place, talked and talked of the past, and many memories were disinterred. Robb reminded Barrie of the special whistle with which as boys they used to signal to one another in Caddam Wood, and this whistle—more grist to that thrifty mill!—was snapped up to be used between David and Jonathan in *The Boy David*. He reminded Barrie, too, of how when they were four they had been told there was a chance of seeing an old man who had committed suicide, and of how fast this news had made them both run.

Robb, to commemorate this renewed friendship, gave Barrie a very attractive canary, named after his giver. Robb the Second became remarkably tame. He would fly about the dining-room of the flat and amuse his master by his habit of alighting on the heads of guests, some of whom were gratified, others excruciated, by being treated as perches.

James Robb came more than once to stay with Barrie in London. After so long a break in their relationship and with such widely different lives behind them, the talk between these two old cronies must, one supposes, have been almost entirely of the 'Do you remember?' kind. Nevertheless, this revived friendship gave no impression of being kept going by artificial respiration. Robb had made his re-entry just at the right moment. Almost, for Barrie the wheel had come full circle, and his old playfellow brought the past back to him, for his imagination to refashion.

(10)

The last figure in my frieze of Adelphi Terrace friends is Charles Turley Smith, a man, to whom, throughout a friendship of nearly forty years, Barrie showed so many different facets of himself. I don't know how to convey the charm 'Turley', as he was always called, had for his friends. Here are a few facts —how little facts tell!—of his life. For years he reviewed a hundred or so books annually for *Punch*; he was an admirable 'coach'; a publisher's reader, and the author of various books, the most successful of which *Godfrey Marten, Schoolboy*, was pronounced by *The Times* critic and others the best book about school ever written. The man himself? He was gentle, unassuming, humorous; he gave an impression of natural inevitable goodness. But what I think I remember best about him is the attractive way his weather-beaten, plain but delightful face, permanently deeply seamed by laughter though it was, broke into a myriad new crinkles whenever he smiled. Turley plays so important a part in the Adelphi Terrace picture, and my own acquaintance with him was slight; so to give an idea of what he was like, I'll quote from a description written by Audrey Lucas, daughter of 'E.V.' and Elizabeth, who had known Turley from her childhood. She always remembered him as 'our favourite visitor' of the many who used to come to stay in her parents' home in Sussex.

'It was not only with me' she wrote, 'that this visitor was a favourite. My father and mother both loved him; and he was, for all his unobtrusiveness a potent bait for other guests; in hostesses' language a "lion" whose particular brand of fame defied fashion; for while superficial enthusiasm might change, nobody, not even the most hypercritical week-end visitor, ever wearied of Turley's courtesy, his gentleness of heart, and that humour, dry, but always kind, which would suddenly, softly and when least expected, hit one between the eyes.... The servants loved Turley too, expressing their esteem in that sound phrase, now so stupidly in disrepute, "he's a real gentleman", and when he walked down our village street people came beaming out from their cottages to shake his hand and enquire after his health. And it was the same wherever he went. Why? I don't know exactly; except that, while many of us contrive, by putting in some pretty hard work on it, to be loved, Turley realised this ambition without any effort whatever. Only, it wasn't with him an ambition at all. He didn't set out to be loved. He grasped at nothing, friendship least of all; yet it is true to say that he was all through his quiet life surrounded by friends who would, given the very smallest encouragement, have sold their shirts, their souls, even, for his sake. It is equally true to say that this encouragement was never once forthcoming. . . . I have stopped for a moment to read over what I have written and I find that I have hardly told you anything about Turley. I have also, after this pause, come to the conclusion that there isn't, just because he was the kind of person he was, anything really to tell. But I can sum him up a little more clearly and suggest this comparison. A dramatist will sometimes fit into his play a character who forms, by deliberate intent, and set against the other characters, a point of rest, a personality who stands entirely though never unsympathetically outside the turmoil, farcial or emotional, in which the rest of the *Dramatis Personae* are involved; someone whose appearances on the stage gives the audience breathing space; a check from too much laughter, a relief from too many tears. Shaped by a good craftsman, this part is neither negative nor dull; its dominant quality is quietude; its duty to pour, either by gentle commonsense or placid irrelevancy, oil on these troubled waters forming the plot. If, then, one may take life in general and the lives of his friends in particular, as a perpetual play, this part, this point of rest, was the one for which Turley, by that God in whom I believed so devoutly, had been cast. While he possessed, I know, quite apart from persistent ill-health, no few griefs of his own, these belonged to another, a strictly private play in which he held by preference the stage alone. In the too rapidly moving lives of his friends his performance was a different one, of extreme value to them, however recessive. Against agitation and distress he had a magic touch; yet, oddly enough, once a trouble had been brought to him there was at once very much less urgency to speak about it. Merely to be with Turley was to feel pain and confusion slipping from one's mind. One had reached the "point of rest".'

I don't think there was any man Barrie liked better to be with than that 'point of rest', Turley. Each seemed to kindle the other's wit and charm. Most relationships have to be paid for in some way, but the long upkeep of this friendship cost neither anything in strain, worry or vexation. As I have said, Barrie's nervous system, as well as his work, prevented him from being always glad to see even those he was most fond of; but in all the twenty years I was his secretary I remember no single occasion when a visit from Turley was not welcome.

Turley, though the most affectionate of men, was, like Barrie, elusive—could, and did, at times disappear from all his friends. ('I'm as lonely as the cry of a plover,' he wrote in a letter to his friend Eleanor Adlard, and this I'm sure was no complaint.) This quality prevented him from ever being a demanding or possessive friend.

The much appreciated fact that from time to time Barrie unlocked to him the doors of his heart, never made him desire, still less demand, permanent possession of a key. Content with intermittent intimacy, each friend respected the other's reticences; neither ever attempted to overdraw on the other's affection or to convert a deposit into a current account.

Letters were exchanged nearly each week. Barrie kept practically no letters from anyone, but Turley cherished every scrap of paper inscribed with Barrie's spidery handwriting. All give the same impression of complete ease.

The friendship between Barrie and Turley was cemented by

many shared interests. The most continuous was cricket. It was this game which first brought them together in the 1890's, when Barrie was captaining his team of cricketing authors— or writing cricketers—called the *Allahakbarries*. Turley loved to make Barrie tell how these once famous *Allahakbarries* had come into being. I remember how delighted the Australian cricketers were by this story. Here is the gist of what Barrie told them. In his early days in London he used often to go with two or three friends for very long walks into Surrey, and one day while they were visiting the lovely village of Shere they talked so much cricket that the ambition to play the game themselves seized them. This ambition was encouraged by the elderly appearance of the Shere Eleven, whom they decided to challenge after letting them grow one year older still. When the day fixed for the first match arrived, Barrie, who had been elected captain, discovered in the railway carriage by which the team travelled to Shere that he must instruct more than one of his players in the rudiments of the theory of cricket. As far as was feasible he also coached them in the practice of the game in the train. While a name for the new team was being discussed Barrie asked one member of his Eleven, the explorer, Joseph Thompson of Maisailand, what was the African for 'Heaven help us' and was told it was 'Allah hak bar'. So, the team decided to call themselves the *Allahhakbars*, a name later changed to the *Allahakbarries* in compliment to the captain. Before play opened, Barrie rashly allowed some bowling practice, and Bernard Partridge sent down a ball which loosened two teeth in the head of the prospective wicket-keeper and put him out of action. Barrie won the toss, to the dismay of his team, until it was explained to them that this did not necessitate their going in first. Instead, he took the field to give his team some opportunity to pick up the general idea of the game. Unfortunately, Shere had a left-handed batsman who was a mighty hitter, which entailed many changes in the field besides those ordered by the umpires. The novices became so hopelessly confused about 'overs' that some of them began to doubt their captain's grasp of the rules. Shere made a large score and, as Barrie said, 'Partridge could do nothing to the teeth of any of the Shere Eleven.' At last, however, they were out, and the once impatiently awaited time arrived for the *Allahakbarries* to go in.

'But', as Barrie has told in *The Greenwood Hat*, 'there was no longer a thirsty desire on the part of any one member to open the innings, but in its place a passionate determination that this honour should be the captain's. I forget whether he yielded to the general wish, but at all events he ordered Marriott Watson to be No. 2, because all the time they were in the train, when others trembled, Marriott had kept saying gamely, "Intellect always tells in the end." For a lovely moment we thought it was to tell here, for Marriott Watson hit his first ball so hard that the *Allahakbarries* were at the beginning of a volley of cheers when they saw him coming out, caught at point by the curate. The captain amassed two. One man who partnered him before taking centre (as they were all instructed to do) signed to me that he had a secret to confide. It proved to be "Should I strike the ball to however small an extent, I shall run with considerable velocity." He did not have to run. The top scorer (as he tells to this day) was Gilmour, who swears he made five. The total was eleven.'

The next time the *Allahakbarries* played Shere, they won because they arrived two men short. They scoured the country in a wagonette to find some extra players, and carried off, despite his protests, an artist whom they found in a field, painting cows. They were still more fortunate in finding a soldier sitting with two ladies outside a pub. He, too, agreed to play for them provided they would also take the ladies in the wagonette, so all three were taken. That unknown soldier won the day for the *Allahakbarries*, and in their last glimpse of him after this famous victory he was sitting outside the same pub with another two ladies.

Shortly after the first match at Shere Barrie brought his Eleven to play against the famously beautiful Worcestershire village of Broadway, and this was where he first met Turley, who, alternately with Monsieur de Navarro, captained the Broadway team. Turley and Barrie sat beside one another at the supper party, given by the American artist Frank Millet, at which the captain of the *Allahakbarries* presented his Eleven with their colours, declaring that they had been selected to play either because he 'liked their wives or because of the oddity of their pairr-son-al appearance'.

The Broadway cricket match was played year after year; each *Allahakbarrie*, according to their captain, being mainly preoccupied by two ambitions—to avoid any painful contact with the ball, and to escape making a double duck.

The hostess at these gatherings was Madame de Navarro, before her marriage the actress Mary Anderson, world-famous for her beauty. With the proverbial animosity of the non-combatant, Madame de Navarro displayed much the fiercest will to win; but despite deep study, she could never learn to follow the game, which, until stumps were drawn for the last time, she still persisted in calling 'Crickets'. Each match she watched, it struck her anew as most unfair that eleven men should play against only two! But whether the *Allahakbarries* were fielding in such brutal force as it seemed to her, or bravely batting against fearful odds, her thumbs were always implacably down for their defeat. Nor were her methods always scrupulous. 'She had,' fondly complained Barrie, 'a way of wandering round the field in the interval with my best batsman, who when his stroll was over would sheepishly tell me that he had promised to play for Broadway in the second innings.'

No matter how irretrievably lost a game of 'Crickets', Madame de Navarro would never accept defeat. Told by Barrie, in a one-innings match, that she need watch no more because his side had already passed the Broadway score, she retorted hopefully, 'Yes, but you still have several more men to go in!'

At the end of one cricket season, which year I know not, the

Allahakbarries drew stumps never to play again. But this melancholy milestone made no difference to Barrie's and Turley's shared interest in the game. County cricket was followed and discussed with breathless concern, and when a Test Match loomed the self-appointed committee of two deliberated far into the night. Weighing the merits of any possible player, Barrie and Turley made a minute analysis of each candidate's form, considering not only his achievement and style as a cricketer but also his moral qualities, charm, manners and tact. While a Test Match was being played, Barrie would send telegrams as long as letters to Turley, so that he should know the worst, or the best, long before the news could reach his distant Cornish home. A bundle of these Test Match telegrams, found among Turley's papers, give detailed bulletins on the changing situation—the number of runs scored, wickets fallen, players injured, records broken—and the facts are interlarded with comments; 'Dreadful delay. Fielding superb. So-and-So in good health. So-and-So hurriedly learning to bowl.'

I can picture both the sending-off and the arrival of these dramatic telegrams: Barrie in the luncheon interval or at close-of-play, diving into a Post Office to growl over the crossed nibs and broken pencils that impede his haste; Turley on the threshold of his cottage, agog to snatch the orange envelope from the hands of the panting boy who has run all the way from the post office shouting its contents through the open door of every dwelling he passed.

Some time in the twenties a sudden misgiving seized the Londoner. These infernal inventions! Had the latest miracle of science linked up Cornwall with Lords? 'Do you get wireless news now, or can I still have the fun of telegraphing?' wrote Barrie, and Turley, being a truthful man, had to give an answer that left Barrie with a grudge against broadcasting which I don't think he ever quite lost. No more telegrams! Letters, however, still carried on a copious running commentary.

'A. was just a stick shoving the balls. . . . B. had no gaiety; he played like a true master of the game, though, and his playing made all others seem clodpoles. They seemed nearly all to be paralysed. C.'s catch was like a line of poetry. D.'s performance made me shiver. The only kindly thing was to look the other way until he was out. I would play E. again because he looked so happy, was grinning all through his innings, and roared with glee when Gregory hit him in the thigh.'

The slowness of the Test Matches of the day is deplored:

'Many thanks for Wisden which I digest as of old. I don't digest the Test Cricket quite so easily though. You will find about the end of the week that Hobbs and Jardine are in again, and towards the end of the month Woodfull will be setting out on another gay adventure. I don't know what is to be done about it. It isn't the fault of the performers.'

Golf, though never for one second regarded as a serious rival to cricket, receives an occasional mention. 'I don't follow golf much,' Barrie wrote, 'but we seem to have made a melancholy show. Perhaps we ought to be too proud to play. Or is it enough to be too proud to win?'

Turley was one of the few friends with a standing invitation to stay in Barrie's flat and, loath as he was to leave his beloved Cornwall for any other purpose, he seldom failed to come twice a year. At each visit the great serial contest on the 'dambrod' (to those born south of the Tweed, the draught-board) would be resumed, the players tossing up with a postage stamp as to who should have first move, because it was 'slower in coming down, thus adding to the suspense'. The draught-board usually resided on a shelf high out of reach of Mrs Stanley's duster: 'The dambrod,' wrote Barrie to his newly departed guest, 'is now returned to its shelf, where it gathers dust between your visits, no one else ever daring to challenge me.'

A day or two before Turley's arrival the board would be taken down and dusted in preparation for the impending contest.

'I think you had black last,' wrote Barrie in a letter welcoming his friend. 'Am oiling the draughts.'

One critic amused Barrie by writing of Turley as 'a Jane Austen in trousers'. I can't say that his lamentably laconic diary in any way reminds me of Jane Austen. It is tantalising to be told that Henry Irving was 'very amusing when he came to luncheon,' yet to be given no hint of what he said or did to amuse. We read that, when A. P. Herbert came to luncheon, 'we laughed and laughed'. I can well believe it, but would like to be given a chance to laugh myself. We are constantly told that someone was witty, but are never told what was said. It is the same with feminine charm. Even when Turley sits besides such sirens as the spectacularly beautiful Ethel Barrymore or Maud Adams, the actress who had created all the Barrie parts in America, he merely states, 'I liked her very much.' He doesn't say why he liked her, let alone describe what she wore. Turley tends to be somewhat more communicative when a meeting with Barrie had been, as he always preferred it to be, *tête-à-tête*. Besides the recurrent 'Barrie in marvellous form' he sometimes mentions what subjects were discussed, now and again gives a fragment of talk—'Dined alone with Barrie at the flat. Most pleasant and interesting, for he told me the whole of the new play (*Dear Brutus*) which he is writing.'

'Jimmy in the exuberance of his imagination has just written a play in three weeks.'

'Talking of *The Admirable Crichton*, Barrie told me crowds of people left the theatre in New York at seeing a star-actor like Gillette play the part of a butler!'

'Barrie said that as far as he can make out his new play is an exceedingly dull one. I wish *I* could write "dull" plays!'

'Barrie says it is a good thing to take out anything one has written in italics.'

'Talking of the youngest Davies boy,' Barrie said, 'painful news. Nico goes into "tails" tomorrow. I begged him to go into one at a time so that I might get used to the idea.'

For all Turley's reticence, his diary and letters do frequently break out in praise—'Soon after we first met, I liked Barrie as much as possible, but as I know him better I admire him more and more.'

And many years later:

'Barrie from first to last, in good times and not so good, has never varied in his friendship, and nothing better than that friendship could be imagined.'

From these tributes it appears that Turley never suffered from those changes of 'weather', which some of Barrie's less unfailingly understanding friends found so trying.

As old age approached, bodily ailments created new ties of sympathy. A friendly rivalry arose between two mighty coughers, and letters, full of solicitude for the delinquencies of one another's bronchial tubes, contain curious bulletins. 'I'm pretty well myself,' writes Barrie, 'and according to my doctor, my nose has done some surprisingly neat thing in connivance with my throat that almost entitles me to favourable mention in the *Lancet*. What it is I don't know, but I am, of course, rather proud.'

There are even references to a troublesome 'extra rib' of Turley's. This unusual affliction necessitated wearing a plaster. Writing to condole, Barrie determined not to be outdone, boasted 'I too was "plastered" years ago when at a dress rehearsal at the Haymarket the gangway I was sitting on gave way and I fell into the orchestra. I had to lie there for a bit and I heard the reporter say indignantly to the Management, "What, no blood?" . . . I suppose they do know things from X-rays, but my throat was once done and I used with complete success to show the photograph as a scene in the Alps.'

Barrie left no diary—by no stretch of the imagination could I imagine him keeping one!—but his letters often express admiration for Turley's qualities as well as enjoyment of his company, and I can testify that these tributes were never, as perhaps were certain passages in his more literary letters, overstatements made in contrition for some real or supposed shortcoming. They were spontaneous outbursts of approval.

Turley, most modest of men, being given to despondency, gave Barrie plenty of scope for one function of friendship in which he had special skill—encouragement. 'And so you were fifty yesterday and knew so little of yourself you feel you have lived so long and done so little. I have known many men, but very few who in my opinion have done so well with their half-century. You have helped others more than anyone I know and there are hosts who bless your name. In fact you are probably Number 1 of the Smiths.'

Barrie's letters to Turley tell little of his own life—only occasional characteristic snatches of autobiography such as, 'Peter Pan is rather bleached bones to me in these twilight days.'

'Yes, I had to go to Buckingham Palace and in *knee-breeches* (closed car and sneaked to and fro like a burglar). My stockings misbehaved and creased like a concertina.'

'I have no skill in stockings,' wrote Barrie to another correspondent. 'Lady Cynthia is looking forward to my having to wear them, but this flat will be denied to her that day.'

In one respect only was Turley a frustrating friend. Barrie liked sometimes to play the part of Providence in the lives of those he was fond of. Now and again his affection, bubbling over like lava, would overflow in a spate of bounty. But Turley had no use whatever for a fairy godfather, and much as Barrie would have liked to supplement his friend's meagre income it was impossible to help him in any pecuniary way. No one respected this sturdy independence more than Barrie, who from earliest manhood had supported himself and others; still he did wish he could break down Turley's resistance, and we often racked our brains to devise a way. When I suggested that money in notes should be sent anonymously, a device to which Barrie had in other difficult cases resorted, he mournfully replied that he had already ascertained that any such offering to Turley would immediately be passed on to some charity organisation. Even such a present as a hamper of good things to eat and drink was liable to be condemned as 'charity' and refused. If the following letter proves that this embargo could be broken down, it also shows how carefully such a gift had to be edited:

Adelphi Terrace,
Strand, W.C.2.

19 Oct. '36

My dear Charley,

Committee formed here to make you vigorous again as quickly as possible. Members present: J.M.B., Mrs Stanley (housekeeper), Frank Thurston. Moved, seconded and agreed unanimously that a member be sent at once to Fortnum and Mason. After motion by Mrs Stanley stating that she was the one for the job, especially good at bachelors, proposed by J.M.B., seconded by Frank Thurston, that she be the member; she sets forth in her black merino in an hour and Fortnum and Mason will doubtless do the rest.

signed

J.M.B., F.T., & M.S.

Whatever Turley's shortcomings as a beneficiary, he had no objection to being helped and encouraged in his writing. In this respect he gave full rein to Barrie, who could be as generous with time and trouble as with money. 'Barrie tells me to send him my MS. for which I am most grateful, as I am worried about the book' . . . 'hugely kind letter from Barrie with most careful and useful suggestions and comments.'

Nor was it only with advice and criticism that Barrie furthered Turley's literary career. By introducing him to Captain Scott he put him into the way of being commissioned to write the *Voyages of Captain Scott*, and this book led to two others about explorers, *Nansen of Norway* and *Roald Amundsen, Explorer*.

Both Barrie and Turley enjoyed the not common good fortune of having made their home in the one place in all the world where they most liked to be, and neither could bear to be long away from his own prized outlook; the one on to the grey green of the Thames; the other on to the deep blue of the Cornish sea. Each, I can't doubt, secretly pitied the other for living where he did. The countryman did his best for the Londoner who was seldom out of his thoughts. Year after year Turley's early Cornish flowers brought the spring to Adelphi Terrace.

To the last the periodical visits to the flat were paid. Very near the end Turley wrote in his diary, 'Dined with Barrie and it was just the same as it has been for so long, and couldn't be better.'

And, on that day when a telegram from Adelphi Terrace brought Turley the much dreaded news, he wrote, 'everything tonight is out of focus. I can't imagine a world without the friend who has never varied with me for forty years.'

Amongst Turley's letters was found one from Thurston who, knowing how greatly, had the order of their deaths been reversed, his master would have missed Turley, was able to gauge the survivor's loss: 'I hope you do not miss too sadly your interchange of letters with Sir James. The early spring flowers of Cornwall will soon be in bloom again, but no more the gathering and posting to your old friend's study. Some of the books are being offered for sale next week, and so the scattering goes on.'

In this letter, Thurston, anxious to convey to Turley a last tribute from the friend who could no longer speak for himself, and not afraid to use a word—as Audrey Lucas wrote, 'now so stupidly in disrepute'—added the postscript; 'Sir James always spoke of you as the most lovable of English gentlemen.'

CHAPTER X

BARRIE AT STANWAY

BARRIE's Adelphi flat was so strongly imbued with his personality—it seemed his very shell—that at first I found it hard
to picture him in any other setting. As time went on, however,
I came, oddly enough, to associate him almost as closely with
a very different place—the Gloucestershire home of my own
childhood.

The neighbourhood had long been known to Barrie, for
Stanway is only five miles from Broadway, where he had so
often led the *Allahakbarries* to defeat. It wasn't, however, until
in 1921, when Barrie came to spend Easter with my parents
that he saw their home and fell in love at first sight, not only
with the gabled sixteenth-century house, but with its atmosphere which—remote, cloistered, yet somehow welcoming—
seemed, he said, at once to enfold him like a cloak.

Barrie—no great stickler for comfort, almost averse from
luxury—was delighted, too, by the lack of any interior grandeur
at Stanway. The restful shabbiness, dignified dilapidation of a
quite unmodernised, much lived-in family home exactly suited
him, as did the informal atmosphere my mother diffused around
her. Her everlasting random hospitality, and the curious con-
junctions this so often brought about, never failed to amuse him,
any more than did her recurrent 'furniture manias', or that
prevailing dog tyranny to which all comers had to submit.

'Everybody here except myself has a dog, or dogs,' wrote
Barrie on a Sunday, 'and every owner thereof takes me aside
to express their surprise at the way the other owners bring up
their dogs. I haven't been bitten yet, but I stay till *Tuesday*.'

132

On his second evening at Stanway Barrie was happily seized by a craze for what, henceforth, was to be his favourite indoor pastime, the medieval game of Shuffleboard or Shovelboard—originally Shoveboard—the great grandfather, I suppose, of Shove-ha'penny. Stanway possesses one of the few surviving genuine shovelboards, an oak table nearly eight yards long, marked at one end with two transverse lines. The game is played with ten brass disks. The player, standing at the unmarked end of the table, shoves off one disk at a time, his object being to send it gliding along the highly-polished length of the table to cross the first, and if possible, also the second line, but stop short of the shallow tray or 'gutter' attached to the opposite end of the table. Exactly how the Tudors scored I know not. This was our method. Disks lying in between the first and second line scored one point each; those in the narrow space (the bull's eye) between the second line and the fatal 'gutter', two; those too feebly despatched to reach even the first line, or so far overshooting the mark as to drop into the gutter, nought; those sent so much askew as to fall off the table, minus.

Shuffles, a very elusive game, requires besides the requisite eye and judgement a special knack of wrist and hand. This Barrie very soon acquired. In a day or two he became so skilful that he constantly scored doubles. However 'pretty' his adversary's disks might lie, none was safe until he had played his last shot. By challenging my father to play for large sums of money, Barrie managed temporarily to inspire with his own passion for the game that inveterate gambler, and so enjoyed many exultant hours at the long disused shovelboard. I heard it said that he looked younger and younger, and, in truth, with each disk sped on its triumphant way he did seem to throw off a year or two.

Stanway, to use an expression Barrie particularly disliked, 'grew upon' him. Smoking his inevitable pipe he would stand for minutes at a time contentedly gazing at the house which, he said, varied like a living face; or, on an impulse, he would wander into the Tithe barn and stare up at the great timber rafters of its roof. Often, too, he would climb the steep grass hill, called, after the obelisk perched on its summit, the *Pyramid*. From that height he would look down onto the golden house hundreds of feet below with its plumes of blue smoke curling up from the chimneys of the gabled roof and, rising behind that, the lovely line of the Malvern Hills.

Barrie loved, most of all, the great Oriel window with its scores of latticed panes, many of these turned by time to the green of deep sea water; others to so amber a hue that whatever the weather may be, to those inside the hall the strange light that filters through the glass gives the illusion of perpetual sunshine.

Years later, Barrie described this Oriel in *Farewell, Miss Julie Logan*; 'The great bow window is said by travelled persons to stand alone among windows, for it is twenty-eight feet in height, and more than half as wide. All who come to look at it count its little lozens, as we call the panes, which are to the number of two hundred and sixteen.'

Barrie's admiration seldom remained purely objective. Stanway soon kindled his imagination. The house, which had become a private residence at the Dissolution of the Monasteries, had before then been the summer residence of the Abbots of Tewkesbury. Barrie, told of this, was soon picturing jovial monks drawing fat trout out of the little chain of ponds on the estate. Moreover—a thought which gave him endless pleasure—Stanway was not far from Stratford-on-Avon. Doubtless, Shakespeare, wandering by, had often halted on this very piece of English earth! Before long, there were several special places near the house where—so Barrie was convinced —Shakespeare had lingered to immortal purpose. Here one deathless line had first come into his head, there another.

Unusually happy as Barrie was on this first visit to Stanway, it never for one moment crossed my mind that I should ever see him established there as tenant and host. But within a few months, this came about.

In May 1921 a terrible tragedy overtook Barrie—'soundless as an arrow of snow the arrow of anguish fell'. His adopted son, Michael Davies, an extremely gifted boy with unforgettable charm, while bathing with another undergraduate in Sandford Pool near Oxford, was drowned. Ever since Michael was a little boy Barrie had specially loved him. For many years now he had made him the chief object of his care, his hopes—his dreams. What his death dealt Barrie in shock and in sorrow cannot—should not—be told.

How was the inexorable future to be faced?—the immediate future? There was Nicholas, the youngest Davies boy, shattered, too, by his brother's death. Somewhere, somehow, his summer holidays must be got through. Barrie, in no condition to make plans, asked if I had anything to suggest. Dormant memories of schoolboy brothers and long-ago holidays stirred in my mind. Had not Stanway much to offer to distract and occupy an Etonian? Was not Nicholas a keen cricketer? Nor did I forget how unusually happy Barrie himself had been at Stanway. I suggested that my old home should be taken for August, when my parents would be in Scotland, and partly to my relief, partly to my alarm, Barrie jumped at this proposal, which hadn't been made without considerable misgiving, for never having seen Barrie in the country for more than four days at a stretch, I had no idea how such a life would suit him.

To my intense relief this venture at once proved a far greater success than I had dared expect. Barrie, as I had hoped he might, took up the challenge of young children to amuse and to charm; the atmosphere of Stanway reasserted its spell over him, and to my delight I found that he whom in London I associated only with a rather perfunctorily-taken constitutional shared my own love for walking and thought nothing of trudging several miles over the hills.

Barrie, as I expected, invited to stay with him at Stanway his sister, her husband and the Davies family; and rather to my surprise he asked various other people as well. Charles Whibley, E. V. Lucas, Lady Guendolen Osborne and my sister-in-law Violet Bonham Carter came; also—unforgettably for this, alas, was to be his last summer—'The Professor', with his wife Lady Raleigh, and their daughter Phillippa. Besides these guests, all of whom I knew, there were two strangers to me, both men for whom Barrie had a great regard—Charles Scribner, the publisher of his books in America, and Hugh Macnaughten, the Eton housemaster. Also two delightful Eton boys, Evan Talbot and Maurice Bridgeman.

Village cricket with all its drama and humour provided, as I had hoped, endless entertainment. Saturday after Saturday found Barrie perched, pipe in mouth, on an uncompromisingly hard bench, keenly scrutinising every ball, stroke, pick-up and throw-in, and always ready with a word of congratulation or commiseration for the returning batsman. He soon knew each player by style as well as by name and would remember this one's top score and that one's bowling analysis. He always specially looked forward to the brief innings of Harry Last, the spirited gamekeeper, whose recklessness made him so likely to run out steadier players that he was seldom allowed to go in to bat before the ninth wicket had fallen, when his dashing hit-a-boundary-or-miss style either promptly brought the innings to an uproarious close or put a lively sting into its tail.

A memorable feature of Stanway cricket was scoring. It was the job of someone—usually a village boy—to hang upon the nails, driven into a small wooden board, square pieces of black tin, on which were painted in white the figures 1 to 9 and some noughts; but as these figures were frequently put upside down (the 6 and 9 almost invariably so) and not seldom in the wrong sequence, spectators—however sketchy their knowledge of cricket—were often puzzled by the published state of the game which might well read:

Runs	-	-	16
Wickets	-	-	9
Last Man	-	-	120

I specially remember Barrie's amusement one afternoon. A tense match was already well under way. A batsman, understandably pleased with his own score, shouted from pitch to pavilion to ask why the devil no figures had been put up on the score board. It was then discovered that, because of some misunderstanding between two alternate scribes, no record whatever of the game had been kept—a discovery greeted with mingled cheers and oaths.

As long as I could remember, a sometime railway carriage (third class) had done duty as pavilion, but in 1925, Barrie, in gratitude for so many hours of entertainment, presented the Stanway Cricket Club with a real, indeed a very imposing, pavilion. This generous gift was greatly appreciated by the Stanway cricketers and their opponents, but, by an irony to which the giver was not unaccustomed, it rather spoilt for himself the natural unpretentious charm of the village cricket ground.

Cricket was not confined to the official cricket field. Barrie had not been many hours at Stanway before he produced some stumps. These, with several little boys dancing around him, he pitched on the lawn quite close to the house. Then, flinging off his coat, he began to bowl left-handed balls at the boys.

After this inauguration, 'lawn-cricket' became an institution. Countless matches were played between the queerest sides picked from whatever children were staying in the house, village boys mustered by my son Michael, and as many guests and members of the staff as could be cajoled into the game. To small children, Barrie would bowl the gentlest, most enticing daisy-cutters, to their elders he would send down those wily googlies for which as Captain of the *Allahakbarries* he had been renowned.

'The reason I bowl so slowly,' he once explained, 'is that if I don't like the ball I can catch it up and bring it back.'

As far as I can remember Charles Whibley was the only guest who contrived to evade any active part in 'lawn-cricket'. Refusing so much as to touch either bat or ball, he firmly appointed himself scorer and referee, and sat comfortably beneath the tulip tree, thus escaping many bruises and grave risk to his eyeglasses.

The keenest of all our players was Millie, the nurserymaid. I've never seen any other fielder take such risks to keep runs down as did this intrepid girl, who seldom used her hands, but would intercept any ball with some portion or other of her anatomy.

BARRIE: 'Why didn't you stop that ball with your hand, Millie, instead of with your head?'

MILLIE: 'My head seemed to come more handy, Sir.'

Stanway lawn-cricket was the scene of many unforgettable spectacles. I have only to shut my eyes and I see two epic batsmen, fantastically contrasted in size, 'The Professor', six foot seven, and Barrie, not much over five foot one, staggering past one another half way between the wickets, just before, by a really remarkable piece of fielding, the bails are off at *both* ends! And how thankful the batsmen were to fling themselves panting onto the grass, for they were running their *fifth* run, and the laces of both Barrie's shoes had come untied. It mustn't be supposed that either the long or the short batsman had had the satisfaction of making a good hit, but a ball swiped at by 'The Professor', and missed, had slipped through the butter-fingers, first of the wicket-keeper (aged six); and then of the long stop (aged four) who, when at long last she overtook the ball, firmly sat down upon it and refused to yield it up.

Having often watched Barrie enjoy himself on the Brighton pier, I knew him, from his success at coconut shies, skeeball and other fascinating pursuits, to possess that mysterious asset, a 'good eye'. How good it was I never fully realised until I saw his almost demonic skill at golf croquet. From the furthest possible distance he would let fly at an adversary's ball and hit it. Successful as he was at sensationally long shots, they weren't his favourites. What he most enjoyed was playing from some heavily-stymied position, from which, pipe in mouth, he would, after taking long and careful aim, so hit his ball as to make it jump high over the other ball and triumphantly sail through the hoop, whatever the angle. These spectacular jumps struck novices at the game as sheer wizardry, and Barrie, as well as his gallery, was quite disappointed if the vicissitudes of a game failed to lay him plenty of stymies.

Rather to my surprise—for I was still young enough to suppose that at over sixty people *felt* old—Barrie occasionally joined in our lawn tennis, a game he had only recently played for the first time; but though he showed agility, and his 'eye' stood him in good stead, this was definitely not one of his games. He played it in inverted commas, so to speak.

'I have a conviction', he declared in a letter, 'that the young secretly think it indecent of me to play tennis. They run about and gather the balls for me and in their politeness almost offer to hold me up when it is my time to serve. By the way, what an extraordinarily polite game tennis is. The chief word in it seems to be "sorry", and admiration of one another's play crosses the net as frequently as the ball. I fancy that is all part of the "something" you get at public schools and can't get anywhere else. I expect that when any English public school boy shot a German he called out "Sorry". If he was hit himself, he cried, "Oh, well shot!".'

Barrie's craze for shuffles proved even more lasting than I'd hoped. Night after night he would scuttle from the dining-room to the board for practice shots; then sides would be picked—usually he captained one, I the other—after which for an hour or so the hall would resound with the clang of misdirected disks hurtling on to the stone floor, whoops of triumph, yells of derision.

Nearly all the guests caught their host's passion for the game. They snatched what practice they could during the day, and lined up tense with anxiety for the evening's contest.

Thanks to his fabulous height, striking appearance and extreme shakiness, 'The Professor' was undoubtedly our Star Turn. I can still see the frenzy of his first innings. He drew himself up to his full height; a look of infinite cunning came into his long Elizabeth countenance; he gave a sort of war-cry, and fired off his first shot. The disk, rising high into the air, crashed into the window; the second, whizzing sideways off the table, hurtled into the fireplace; the third struck me on the forehead; the fourth flew over his own head.

As next morning I passed through the hall on my way to breakfast, I found 'The Professor', hurling disks east, west, south and north. He looked like an immense windmill in a hurricane. 'Glory, glory, Hallelujah!' he shouted, far too exultant to notice how badly his last missile had hurt my shin, 'I've reduced my minus to six!!!'

The record minus was two, and he had been practising since seven o'clock.

The keenest of all those whom Barrie initiated into shuffles was the then Lord Chancellor, Lord Cave. This—with his close-clipped moustache and almost military carriage—rather unlawyer-like figure instantly developed such a passion for the game that he could scarcely be dragged from the table even for meals, and after his first visit to Stanway, he had a set of disks and a miniature board constructed for his London home. 'Cave is convinced,' said Barrie, 'that the Stanway table was the favourite resort of Henry VIII, and that each disk represented a wife past, or to come. I cannot undeceive him, so no doubt in time we shall all come to believe so.'

The shovelboard was not the only attraction Stanway's hall held for Barrie. The height of its ceiling gave splendid scope for his favourite parlour trick. By throwing up with one another a licked stamp and a penny, he could make the stamp stick to the ceiling. Before long, the ceiling of the hall was thickly sprinkled with stamps.

*   *   *

What—that long ago August, when he was not playing lawn-cricket, croquet, shuffles, or chucking stamps on to the ceiling—was Barrie like as a host? On the whole remarkably

good—courtly and charming. But, of course, there were hours
—days even—when he seemed, all of a sudden, to wonder why
he had invited his guests. I can't doubt that there were times
when they wondered, too. As always, he was fluctuating, unpredictable. Now, he would put others on the best possible
terms with themselves; now, lower the temperature for miles
around. But why should I attempt to describe what he so
well described himself—his manner at its least 'happy'? In an
anonymous article which, to the great offence of his 'fans',
appeared in *The National Observer*, he wrote:

Barrie was evidently anxious to please. The way in which his arm shot
out, like a pirate lugger from its hiding place, was proof of this. The natural
solemnity of his face is a little startling to one who has come out to dine,
but there is no doubt that he made several gallant attempts to be jolly.
When a joke was made you could see him struggling not with his face alone,
to laugh heartily. It was as if he tugged the strings that work the organs
of risibility, but either the strings were broken or he had forgotten to bring
the organs. Only once did he manage a genuine smile. He sat hugging
this smile. . . . He might, so careful was he, have been balancing something
on his head. . . . I was too far away to hear what he said when he engaged
in conversation. Obviously he was very anxious to be sociable, for when
those near spoke to him he listened with an attention that must have been
painful to them if, as is probable, they were speaking only of the weather.
Sometimes it seemed to be a good story for they laughed and he flung
himself back in his chair and waggled his head and slapped his knee and
went through all the mechanical business that accompanies a laugh, but
is as a suit of clothes without a man in them when, as in his case, the laugh
itself won't come. . . . His favourite remark is 'H'm' with which he expresses
surprise, thankfulness, indignation, delight, grief. He also asks questions
with it, and he has a 'H'm' that is final.

As a host Barrie was undoubtedly at his excellent best the
day the Australian Test Team, then playing at Cheltenham,
paid us a visit. Our house party fortunately included E. V.
Lucas, whose encyclopaedic knowledge of cricketers, as well as
of cricket, qualified him to coach us in the *Who's Who* of Test
Matches, and to decree who should sit beside whom at the
Homeric luncheon laid on the shovelboard. Barrie, looking
'tremendously wee', sat beside the huge, amiable, invincible

Armstrong; I, to the dazzled envy of my small son, between Collins and Gregory, each of whom profanely told me that he preferred lawn tennis to cricket!

I hadn't expected to have to provide more than one meal on so large a scale, but, to Barrie's delight, our guests stayed on to tea and then to an improvised dinner. They had fallen under Barrie's spell, always, it seemed to me, specially potent with cricketers. They were also volubly appreciative of Stanway, and Barrie was amused, if somewhat alarmed, by their assumption, impossible to dispel, that he was its owner.

'Say, Sir James, and when did you build this shack?' asked one overseas guest—not a member of the Team—pointing at the rafters of the Tithe Barn, which, mentioned in the Domesday Book of William the Second's reign, must at least be nearly a thousand years old.

It was a strenuous Sunday. First—Barrie, followed by a string of excited children, conducted the Australians, who had arrived betimes, to the cricket ground, where they gave some dazzling exhibition play, and then Barrie wafted my small son into heaven by arranging for him to bat—tremendous ceremony over his 'taking centre'—while Mailey bowled him googlies, and Gregory kept wicket.

Next, Barrie initiated his guests into shuffles, for which, though they played it with enthusiasm, they showed no particular aptitude. There followed hours and hours of golf, croquet, and lawn tennis. A long day—one of the longest I can remember, but great fun.

Each member of the Eleven good-naturedly wrote his name on my son Michael's bat. I thought he would be overjoyed. Far from it! Not yet autograph-minded, he was, to Barrie's great amusement, deeply displeased. 'But Mother, isn't there any writing paper in the house?' he indignantly demanded. 'Why did you let all those men spoil my beautiful new bat?'

The temporary tenant of Stanway soon made friends with several of the entertaining 'characters'—survivals of a fast-vanishing age—in whom the village was blessed. 'The atmosphere around Stanway fosters idiosyncrasy,' declared Barrie approvingly.

There was the silent, clock-work punctual postman, who one day tramped in a blizzard the eight bleak miles of his beat, to arrive on the stroke of the appointed hour, but without his bag!

Another memorable figure, lumbering of speech and of gait, was the old village carpenter. My mother once met this good man trudging up the hill with his empty hands held out in front of him at some distance apart from one another. The expression on his large red, whiskered, ham of a face was intent as a tightrope-walker's. 'Would Her Leddyship please not speak to me,' he mumbled, 'I be carryin' the measurements of a door.'

In a little gabled cottage very close to the house lived a wonderful anachronism, the old ex-coachman, James Prew, an uncouth, but spectacularly picturesque figure with a rugged Rembrandtesque countenance, furrowed like the bark of an elm. Barrie spent many hours smoking with this other 'James', and lending a sympathetic ear to his condemnation of 'Progress'. Prew was an unforgettable talker; his raucous words being few but memorably different from those in general use, and all repeated at least five times with the vehemence of a Greek chorus. Prew specially enjoyed telling Barrie how in the early days of 'them motor cars'—contraptions, which he still hoped, and I think believed, would prove no more than passing follies—he had constantly been summoned to drive the 'Old Mare' to the rescue of stranded motorists. ''Osses is best. 'Osses is best,' he would scornfully chuckle.

Another favourite crony was the corduroyed gamekeeper, whose impetuous cricket Barrie so much enjoyed. Harry Last, a man of great charm both of looks and of manner, was as great a reactionary and carper as Prew. He, too, never knew 'what the country was coming to'; and whatever government was in power was blamed for everything—even the weather;

but the gamekeeper was far more articulate than the old coachman—able, indeed, to voice his violent prejudices with a trenchancy that made his talk as entertaining as his batting. From time to time, Last could be persuaded to tell the story of his gallant encounter in early youth with a desperate gang of poachers, who had left him lying for dead in a wood with I don't know how many pellets of shot in his arm.

*   *   *

Long before the end of August 1921, Barrie had decided to return to Stanway the following summer. Most of the same visitors came again, and many more; amongst them Bernard and Barbara Freyberg, Lord and Lady Dufferin, David Cecil, Patricia Blackwood and Audrey Lucas. This time Barrie, who evidently felt more at home than ever, settled down to something of a routine. The forenoons he usually kept to himself. When 'C. Greene' had forced him to attend to as much of his correspondence as was imperative, he would read *The Times*, and then write letters, or, possibly, sketch out a little play for the children to act or the scenario for a charade. After luncheon, except on Saturdays when he watched the cricket match, he invariably played croquet. This was followed by a brief siesta from which he would resurrect for tea. He would then, perhaps, play cricket with the children, perhaps saunter with some chosen companion in The Sling, a nearby little wood of which he became very fond. Or, if there were no guest who couldn't be left, he and I would go for a long walk together. After dinner, over which, when there were good talkers—or at times preferably good *listeners*—he liked to sit and smoke for a very long time, came the inevitable Shuffles, followed, possibly, by some reading aloud, or if, happily, he was in the mood, by charades, at which he was past master. No one could be funnier: no one more curdling.

Sir Edward Marsh, in his book *A Number of People*, gave a description of Barrie's acting:

I am sure a great actor was lost in Barrie. One evening at Stanway we

Barrie playing croquet with H. G. Wells

played Charades, and he enacted in dumb show with Cynthia Asquith a husband consumed by a murderous hatred of his adoring wife. Our blood froze as once and again he crept up behind his unsuspecting victim, paper-knife in hand, with a look of fiendish malignity, and when as she always did she looked round at the last nick of time in confiding sweetness, jerked his features into a ghastly grin of uxorious fatuity.

On the Friday of our second week at Stanway, 'C. Greene's' efforts to make Barrie attend to the morning correspondence were interrupted by the sudden appearance of a bulky police sergeant, who loftily informed us that he had come over to make arrangements 'in regard to Her Majesty the Queen's visit to Stanway next Monday'. Her Majesty, he added, would be bringing a party of twelve. This was the first we had heard of Stanway's impending honour. Panic-stricken, I at once sent an S.O.S. telegram to my mother imploring her to come back to her own house. Next I held, by request, a curtseying class for an Alice-in-Wonderland-like assortment of flustered guests.

Monday was a lovely day—'Queen's weather' the cook pronounced it. This was very fortunate, for my mother had made a fair-weather plan, from which nothing—not even a cloud-burst—would have deflected her. Determined that the village should be given the closest possible view of Queen Mary, she had arranged for a crowd to gather at the top of Cockpit Hill, where Prew, the old coachman, swathed in a Union Jack, would be standing by the War Memorial, to which, at the appointed hour, Her Majesty was to be conducted on *foot*. Had the weather been less loyal, Queen Mary's pilgrimage would have been unpleasant, for the Cockpit is a high steep and, in rain, slippery hill to climb. As it was, everything went beautifully. The knees of my older pupils cracked like pistol shots, and their curtseys were very tottery, but no one toppled over.

Barrie, whose manner from first to last was most courtierlike, gave precisely the regulation Court bow, and while he was showing Her Majesty the barn, she graciously remembered to ask him for the solution to his unfinished play *Shall We Join*

The Ladies? No one but the questioner overheard his doubtless mystifying reply, but it appeared to give satisfaction. Queen Mary smiled, and looked pleased.

Barrie's second tenancy of Stanway ended with a great Cricket Week for Nicholas Davies. The whole, or very nearly the whole, of the Eton Eleven came, with girls to applaud their prowess in the field, dance, act or play games with them in the evenings; and Barrie, at his most masterful, in command of all the revels. At the last dinner each cricketer was compelled to make a speech; the worse he spoke, the better pleased was his host, whose own speech, a little work of art, came last. Not for the first time, I was struck by Barrie's obsession with Eton— Pop and the whole caboodle. Half beglamoured, half resentful, he could scarcely keep off the subject.

I told him he had a Scotsman's complex about English public schools, and then had no little difficulty in trying to define the word 'complex', one which he, like Arthur Balfour, refused to add to his vocabulary.

Again and again Barrie reverted to that mysterious 'something' instilled at Eton, about which, in a speech recently made to Wallasey High School, he had said:

You just become enrolled a member of that school, and gradually you acquire that Something. So far as I can understand, it oozes out of the historic walls and penetrates through your clothes. . . . Many are after that Something. Will the old walls that provide it hold out? Let us hope so— but life is becoming more strenuous. Some day, somewhere, somehow, somebody will have to submit a piece of that Something for scientific examination. . . . Don't think I am saying one word against these great institutions . . . all I'm arguing for is, that if they are so splendid, a way in should be found for the boys outside.

*   *   *

After the second successful experiment, Stanway at August became an institution. For ten more years in succession, Barrie 'took' the house, and I—acting as housekeeper, secretary and hostess, ran it for him, with my children staying there all the time and my husband coming down from his job in London each Friday to Monday.

On Barrie's first visit to Stanway, chance had put him into the smallest, most uncomfortable room in the house, nick-named, because of the habits of its chimney, the 'Smoke Room'. Choice made him always return to the same uncoveted room. He never would consent to have any other.

As the house was perpetually full, there was a great deal of work, but we had very little 'staff trouble'. The incomparable Thurston migrated from London, bringing his dictionaries with him. Silently, efficiently, this erudite butler took over the Stanway pantry, presided in the dining-room and, generally speaking, ordered our days. Goodness knows, he had plenty to do, but it wasn't long before he knew far more about the local archaeology than did any of those whose wine-glasses he filled and whose clothes he laid out.

Except for Thurston and one or two other importations, we were 'done for' by the usual Stanway staff, and much beholden to them we were—particularly to Katie Acheson, the smiling, still-room-trained Scottish housekeeper, as dependable as the delectable scones she baked; and to Mrs Sapcot, quite as fat as the proverbial cook, but unlike her, inexhaustibly good-humoured. Devoted to children, Mrs Sapcot was revered by them for the peculiar lusciousness of the chocolate éclairs with which she loved to ply them.

For entertainment, if not for utility, we were also much indebted to Esther, the witch-like head housemaid with a nose like a radish, and an addiction to cowslip-wine. Esther was famed for her ubiquity. This really was uncanny. No one could ever go into a room without finding her in it. At what-ever time I might happen to look into my bedroom, there unfailingly would Esther be. As I opened the door, she would spring into sight, looking as guilty as if I had surprised her in some nefarious deed, and flapping her duster—no one ever saw her without a duster—in my face, dart towards me and splutter out some explanation for her presence—'Please, I only just come in to see as everything was all right!' or (pointing at the empty August grate), 'Please, I just come in to look at the fire.'

Barrie used to say one of his reasons for preferring a small bedroom was that it made it so much easier to make sure that Esther wasn't in it! Further testimony to her omnipresence was my father's cry to my mother, 'That's the *third* time this week I've locked myself in the bathroom with that woman!'

Another memorable figure was Fred, in years a man but in status still the Odd—very odd—Boy. For two reasons, Fred was a local celebrity. First for his really remarkable resistance to education. Though he had attended school regularly for the usual number of years, he was unable to read one word! Secondly, for his power to practise, without becoming a total abstainer, the most extreme moderation. It was common knowledge that in the whole course of the year, Fred indulged in *one* bath only, this annual rite being enjoyed—or endured— on the eve of departure for his annual holiday. Told one day that most of the other people in the house had a daily bath, he exclaimed, 'My! they must be dirty!'

Each year, Barrie's stay at Stanway was wound up with 'sports', mostly of a highly undignified nature, for the 'staff'. The winners—there was always a surprisingly large number— were presented by Barrie with prizes—dresses chosen by me in Cheltenham. One very popular 'event' was the pell-mell race all the long, slippery grassway from the top of the Pyramid hill. But the great feature was the croquet tournament. I can still see Barrie partnered by Esther. Flown with cowslip wine, that ubiquitous housemaid proved too heavy a handicap for even his skill to drag to victory. With the inevitable duster draped round her arm, and wielding her mallet exactly as though it were a broom, Esther looked for all the world as if she were about to 'do' the lawn, and then give her partner's dusky face a good 'rub up'.

CHAPTER XI

TEN AUGUSTS

THOSE long-ago Augusts at Stanway have blurred in my memory. Looked back upon from this distance of time, they fuse into one summer—a single summer; but a mysterious one; in whose slow, unbroken course, babies surreptitiously turn into children; children into boys; the muzzles of young dogs whiten; and, almost imperceptibly, Barrie's step grows slower, until, all of a sudden, I realise with a pang that instead of joining in the lawn-cricket he sits beneath the tulip tree and watches others play.

My selective memory serves a wishful thinker well, so flatteringly does it sift and delete. It gives me the illusion that the weather was perpetually fine, and that Stanway was an enchanted place where it seemed, not, as in the Island of the Lotus-Eaters, 'always afternoon', but always evening—a magic evening, in whose lucent atmosphere the house glows apricot-coloured. The elm trees are rimmed with gold; the air is filled with the coo of wood pigeons, the tock of ball on bat, the shouts and laughter of children.

And, just as I remember the loveliness of a radiant day—forget its glare, its midge-bites—so with my memories of those who walked the Stanway stage.

Seen through a golden haze, all seem happy in their different —very different—ways.

Needless to say—as passages in my diary vividly remind me —reality was often glaringly at variance with this illusion. Inevitably there were many days when the weather was vile, the house overfull, the staff disgruntled, the guests so many parodies of themselves, their hostess exhausted.

And the host . . .? Again, my first glance falls only on happy pictures of Barrie. I see him at dinner, spirals of smoke rising above his head as he holds the table, or contentedly listens to, say, Augustine Birrell, Charles Whibley, Stephen Gwynne, or some other kindred spirit. His hands clasped behind his head, he lolls right back in his chair and, cigar in mouth, gazes straight in front of him, as though he could see, actually happening before his eyes, whatever he is remembering—or imagining! . . . Now, I see him alert, and elated at croquet or at shuffles; or intently packing his pipe before we set off for a long evening walk. . . . Most vividly, I see him with two red-headed, freckled boys; now on the lawn, bowling them ball after ball, aimed, not at the wicket, but at the bat; now in their nursery, telling evening after evening an unending story, or juggling with pennies, or doing funny things with his eyebrows until the littlest boy topples off his chair with laughter.

But Barrie, of course, was never 'Set Fair'. My diary reads absurdly like a weather report—'Barrie at his best'; 'Barrie at his worst', and when the second condition prevailed 'an associated trough of depression' was likely to affect the entire company. These dark moods, thank goodness, seldom lasted long. 'It is one of the hardest things in life to remain miserable for any length of time at a stretch,' Barrie had once written. Fortunately he seemed to find it so.

At other times, though, apparently neither consciously depressed nor annoyed, he would just fade out—perhaps tell one funny, very funny, story, and then subside into silence—Trappist silence—for the rest of dinner. On such occasions, I sometimes felt prompted to quote to him his own words in *Sentimental Tommy*: 'In dinner talk it is perhaps advisable to fling on any faggot rather than let the fire go out.'

I have heard it said that Barrie did not like anyone else to be funny. Utterly false! No one could be more delighted by the wit or humour of others. It was, however, true that when his receiver happened to be off, other people, if sensitive to atmosphere, were likely to be discouraged.

*   *   *

Since I find it so difficult to sort, sift and summarise the tangled memories of ten separate Augusts, and can never—so flattering a veil does time hang between my eyes and the past —see long-ago things with objectivity, much of this long Stanway chapter of Barrie's life will be better told by my once immediate impressions than by anything I could write now. So, I will freely lift from the diary which, from nightly jottings-down, I usually wrote up at the end of each tenancy, and from my long letters to my mother.

These excerpts demand a brief *Dramatis Personae* of our guests. Those referred to as Annuals, came, like my brother Guy, Charles Whibley, Elizabeth Lucas, E. H. Coles, and my friend Dorothy Barnard, each year—some for a fortnight, some for a week.

Our 'Annuals' included Barrie's much-loved youngest sister, Margaret Winter, a very remarkable woman. 'Maggie', as her brother always called her, had to some extent, I believe, been the original of Elspeth in *Sentimental Tommy*, and had a distinct look, especially in her very fine eyes, of her brother, whom she loved to idolatry. With Maggie came her devoted husband, William Winter, a transparently good, touchingly selfless man of a charming simplicity. Mr Winter, a Senior Wrangler, was an admirable mathematical coach. He had, also a great gift for chess, a gift handed on with interest to his only son William, who, having at the age of six shown his future form by defeating his father, subsequently became an international player and champion of England.

The Winters were what we called 'Fortnighters'. So was Barrie's adopted son Jack Davies, a very good-looking young Naval officer. With him came his lovely wife Gerrie and their two children, Timothy and Jane.

Another 'Fortnighter'—the only one equally popular with fellow-guests, staff, children, dogs and hostess—was E. H. Coles, a son-in-law of George du Maurier and, thus, uncle by marriage to Barrie's adopted sons. 'Coley' was indeed the perfect guest, for though self-declared a very shy man, he possessed more, I think, than anyone I've known, the gift for putting others at their ease. Innate kindliness, tolerance, unfailing understanding, made 'Coley' the most comfortable friend in the world; his curiously individual approach to life, his wit of a quick, unexpected kind—always delightful and usually at his own expense—made him one of the most amusing. 'Coley's' sympathy was as ready, as supple as his sense of humour. You could rely on it, just as surely as you could rely on his ability to provide the missing word in any crossword puzzle, or, under strong compulsion, to repeat by heart almost every poem in the Oxford Book of Verse and every sonnet by Shakespeare.

Barrie used to say that 'Coley' who, admittedly, had a certain endearing indolence and was essentially a private, not a public, person, seemed all through life anxious to conceal, rather than to display and exploit, his remarkable natural gifts. From time to time he was, however, foiled of this ambition. He didn't fail to win a scholarship at Oxford, take a First in Greats, become a recognised expert on English Water Colours, of which he made a very fine collection. While working at the War Office, for which he left the Bar to be Controller of Lands, he so greatly impressed his chief, Lord Haldane, that I heard this statesman declare him the ablest man who had ever worked under him. Unlike most men, 'Coley' couldn't have been more glad when the time came to retire from public life. Nor did the luxury of unlimited leisure ever begin to pall on him. No day in which 'Coley' was free to do what he liked could possibly seem one moment too long.

He remained preternaturally young for his age, and his nearest approach to anything even remotely akin to vanity was his pleasure when strangers refused to believe how old he was.

No 'Annuals' were more welcome than Algernon Cecil, the historian, and his wife Lady Guendolen. Both ideal guests, they invariably made themselves superlatively pleasant to all their fellow-guests as well as to their host and their grateful hostess. In the soft radiance of Guendolen's presence, duller minds became brightened out of self-recognition, and the lovely way she had of listening gave others the pleasing, however transient, illusion that they were contributing their share to the quality as well as to the volume of the talk. Barrie delighted in Guendolen's fluttering grace, exquisite manners and the delicious ironical twinkle of her wit.

One formidable 'Fortnighter', who shall be given the name of Mrs Grum, the widow of a great friend of Barrie's, was a solemn duty. Year after year, this Gorgon, nicknamed 'The Dinner-Table Bunker', proved the rock on which many guests foundered. She stumped even the most deft conversationalists; drove even the best-mannered children to giggles. No wonder, for her rare utterances were preceded by a noise like a running-down clock clearing its throat to strike, and many of her sparse remarks were as disconcerting—as unplayable—as those of 'Mr F's. aunt'. She suffered, too, from extreme 'delayed action'. Just as general conversation had got going, she would suddenly stretch across the dinner-table and in a voice like the cry of a seagull, urgently—usually to some far-off seated guest arrived at least three days ago—put the question, 'Did you have a good journey?' Having shot her bolt, she would then lean back with the air of one who has brought off a dazzling conjuring trick.

Mrs Grum was an emotional vulture. She hovered over the newly-bereaved, and though so bafflingly silent in general company, she could be dismayingly forthcoming and intense tête-à-tête. What she liked was to 'get one gentleman to herself' for what she called a 'heart to heart'—in reality one-way-traffic talk. With this object in view, she used every morning to scuttle down very early to breakfast. If she found a satisfactory prey—preferably a widower—she would first explain that she was 'terribly psychic', and then tell her victim, over his bacon and eggs, that she had during the night 'got through' to his wife and had a message for him. Morning after morning I would come down to find one man waiting outside the door for a chaperone before he dared enter the dining-room where Mrs Grum chumped her solitary breakfast.

Our most indispensable 'Annual', my invaluable Nannie— 'Nannie Faulkner'—who for nearly thirty years, stood between me and all the harsher winds of life, presided beamingly over the nursery party. Unrivalled at winning, and keeping, the love and confidence of children, and providing them with endless fun, she made Stanway a blissful temporary home for the various boys and girls who came to stay with Barrie. Grown-ups vied with one another in coveting invitations to that uniquely happy nursery atmosphere.

Never since I had known Barrie had he owned—or wished to own—a car, but station work made it necessary to hire one for Stanway. Harry Faulkner, a brother of my Nannie's, came each year to drive this car, and with him came—great addition to our company—his charming, gifted wife, 'Tib', and their two delightful boys, Dick and Bobbie, much the same age as my two sons and their inseparable playfellows. Dick and Bobbie Faulkner, both keen cricketers, became great favourites with Barrie.

Nearly every year, in celebration of my son Simon's birthday, Nannie and 'Tib' got up a delightful variety entertainment of songs and acting.

My diary tells how Barrie, who took great delight in these performances, himself took part in one:

Our annual celebration of Simon's birthday was the best we've ever had. He and Judy Wood did lovely Romeo and Juliet balcony scene; Bobby Faulkner sang, in his sweet throstle's pipe, some of Beb's poems set to music by Norman O'Neil; Dick Faulkner played the violin, and Barrie, in real

Charlie Chaplin vein, brought the barn down with a 'turn' devised by himself, in which he and Harry Last, as a pair of crazy batsmen, fought a duel with stumps, and he spat out dozens of teeth (cherry stones)—tonk tonk, tinkerty tonk—into a tin basin. . . .

Full to overflowing though the house was with 'boarders', various neighbours, eager to see Barrie, constantly added to our numbers. Of these, the general favourite—he came to dinner at least three times a week—was the vicar. The Rev. H. B. Allen, ironically—because so unlike anyone else in Orders—nicknamed 'The Priest', at one time headmaster of a well-known private school, was a renowned 'coach', able by his great gift for teaching to get into Oxford and Cambridge boys who, without his help, could never have passed their examinations.

'The Priest' seemed to understand Barrie by instinct. Barrie, who took to him at once, never ceased to delight in his enlivening company. 'The Priest' enjoyed perpetual youth, and a sense of humour so irrepressible that it constantly threw him into paroxysms of laughter, positively alarming—as his heart was known to be weak—to his friends. Barrie was particularly impressed by the adaptability of this nimble-minded man, who, though a scholar with such a love of the Classics that he felt deeply sorry for anyone so unfortunate as not to know Greek and—forgetting his congregation was no longer a school—sometimes harangued ploughmen in Latin, could nevertheless get on just as well with the unlettered as with the learned. Like Falstaff and other lovable characters, 'The Priest' was a life-long sufferer from 'consumption of the purse', in his case an incurable disease, for he was constitutionally incapable of saying no to any undeserving person who might ask him for money. Another heavy drain on his small resources was his love for animals. This compelled him—an extravagance that delighted Barrie—to buy any horse, whatever its age, who struck him as looking insufficiently cared for. His stables and paddock were filled with these pensioners, all years past earning their keep, but for ever munching oats, carrots and sugar.

Another ever welcome visitor was Eliza Wedgwood. This much-loved Cotswold character, a great, great grand-daughter of the famous potter, lived in the nearby village—one of the loveliest in England—of Stanton, to the welfare of whose fortunate sons and daughters she all through a long, intensely active and quite selfless life, devoted her very rare qualities of heart and mind, and remarkable initiative. It became an institution that all Barrie's guests should be taken to tea with 'Eliza' in her home, an orchard-set grey gabled cottage, famous for its charm and hospitality.

Within very easy reach, too, was the Stanley Wood family with four delightful daughters to take lively part in all the games and theatricals at Stanway.

Various friends came over from Broadway. Some, like the Navarros, dating from Barrie's *Allahakbarrie* days; others, Londoners only recently settled there. Among these were two very old friends of Barrie's, both excellent company, Lady Lewis, the widow of the famous solicitor Sir George Lewis, and her daughter Kate. Lady Lewis's house in Portland Place had been celebrated for its musical, and other, parties, and it was at one of these gatherings that Barrie had first met the beautiful daughter of George du Maurier, Sylvia Llewellyn Davies. But for that meeting there would, according to Barrie, have been no *Peter Pan*.

'I made Peter by rubbing the five of you violently together, as savages with sticks produce flames,' explained Barrie in his introduction to the published play, which he dedicated to his three surviving adopted sons.

To return to my narrative. In 1923, all the guests of the previous year came again, and many more, including the rightful owner of the house, an exemplary guest, for he lost several games of draughts to his host. Golf-croquet—often much too solemnly played for my taste—raged again. As Barrie was a master of its tactics as well as its play, it did not behove his partner to have views of his—or preferably her—own. What he liked was an utter 'rabbit' at the game—a docile rabbit, dazzled by his play, who, if shown precisely how to hold her mallet, could be hypnotised into bringing off a sufficient number of shots to enable him to carry her to victory. He always obdurately insisted on a game immediately after luncheon, however hot the day, and quite regardless of his guests' digestions—or of their addiction to a siesta.

Newcomers included an extremely nice, enthusiastic American family, Mr, Mrs and Miss Garland; Gilmour, mercifully without Income Tax forms!, Nicholas Davies's housemaster 'Tuppy' Headlam, David Cecil, and A. B. Walkley. Also that dainty judge in porcelain, Lord Darling. Barrie was much amused to find the children waiting white-faced on the doorstep to see a 'real live judge' arrive in the Black Cap. Darling, who was excellent company, brought with him his adored daughter Diana, and Barrie was much touched and tickled by his fatherly devotion. While Diana, in charmingly Victorian fashion, warbled us ditties, the Judge gazed dotingly at her just like the father in the picture *Her Mother's Voice*.

The chief luxury among the year's 'New Boys' was David Cecil, whose darting, responsive mind bridged all age-gulfs. My only slight trouble was Walkley, whom—my own fault, no doubt—I found difficult at first; deflating. He seemed offended. But probably it was only his manner. At all events, he thawed before he left.

A complication this year was that, to Barrie's embarrassment and annoyance, his sometime wife, Mrs Cannan, who, according to Elizabeth Lucas—deaf to the lesson of Dear Brutus—hankered after a 'Second Chance', had taken up for the summer a strategical position at Broadway. Consequently, Broadway, which is only five miles off, was put strictly out of bounds. In no circumstances, Barrie adjured me, must anyone from Stanway ever go there. Very awkward, for most visitors clamoured to see the famous village, and I grew tired of telling them unconvincingly that it was utterly 'spoilt'. One day, Barrie, on his way back from a funeral, forgot to lay this embargo on the driver, and was driven home through Broadway. During dinner one of the others in the car told me of a terribly narrow escape they'd had at Broadway corner. They had only missed by a hairbreadth running down an elderly woman. After dinner, Barrie, white and trembling, told me *who* that 'elderly woman' was. What a fantastic might-have-been!

Our 1923 season's house-party culminated in another mammoth Cricket Week. A match each day; dancing or charades until all hours, and, in the interludes, every conceivable and inconceivable game—including croquet by moonlight. My diary, written just after the departure of the cricketers, tells of their stay and describes Barrie as host to them and to others.

Sept. 10th, 1923

The last motor-bike has just spluttered away. A wonderful hush has fallen. The house feels like a great empty shell; silence a positive thing. Only self and sons left with Barrie.

He was in marvellous form all through the cricket week, and in his most masterful mood—presenting the Eleven with special caps at a speech-making dinner, and summoning from London a 'camera-man' to film a fantasy called 'Nicholas's Dream', into which he'd woven a part for everyone—a bicycling one for me. He also wrote a duologue for me and sister Mary. It was great fun having her here to beguile the Etonians. Pamela Lytton, as lovely as ever, came, too, with her daughter, Hermione. Barrie was delighted by her cricketer son Anthony, who, engagingly light-hearted, delightfully articulate, and endowed with the most glorious laugh, seems able to make his friends share his own uproarious exultation at being alive. No wonder they all love him.

Nicholas, also in delightfully contagious high spirits, was great fun, too.

Barrie has been remarkably near to 'set fair' this year. Really, only one bad lapse when—extenuating circumstances—the So-and-So's invited themselves and several friends to dinner. Anyone who hoped (or feared) Barrie would be 'whimsical' was certainly in for a disappointment that evening. To quote his own description, he 'sat very mouse', and his silence put a brake on everyone else. Mr So-and-So, like the man described by Barrie in *My Lady Nicotine*, was 'the kind of talker who draws a map with a fork on the tablecloth', and poor Mrs So-and-So, who has literary ambitions, *would* ask Barrie how his writing 'CAME'!

'She found me as hopeless as a sulky drawer,' croaked Barrie.

Our only other trouble has been Barrie's recurrent grumbles about people not talking enough to our 'dinner-table bunker', Mrs Grum. Whenever he does this I put her beside *him* at the next dinner, whereupon scarcely one word passes! But then he's been skilful enough to establish the convenient legend—or can it be a fact?—that the understanding between him and her is so complete as to make mere words unnecessary?

For all Barrie's lip loyalty, he didn't make too good a job of trying to conceal his relief when Mrs Grum's fortnight came to an end. Perhaps this helped him to play up so splendidly for the cricket week.

*   *   *

The Stanway season of 1924 was a specially strenuous one. Besides all the 'Annuals' there were innumerable newcomers. These included Bernard and Barbara Freyberg, Joan Peake, my youngest sister, Irene Plymouth, my nephew Martin Charteris, Stella Beech and her son, Denis and Diana Mackail, the Granville-Barkers and Augustine Birrell.

If their hostess remembers quite a few difficult moments, there is no doubt which was the worst. One evening before the men had joined the ladies I was sitting in the drawing-room with Mrs Grum and a certain young woman with whom she had fallen in hate. I was aware of thunder in the air but did not expect the storm to break. All of a sudden, Mrs Grum sprang to her tiny tightly-shod feet, burst into tears of rage and ran amok. 'I can't stay in the room with that young woman!' she screamed; then rocketed through the doorway and upstairs to lock herself into her bedroom, whence it took me nearly half an hour to coax her down again. Then I wished I hadn't. . . .

Another crisis ended in acute disappointment for me, but to the intense relief of my husband. Two film magnates who had temporarily persuaded Barrie to go to Holly-wood in September for the 'shooting' of *Peter Pan*, at sight of Simon, set their hearts on deporting him to play the part of Michael. Would I come too, and play Mrs Darling? Long dormant ambition flared; thrilled, I started to pack. But, in mid-cough, Barrie changed his mind. Nothing, he decided while re-lighting his pipe—nothing on earth—would induce him to go to America. As for Simon and me going without him? Out of the question! Shattering collapse of my towering castles in the air!

The 1924 cricket week—the last we had—was enlivened by the ostensibly secret, but really charmingly evident, romance between Nicholas and Lord Northborne's delightful daughter, Mary James. Also, by some sensational cricket. Worthington made 139 not out. Barrie clapped on one of the boy's caps, went out to field for half an hour, put himself on to bowl googlies and DID THE HAT TRICK! With how much co-operation from batsmen, wicket-keeper and umpire I know not—possibly some—but at all events, it gave great satisfaction all round and provided excellent ammunition for the last-night speeches.

This year was memorable, too, for a shocking new development in Mrs Grum, of which my diary tells:

Mrs Grum, presumably anxious not to commit that rare sin

of hiding a talent in a napkin, has taken to singing olde English songs! 'There is no doubt,' as some music teacher said of a pupil!—'there is no doubt that she has a very small voice, but it is very bad.' Neither has our siren any ear. What, unfortunately, she has got, is Lorelei-like staying power. She can go on and on and on. She likes her audience to be one gentleman at a time, and tries to pin at breakfast each morning a victim to book for a private evening recital. So far, her host has not felt 'so dispoged'. . .

Barrie, so my diary reminds me, was in good spirits most of this August. In one of his Impresario moods, he inspired the most unlikely people to act, then froze their blood with his own famous imitation of Henry Irving in *The Bells*.

He greatly enjoyed some of the dinner-table talk, especially when Granville-Barker and Augustine Birrell were there. A letter to my mother describes these two guests, and their host.

Sept. 1st, 1924

Granville-Barker has not—as I'd heard said that he had—lost his charm and personality—how could he?—but he *does* strike me as the worse for wealth. A certain sleekening of spirit and mind, as well as of body, doesn't become him. He looks less like a poet, and not wholly unlike a butler. According to Barrie, and Elizabeth Lucas (who has just 'decorated' his house), his daily life is over-organised by his wife, Helen. The notice 'WORKING HOURS NINE UNTIL ONE' hangs on the door of his writing-room, but apparently nothing much gets written. I'm sure he would have written much more, however snatchedly, under the continued stimulus of stage production. But Barrie tells me Helen is determined not to let him have anything to do with the theatre. Incidentally, she has entirely cut him off from Bernard Shaw.

Birrell, 'benevolently trenchant'—Desmond MacCarthy's description of him—has mellowed beautifully with the years. He and Barrie sat up talking until all hours, exchanging, I assume, memories rather than opinions. Mentally, he's as vigorous as ever, but he now walks so slowly that he's difficult to keep back with. I want to run round him in circles, like a dog. He and Whibley got on almost disappointingly well. Barrie and I had looked forward to some sparring.

Barrie has been an intensified edition of himself; now as executive as Prospero, making everybody do things they'd never dreamt of doing before—and enjoy doing them; now completely fading out, behaving as irresponsibly, participating as little, as though he were the victim of a press gang, instead of officially the captain of the ship. Difficult, indeed, impossible not to be angry with him at times. Still more impossible to be angry with him for more than twenty consecutive minutes. How unfair on the less articulate is that gift of being able to put everything right with a word or two, or by a little note—two lines of literature—pushed under the door!

*   *   *

In 1925, the Granville-Barkers, Birrell and David Cecil came again, and there were plenty of newcomers, notably Walter de la Mare, with his very pretty daughter Jinny, Irene Vanbrugh and her husband Dion Boucicault, Lady Desborough —marvellous with Mrs Grum!—Horatia Seymour, Sir Douglas Shields, and a brilliant young Cambridge don called Barnes, whom Barrie particularly liked. My diary this year was extremely laconic, but a long letter I wrote to my mother gives various house-party incidents, and my first impressions of John Galsworthy.

Sept. 8th, 1925

No Cricket Week this August, but what with Simon's operation and poor Mrs Winter's broken leg, both of which threw Barrie into a 'state', by no means too tranquil a time. Besides the house being over-full of 'boarders', we were much infested by day-guests. I did, however, manage to finish *David Copperfield*. Barrie and other grown-ups attended the readings as well as Michael. In fact they attended more closely than he did. One day while I, deaf to all around me, was reading myself to tears, he crawled Red Indian-wise out of the room. Unaware of his departure, I droned on and on until I'd finished the description of Steerforth, drowned—'there I saw him lying with his head upon his arm as I had so often seen him lie at school.' Raising my swimming eyes from the page, I looked up, hoping to see Michael's face bathed in tears, only to find that, but for Barrie, shaking with silent laughter, the room was *empty*. Michael had been at the top of a distant elm tree for quite ten minutes!

I wish you could have seen Simon and Irene Vanbrugh as Hamlet and Ophelia. Better still, the revival of Barrie and Simon's famous rendering of *Mary Rose*, which has been in their repertory since Simon was four. Usually, they divide all the characters between them. This time, to furnish Irene Vanbrugh with a part, a parlourmaid was added to the cast. . . .

I don't think you've ever met John Galsworthy? Upright, correct, immaculately dressed; he looks the very personification of integrity, rectitude, 'good form'. But Barrie declares this conventional and imperturbable exterior is most deceptive. It conceals, he assures me—seething inner turmoil. No one, says Barrie, is more genuinely distressed, torn—tormented—by injustice, social distress and the general disjointedness of things. He appears to see nearly everyone as a 'case', and to divide the human race into 'top'- and 'under'-dogs. No wonder the philanthropist at times predominates over the artist. I liked his compassion, and scrupulous fair-mindedness, but found his almost portentously good manners a little oppressive. Socially, he is as predictable as Barrie is unpredictable.

Had Galsworthy's manners always been so ceremonious? I asked Barrie.

'Yes,' he replied, 'once when he was flung out of a hansom he alighted on the doorstep as decorously as though leaving a card. However, don't get the wrong impression and label

John limited. Though he looks so conventional, so Man-about-Town, there's really precious little he hasn't done, and few places to which he hasn't been.'

Fascinating conjectures chased one another through my mind. What *could* Galsworthy have done?

'Has he been in prison?' I asked hopefully.

Anticlimax! 'I believe,' Barrie rather proudly replied, 'I believe he was once a cowboy and I have hopes he was once a pirate.'

'Was he always as earnest, ethical and high-minded?'

'When he was young,' answered Barrie, 'he appeared to care about nothing but racin', huntin', shootin', Bridge and so forth, and what turned him from a man of pleasure into one almost ponderously earnest I've no idea. But', he added, a little on the defensive, 'whatever it was, I'm very fond of him.'

I remarked that Galsworthy seemed to enjoy enviable certitude.

'Yes, indeed, he does,' said Barrie, 'and I promise you he would go to the stake for any of his convictions, but he would go immaculately dressed—probably in a grey top hat and spats.'

Evidently he is one of the best and nicest of men.

Mrs Grum has been particularly difficult and 'dumbing' this year, but Barrie more sustainedly at his best than ever before; neither scowling, nor growling—even, like the audience at a good play, coughing less.

Beb, Bibs and I had a lovely ten-mile all-night walk over unshared, moonlit Cotswolds. Barrie, one part disapproving, three parts envious, attended our preliminary midnight meal in the stillroom, and we left him dancing—in his moss-green dressing gown—on the black beetles.

*   *   *

My diary of the following Stanway season, in which the Australian cricketers visited us again, needs no amplification.

Sept. 1926
Very sorry to leave this year. It has been a particularly happy time. Barrie on an unusually high level of spirits, held the stage, with a strong 'Supporting Cast'—our usual stock company, all at their best, and various visiting stars: Desmond MacCarthy; Karsarvina and her husband; Margaret Mackail; the 'Lord High Shuffler', Cave, and Galsworthy.

Barrie much enjoyed taking the boys—Michael, Simon, Dick and Bobby Faulkner—to Stratford-on-Avon plays, and, also telling them in nightly instalments an endless tale about their own adventures on a desert island, where they've been wrecked and perform prodigies of valour and slaughter.

Another great pleasure for Barrie has been his rediscovery of a delightful godchild, Quiller-Couch's daughter, Foy, who came to stay and is, I hope, henceforth to be an 'Annual'.

Grand charades one night. Barrie excelled himself in what I think his best part—a bashful young Scotsman who, leaving home for the first time with instructions not to speak to any stranger in the train, finds himself alone in a railway carriage with an alarmingly pretty girl, and after long, slowly-crumbling resistance, is vamped.

Plenty of reading aloud this year—mostly *Pickwick Papers* under the tulip tree. Also, many lovely long walks with Barrie, whose pace still shows no sign of slackening—not bad at sixty-six!

Simon's birthday entertainment was better than ever. Barrie wrote a delicious duologue for him and Michael. Just as I was conducting a last moment rehearsal, Margot[1] arrived for luncheon with SEVEN people, none of them expected! A drowning look came into Barrie's eyes. While I flew to placate the kitchen and pantry, he entertained the invaders by throwing stamp after stamp on to the ceiling (I regret to say Michael has been tactless enough to master this accomplishment of Barrie's!) but Margot, dissatisfied with the role of spectator, soon leapt onto the shovelboard and, clicking

[1] Countess of Oxford and Asquith

imaginary castanets, performed a Carmen dance. They stayed till half-past four when fifty-two people came to tea on the shovelboard.

The Australians honoured us again. The entire Eleven came to luncheon, tea and dinner, and Collins, the captain, Mailey and McCartney stayed the night. McCartney clean bowled by Barrie—I've never seen anyone more under his spell. He followed him about like a spaniel. Rag game on the cricket field, each of us in turn given the privilege of being bowled out by Mailey. Hours and hours of shuffling, tennis and golf croquet. McCartney brilliant at all three. He and I enjoyed defeating Barrie and Guendolen at golf-croquet. Barrie disappointed because he wasn't set a single stymie to jump. Brother Guy an invaluable help all through the long, long day, and in the evening, when he and Beb played not over-serious Bridge against Collins and me. Collins delightful.

Barrie charmed by McCartney, who, invited to stay the night, at first said he couldn't because he'd promised himself that he'd finish a long letter—he spoke of a letter as though it were a book—to his wife to catch the Australian mail. Barrie said he would write this letter for him, and he did. Then a cable was sent to Dion Boucicault, now on tour in Australia with Barrie's plays, instructing him to give Mrs McCartney free seats for every performance.

*　　*　　*

The August of 1927 was badly over-congested. Besides all the 'Annuals' in full force, we had about fifty other guests, and the Broadway invasions were unusually heavy. Furthermore, Barrie's health was much less stable than the year before, and his spirits consequently lower.

One very welcome newcomer was Ruth Draper, who, to the delight of the assembled household, angelically gave a performance in the hall. Others were Horatia Seymour, Angela Thirkell, Jose Grey, Violet Leconfield, David Cecil, Owen

Seaman, a brilliant exponent of golf-croquet, but frugally saving up his wit for *Punch*, and—unforgettably—Robert Nichols!

I was so busy writing a book against time that my diary remained a total blank, but a letter to my mother, written after the house had blessedly emptied, describes an absurd picnic, Barrie at The Wharf, and Robert Nichols's visit.

Sept. 4th, 1927

I took your advice and organised a picnic, but no one could have called it a success. It was never nearly warm enough, and things began to go badly wrong when some pigs joined our party, and my instinctive hospitality compelled me to offer them sandwiches. Unfortunately the sandwiches were made of HAM! The ensuing outbreak of cannibalism upset poor Barrie terribly. I need not tell you that no other guests, bidden or unbidden, could have been more popular with the children of the party; but alas, just as cats will unerringly rub themselves against anyone who dislikes them, so, with one accord, did the pigs make a dead set at Barrie, grunting and rootling around him as though he were a truffle.

As soon as our unbidden guests had guzzled up every morsel of fellow-pig, they floundered ungratefully away, and Barrie had just begun to recover from their visitation when, by ill luck, someone began to talk—of all topics in the world—about RATS! Have I told you that Barrie has a rampant rat-complex? Mere mention of their name drives him white-lipped from any room. But, this time there was no room for him to leave.

After a pipe or two, he rallied and when conversation turned on etymology, began quite happily to rhapsodise upon the beauty of the word 'star', which he maintains to be the loveliest in the English language. So, our 'pignic' might after all have ended on quite a pleasant note had not some cursed compulsion made me tell him to spell 'star' backwards!

One day, Barrie came with me to The Wharf. He was much hoping for some talk with Lord Oxford, whom he loves, but

Margot annexed him for the whole time. Using him, he said, like a crutch—he complained that his shoulder was badly bruised—she walked him up and down the lawn, curdling him with her confidences.

'Shyness,' he remarked on our drive home, 'shyness is my favourite quality in a woman. Shyness—and reticence.'

I must tell you about Robert Nichols, whom Barrie and I hadn't seen since we attended his wedding. Of all human beings I've ever met he's the most wire-taut and quivering. Every nerve in his body seems exposed. Interesting, touching, lovable, disarming, but exhausting in the extreme. His ego-centricity—probably quite unconscious—can seldom have been equalled. He arrived with a five-act poetic drama in his trembling hands and was visibly injured because Barrie didn't instantly sit down to read it straight through at one go. When I took him for a walk he interrupted his non-stop soliloquy to complain that the Cotswold Hills didn't appear to 'take any notice' of him!

His over-wound-upness disturbed, even alarmed, us. After our too-long walk he exhausted himself playing frenzied cricket; collapsed, and had to go to bed. But can he, I wonder, ever get to sleep? Difficult to imagine him insensible.

He left us feeling, it must be admitted, very tired; but when I read aloud his lovely war poem about the yellow hammer Barrie told me to telegraph to beg him to come back again at once.

*   *   *

August 1928 I enjoyed, I remember, more than any other year. Having no book to write gave me a luxurious sense of leisure, and all were at their best. Barrie's spirits were good. I noticed, however, with concern that he seemed to feel less well; had taken to lying down at odd times, now and again leaving the dining-room before the meal was over; but he nearly always came to life towards the end of the day, and then liked to sit up and talk until two in the morning. He had

two rather heavy 'holiday tasks'. Charles Scribner had come
to discuss the new complete—horribly final that sounded!—
edition for America; and Mrs Hardy, who came with Sydney
Cockerell, brought her biography of her husband for him to
criticise.

Barrie particularly enjoyed having Donald Maclean, to
whom he was devoted, to stay, and there was some very good
dinner-table talk from Birrell, Whibley, Stephen Gwynne, A. P.
Herbert and L. P. Jacks. A. P. Herbert very amusing at the
piano—away from it too.

This year, I had plenty of time to keep my diary—time
enough even to give the gist of some of Birrell's talk, and,
captiously to complain of Galsworthy's good manners. I wrote:

Birrell, his jutting chin more stubbly this year than ever,
was at his emphatic best. He was interesting last night talking
to Whibley, Coley, The Priest and me about the hit-or-miss
character of Barrie's writing—the J.M.B. tendency to inspire
either blind idolatry or equally blind prejudice. How seldom,
he complained, was Barrie dispassionately judged. People were
either 'potty' about him, or else, because put off by the
'whimsey-whamsey' element, blind to his remarkable originality and artistry—not to say genius. To give an instance,
Birrell then told us how widely divergent had been his own and
his son's reactions to Barrie's speech at the Printers' Corpora-
tion Dinner, when he spoke of his imaginary meeting with a
young man of 'exceeding tenuity of body wearing a velvet
jacket', who turned out to be Robert Louis Stevenson.

'I thought it as good as anything I'd ever heard,' declared
Birrell, 'a work of art. It made me laugh. It made me cry.
I would have liked it to go on and on. But my son who, I
flatter myself, is deficient neither in head nor in heart, declared
it made him feel sick!'

'Surely,' said someone, 'nearly all markedly individual
writers have this provocative effect on readers who don't fall
under their spell?'

'Yes,' snorted Birrell, 'even Charles Lamb made some people feel sick!'

It was agreed that nothing irritates so much as idiosyncratic charm that doesn't charm; but that, on the other hand, writers who are free from any mannerisms—defects, if you like—which could possibly offend anyone's *taste*, are seldom loved, however much they may be admired. Lastingly popular authors—both the good and the bad—are all parodyable.

Galsworthy, whom I like more and more, was looking specially like the ideal stage schoolmaster, and his manners were as sedulous as ever. The way he springs to his feet at breakfast the instant his wife enters the room, and darts to the sideboard to help her to food had a highly disturbing effect on other husbands. Feeling they ought to follow his example, they pretended—unconvincingly—that this was quite usual behaviour. Result of their unpractised zeal: much clattering of dish-covers and upsetting of coffee cups. Most tiresome! But I had little fear that this epidemic of excessive good manners would long survive the chivalrous Galsworthy's departure. I was right. No sooner was example removed than everyone relaxed and relapsed into casualness—it was like 'Fall out the Officers' on parade. To do Barrie justice he hadn't succumbed. I couldn't bear it if *he* took to Jack-in-the-Boxing out of his chair and sprinting to open doors. He is hard at work on some kind of a book based on hundreds of his very early articles, photostats of which have been procured from the British Museum. Nannie is typing for him. He has often been offered vast sums for republication of his old articles and stories, but has always refused; once in a letter to a pleading editor in rhyme:

> They had their day and ceased to be,
> But oh the meals they meant to me.

I gather his latest intention is to have fifty or so copies, of whatever book[1] may result, privately printed to give, glamorously-bound, as glorified Christmas presents.

[1] *The Greenwood Hat*

Of the next two years my diary tells all that I remember.

Sept. 1st, 1929

End of the NINTH J.M.B., Stanway August. Difficult to
believe, yet some of the Cast *do* begin to look older; others,
alas, less young. It has been the quietest, easiest season we've
ever had. Fewer visitors and no staff trouble, except when
Comus[1] further endeared himself to Barrie by, as P. G. Wode-
house would say, 'wrapping himself round' an entire ham
snatched from the larder!

Our only slight social strain was visit of Mrs Thomas Hardy,
with whom I fear Barrie in the first emotion over her husband's
death, pitched his relationship—a vicarious relationship—too
high. He now finds he has taken no light burden on his shoulders. As long as she had Hardy to look after, she was admirable,
but, with her occupation gone, she has become, perhaps, a
little portentous, and rather inclined with a sort of gloomy relish
to make the worst of things. When Barrie was ill in London
she stalked Mrs Vincent Crummles-like about the flat as though
already, as chief mourner, following his coffin to the grave. She
is rather proprietary too, and obviously thinks that neither
Elizabeth Lucas nor I speak to, or of, Barrie with sufficient
reverence. In fact, she actually reprimanded Elizabeth—a friend
of at least twenty years standing—for calling him 'Jimmie'.

Fortunately Mrs Hardy has struck up a great friendship
with Barrie's beloved sister.

Conan Doyle has been our chief newcomer. Burly, unpretentious, lovable, ingenuous, he looks like a country doctor—
he is a doctor. I'm sure the reason why people so readily accept
his word on Spiritualism is that they confuse him with his own
creation. Surely, they think, Sherlock Holmes would be able
to sift evidence. So, crediting Conan Doyle with the faculties
of his hero, they are confident that he couldn't be imposed
upon by frauds; whereas, really, he is, I'm sure, a touchingly
credulous man—a King Gull!

[1] A golden retriever

Apparently, he can't believe that any intelligent person, who seriously investigates Spiritualism, can fail to be converted to its truth—professional mediums and all. That's why he won't forgive Arthur Balfour for failing publicly to testify his belief. I did attempt to explain that Arthur Balfour hadn't ever really been convinced. No use! Whatever I said was pooh-poohed. Arthur Balfour's culpable silence came, insisted Conan Doyle, either from lack of moral courage or from indolence.

Alas, for the vanity of all human success! Conan Doyle declared that he often wished he'd never invented Sherlock Holmes, a blasphemy that turned Beb quite pale. This, Barrie says, is perfectly true. Conan Doyle feels the glamour of Sherlock Holmes—with the exception of some Dickens characters, the most widely-known character in English fiction—stymies from the public what he himself regards as his 'serious' work. The book he prides himself upon is one I've never read —*The White Company*.

If Conan Doyle's presence attracted to Stanway any of those very mundane-looking fairies of whom he showed me photographs, none showed her horrid self to me. (How fortunate that he did not put the question 'Do you believe in fairies?' to the author of *Peter Pan*!) The only unusual thing I *did* see while he was here was an enormous rat galumphing upstairs after Mrs Hardy, a portent I kept from Barrie. . . .

Dear Birrell perceptibly aged this year, but quite as vigorous —and ribald—in talk as ever, and able to read us a quantity of Browning, including with great gusto, *The Bishop Orders His Tomb*. He has, however, given up even trying to talk to Mrs Grum.

Only newcomers this year: 'Goonie'[1] to whom Birrell is devoted, with her lovely little daughter, Clarissa[2], and her son, Peregrine.

To Barrie's disapproval, ritual of my annual night walk was religiously kept up—this time the ten miles over Cleeve Hill into Cheltenham with 'Coley', Michael and Dick Faulkner.

[1] Lady Guendeline Churchill   [2] Mrs Anthony Eden

No visit from Margot this year, but Barrie much amused by the telegram she sent me the day I was going to luncheon with her: 'Bring sixteen magnolias.' At that time there were exactly two magnolias in bloom. . . . Now, I'm enjoying a few very happy last days alone with Barrie and the children. Good-bye visits and long walks with Barrie, this year again in much better walking form, and in every way at his best, despite considerable toil over proofs of the American edition of his books and plays. 'Oh, the re-reading of one's own works!' he groaned. Can what he says be true—that he never looks at any of his published writing except before a re-print or a revival of a play?

Sept. 3rd, 1930
Our first August here without Whibley—'turn down an empty glass'. Six months now since he died. . . . Barrie has been very well, and but for a few minutes after a hapless guest innocently mentioned rats at dinner—wonderfully 'easy'.

Several cricket matches for the boys; torture for me, because despite my insistence on the under-fourteen rule, the one inevitable giant—obviously at least sixteen years old and, of course, a fast bowler—inevitably turns up to reduce me to a jelly of terror for Simon's nose and teeth. No one could be more sympathetic than Barrie about this particular variety of anxiety complex.

Violet Bonham-Carter came with three delightful children —Cressida, Laura and Mark, all mad keen on cricket. Barrie much impressed by Mark's batting style.

Amongst various other young people, we had the lovely, blue-eyed Beatrice and Rosemary Grosvenor, who at first sight and sound of Mrs Grum both engagingly succumbed to giggles, thereby disastrously releasing Simon, 'Coley', and 'the Priest's' long pent-up guffaws.

Plenty of 'parlour games' this season. Barrie much amused by Rosemary and Simon's impersonation of Ramsay MacDonald and Snowdon debating Capital Punishment. The fashionable new game—the 'Murder Game'—first played one night when 'Shakes'[1] and Alison Morrison came to dinner, became a craze.

Post-prandial croquet still inexorably played, however grilling the sun, and even if three out of the four players are aching for a siesta. Epic duels between Barrie and Lord Desborough, who've taken an immense liking to one another. McCartney came again, this time a man of leisure, for, as he brought his charming wife with him, he didn't have to write to her. He put the boys into seventh heaven by first bowling at them, and then with great skill allowing them—quite convincingly—to bowl him out. I played tennis with him, rather with than against, for his service is fiendish.

Maud Valerie White came over from Broadway one day and sang to us in that pathetic little husk of a voice, the tears coursing down her cheeks as her soft squat fingers flew over the keys. Alas, I doubt whether Barrie would agree with Dr Johnson's dictum that music is the 'least disagreeable of all sounds', because of obligation to make some comment when the 'sound' stops.

Several 'bright, particular stars' this year. Walter de la Mare, who brought his charming son, Colin, L. P. Jacks, G. K. Chesterton, and one newcomer, Leslie Hartley, a great addition, a delightfully leading-on talker with that blessed knack of making his interlocutors feel pleased with themselves. He came through his ordeal by Mrs Grum with flying colours, listening to her caterwauling with as much seeming deference as if she were a prima donna.

Lady Desborough more and more delighted with Barrie. 'You don't know what charm is until you've met that little man,' she declared, and then quoted word for word what the heroine of *What Every Woman Knows*, says about charm: 'If you have it, you don't need to have anything else; and if you don't have it, it doesn't much matter what else you have.'

Chesterton was a delight to everyone, and his great popularity with the children, whom he not only entertained but

[1] Mr W. S. Morrison, now the Speaker

treated with the most charming courtesy, suffered no decline when he got stuck—literally stuck—in a doorway, a predicament he seemed himself to enjoy as much as the onlookers. He's even larger than I remember—an absolute mountain of a man! I'm afraid Mamma will find some pretty deep depressions in her bed, for thereon was stretched 'the solemn slope of mighty limbs asleep'. I wonder how much he minds having that ardent spirit, and agile—not to say acrobatic—mind encumbered with so vast a deal of flesh. Each wheezing breath is drawn with a conscious effort, and heaving himself up from the depths of an easy chair appears an exertion equivalent to an ordinary human being climbing a high hill; yet he does invariably struggle up every time anyone—even a child—comes into the room. His wife's chief anxiety was that he might sit down upon some chair which couldn't bear his weight. Having thrice noticed her restrain him from incautiously lowering himself into a deck chair, I had an *iron* bench brought out to the croquet lawn. Barrie tells me this devoted woman looks after her husband in all practical ways, doling him out pocket-money, and so forth—above all making him keep his engagements. This was confirmed by a charming story she told me. While Chesterton was away on a lecture tour, he sent her the following telegram: 'Am in Birmingham. Where ought I to be?'

Chesterton engagedly put into practice on the croquet lawn his admirable maxim that 'whatever is worth doing is worth doing badly.' Totteringly poised on his disproportionately small feet, with his pince-nez insecurely perched on his nose, he wielded the craziest mallet, losing every hoop but winning tremendous applause from the gallery.

He's a grand sight at the dinner-table with a glass of red wine in his hand, and a napkin tucked under his chins. I love his wide-ranging, affluent talk; the long sentences welling out with equal ease, whether he speaks of 'tremendous trifles' or of transcendentalism. His bubbling voice rises almost into a squeak at times, and, Belloc-like, he quite often breaks off in mid-sentence to gurgle into song—usually some snatch from

one of his favourite music-hall ditties. I wish Mamma could
have heard the roistering enthusiasm with which he spoke of
her brother, George Wyndham. He gives me the impression
of enormous, inevitable goodness. I don't wonder he makes so
many converts.

I was amused by Chesterton pronouncing Barrie 'the shyest
of men, and the most impudent of writers.' They get on
wonderfully well together and make a spectacular combina-
tion. Walking side by side on the lawn, they looked just like
two figures out of a fairy tale—a genial giant and a kindly
gnome.

Chesterton sealed his popularity with the children by writing
in my visitors' book:

> When we goes up to London town,
> We likes to drown our sorrers:
> We likes to go to the waxwork show,
> And sit in the Chamber of 'Orrers.
> There's a lovely image of Mother there
> And we do enjoy it, rather:
> We likes to see her 'ow she was
> That night she strangled Father.

*   *   *

Barrie and I agreed that Walter de la Mare must be the
most undisappointing poet that's ever been. He enchanted
every man, woman and child. As someone said of Blake, he
makes you feel you 'have entertained an angel *not* unawares'.
His extraordinary charm is instantaneously felt, and I don't
believe even the veriest dolt could be one moment in his company without realising how different he is from everyone else.
Yet, for all his otherness, he never makes you feel left behind.
Some magic empowers him to lend his companions the freedom
of the different air he breathes—to take them with him into
that mysterious region of which he is a denizen—a region of
fantasy, enchantment—and fear.

However profound his talk, his touch is always light; nor
does he ever seem out of kin with the 'work-a-day world'. He

specially loves talking about murders. We never meet without discussing the latest.

I love his questing, marvelling mind, and his refusal—or rather inability—to waste one second's time on small talk. No sooner has he said how-do-you-do? then—like a jackdaw darting at a gem—he's on to some subject which interests him, and, hey presto, everyone else in the room—even the least likely person—is enthralled.

*   *   *

My diaries of 1931 and 1932 give little beyond the names of our guests at Stanway, but the following letters to my mother recount all that I can remember, and much that I had for-gotten, about the Augusts of those two years.

Sept. 3rd, 1931

. . . You will be glad to hear that my innovation of two small dinner-tables instead of one large one, has been a great improvement. Husbands and wives are temporarily divorced, and I can talk as much as I please without Mrs Grum glaring at me for interrupting Barrie.

We've had some newcomers—Lawrence, the editor of *The Cornhill*, very likable; Anne Charteris, Priscilla Bibesco, Bruce Ogilvie, Jimmie Smith, and the Hartingtons with their son, Andrew. 'Mowcher'[1] lovely with that delicious eager look.

Sir Reginald Poole, Barrie's solicitor, came to draw up the Deed of Conveyance for Barrie's staggeringly generous gift to the Great Ormond Street Children's Hospital of the perpetual rights in *Peter Pan*—all of them, the books as well as the plays! Sir Reginald and I thought Barrie should leave control over the production of the play to some disinterested person for fear the hospital might come to consider only the commercial side, but Barrie prefers to make his gift unconditional.

This year our Principal Boy was George Moore, whom I hadn't seen for years, not since we used so often to meet at

[1] Mary, Duchess of Devonshire

Tonks' wartime kitchen-dinners, and occasionally at Mrs
Charles Hunter's, where I remember his being huffy one
Friday, because his hostess hadn't placed him beside her at
dinner; so huffy that he ordered a car to take him back to
London on Saturday morning. Tonks only just managed to
soothe him down in time to prevent his going.

I've never seen anyone so much altered. For one thing, his
appearance—except for the sloping shoulders and baby-blue
eyes—is almost unrecognisable. D'you remember how tallow-
pale he was? Now, for what reason I know not—diabetes
perhaps—his cheeks are rose-pink. His disposition too, seems
transformed. Instead of attacking practically every painter and
writer, dead or alive, he is almost fulsomely laudatory, and
only once did he revert to his old gambit of provocative literary
paradox. He said that Anne was the only genius of the Brontë
family, a sally which didn't amuse Barrie, an Emily-idolater.

George Moore's visit was entertaining, but far from a rest-
cure, thanks to a series of incidents, some of them alarming, as
he hasn't yet recovered from a serious operation, and Tonks
had enjoined me to 'take great care of him'.

I sat beside him at luncheon on the Friday he came, and it
was arranged that at three o'clock we should go for a walk
together. Punctual to the minute, I arrived at the appointed
meeting-place only—most disconcerting—to find him curled
up on the sofa—unconscious! He was sleeping just like a very
well-to-do baby; apple-blossom cheeks, gentle, regular breathing—no suggestion of a snore. Dilemma. Should I wake him?
I hadn't the heart. Neither did I want him, not finding me
there when he awoke, to suppose me faithless. Counting his
respirations like a hospital nurse, I sat motionless by his
slumbering form. Barrie appeared; laughed silently at my
plight, and basely tiptoed out of the room. At last, George
Moore awoke without so much as a snort in immediate possession of all his faculties. 'How long have I been asleep?' he
asked, opening wide his sleep-brightened eyes, 'and why didn't
you wake me?'

While, talking of this and that, we toddled round the garden,
it was, for some inexplicable reason, arranged that after dinner
I must read to him *Lycidas*, a poem which this Man of Letters
declared—can it be true?—he'd never read.

As I hurried along the passage on my way down to dinner,
I heard a sickening little plop just in front of me. Looking
down, I discovered to my horror that the curious object lying
at my feet was George Moore! He had fallen face downward
over that booby-trap single step, against which I'd so carefully
warned him. Terrified, I scooped him up and, like a Nannie,
practically carried him down the stairs, but he managed to
wriggle out of my clutches just in time to fall over the single
step in the hall, this time to lie in a little heap, like a lump of
lard, at Mowcher's feet, whereupon she and I—and who shall
blame us?—both succumbed to bad attack of giggles. Mercifully, George Moore seemed none the worse for either mishap.
He can't have a bone in his body—must be pneumatic!

After dinner, while the rest of the party 'shuffled', I was put
through my *Lycidas* ordeal. 'I'm converted to Milton,' said
George Moore, with a gracious wave of his boneless, wax-white
hand.

Not long after I'd gone to bed, an eldritch scream and a
scuffle brought me out into the passage. Tremendous com-
motion. George Moore, confusing two doors, had opened the
one leading down to Esther's room and would inevitably have
fallen headlong down that deathtrap flight of stairs and almost
certainly have broken his neck had not Nannie, who fortunately
was patrolling the passage for errant children, caught him just
in time by the cord of his magenta dressing gown. 'Esther
Waters', as, of course, your housemaid has now been renamed,
was much upset by this tallow apparition. In fact, she 'came
over all queer', and was 'took bad'.

Early next morning, I saw George Moore slinking out of the
bathroom with 'Esther Waters' coming out of it *behind* him,
flapping—like an old hen flapping its wings—her duster at his
retreating form. Whether that ubiquitous witch had been

locked up in the bathroom with George Moore while he was in his bath, or whether, baffled by finding her in the room, he was retreating unbathed, I haven't liked to ask. Washed or unwashed, he regaled Barrie, Mowcher and me for hours with tales of his 'affairs of the heart', particularly of one with a siren called, if I remember rightly, 'Opal', who he alleged, had been 'taken from him' by a certain Pro Consul. Then he made me read the whole of *Adonais*, and spoke quite kindly of Shelley.

From first to last he was sweet as barley sugar, and I'm booked to lunch with him in Ebury Street, when I'm to read him an unpublished story by himself and tell him if I don't think it 'as good as anything in Chekov'.

Birrell—shakier on his legs than last summer, but no whit less alert-minded, and even more mellow.

Galsworthy's courtesy has not moulted a feather. His wife embarrassed me by telling me in front of him that the description of Dinny, the girl in his latest novel, *Maid in Waiting*, had been taken from me, whereupon he made me a courtly little bow. I told Barrie I'd had no idea what to say to this, or what to do with my face. 'Of course you should have curtsied,' he said.

Barrie was well disposed to the revised version of George Moore, former editions of whom he hadn't wholly liked, but he has tended this year to be a detached host and to wander off and sit with Prew! His cough, worse than ever, is now often escorted by an angry shout—a sort of jungle roar. Otherwise, he has seemed well and content.

Sept. 2nd, 1932

This year I must, alas, admit that I'm glad the last day has come. It has been such a strain that we're all exhausted. So much worry about poor Beb's eyes, and Barrie, who arrived having just been ill with a feverish cold, the effects of which he never shook off; very low most of the time. Some days, he has just lain in bed, a mere hump of misery, but sending out such powerful black rays that their effect is felt all over the house. When he's ill in London I imagine that I feel the influence of these rays as soon as I step off my 'bus in the Strand. Yet, I don't suppose he really surpasses other men in self-pity, or in failure to make just that little effort which practically every woman—so invaluable a quality is feminine vanity!—makes when anyone comes into the room. No, it is just that abnormal power he has to communicate his feelings.

Now and again he would revive, soar into a brief exultation, in which he would over-exert himself and then collapse again; so that, quite often, he had to go to bed before dinner. One symptom was aching legs, for which I persuaded him to have some electric treatment. He was very sceptical about this, and consented to it only, I think, to please Dr Leslie, of whom since Simon's operation he's very fond. Just for a day or two, he did appear to be better for it, and brisked up, only to relapse into blackest gloom. Poor 'Saul'! And I'm afraid his 'David' is no longer quite young enough to play the harp with magic effect.

There were, of course, fleeting truces with affliction. One evening, Barrie read us his one-act skit on Ibsen, *Ibsen's Ghost*. This, his first publicly performed play, acted in 1891, by Toole, has just been privately printed. Scene: 'Hedda's Shooting Gallery'!

Another day he blithely conducted a large party, including the Galsworthys, to his favourite village, Bibury. And he was able to enjoy the company of some of our visitors. He specially loved having Mowcher[1] here, was always delighted to see the Morrisons, dear 'Priest' never palled, and he was very pleased when Wells came to stay. 'H.G.', chubby and blue-eyed as ever, was in grand form and threw himself into every game. He is our only guest who has arrived with a special kit for croquet. 'Now I must go and change,' he announced, scurrying from the room, soon to reappear, armed with a mallet, in shorts, a sleeveless zebra shirt and a beret.

At dinner one evening Wells publicly acknowledged a very old debt to his host by declaring that he had only found the

[1] Mary, Duchess of Devonshire

secret of the 'true path to journalism' through reading *When a Man's Single*. (I forget if you've ever read that strangely uneven and carelessly architected early book of Barrie's? It contains one brilliantly drawn character, the journalist, Noble Simms, who, like his creator, can write an article on anything—or nothing.) 'For years', said Wells, 'I'd been straining after lofty and original topics. The more articles I had rejected, the higher I aimed. All the time I was shooting miles over the target. Noble Simms, bless him, taught me that all I had to do was to lower my aim—and hit.'

Very few newcomers this year (just as well), only Harold Baker, Lady Winifred Gore, Donald Maclean's good-looking clever son, Ian, Mary Rose, Barrie's very nice young nephew, Alec Barrie, and some schoolboy friends of Michael and Simon's. For the first time no Mrs Grum! I had expected this revolutionary change to make everything, particularly the arrangement of the dinner table, so much easier; but, by a curious irony, her absence produced a distinct sense of flatness! It was like playing golf on a links without any bunkers. We all missed the getting-together in corners to talk about her, our struggles against laughter and the camaraderie inspired by difficulty shared and partially surmounted.

Far our best time was Chesterton's visit, for which Barrie resurrected after three sombre days in bed. Chesterton devoted an entire day to preparing an elaborate game for us. Early one morning, he set off with his wife on a shopping expedition into Evesham, whence they returned laden with various parcels of challenging shape. All that afternoon he remained closeted in the Old Library, emerging at tea-time to announce that he'd invented for us a new kind of Murder Game, the object being to find, not the murderer, but the murderee, who turned out to be Lord L. . . . , for whom Chesterton has no love. He had drawn, painted, and cut out in cardboard, a wonderful caricature of this 'Wicked Nobleman', which he then dismembered, hiding the fragments all over the house. He had also written clues in rhyming couplets. These clues, besides guiding the seekers in the hunt for the dismembered baron, provided curdling sidelights on his personality and public career. A long search, in the course of which limb after severed limb was gradually found, ended in the discovery, in a very difficult place, of the missing head complete with coronet.

CHAPTER XII

BACK TO SCOTLAND

IT never occurred to me, while writing to my mother at the end of our 1932 'Stanway Season', that that year—the twelfth —would be the last, but so it proved to be.

Barrie as a guest constantly returned to Stanway—I think he spent all his remaining Easters and Christmases with us— but as host he came no more. Because, in the spring of 1933, he had been very ill at Stanway, it was questioned whether it would be wise for him to return so soon to the same place; and various other reasons prompted a change of plans. The strongest was perhaps, that Barrie, like others, as he neared the end of his life, found his thoughts turning back to its beginning. The place where he had been born, the place where he was to be buried, began to beckon him back—to pull at his heartstrings. It was decided that a house in Scotland should be taken somewhere quite close to Kirriemuir.

In retrospect, that last August at Stanway stands out as one of those momentous milestones, not recognised until far behind. From that time on the stage began to darken, until, some four years later, the curtain fell.

'When you are over sixty life becomes like a bloody field of battle with friends falling all around you.' The truth of that lament was forced upon Barrie as, one by one, so many friends died—Galsworthy, Anthony Hope, Birrell, Kipling, Fred Oliver, James Robb, Margaret and William Winter—finally his lifelong comrade the devoted Gilmour. During these last years Barrie suffered too—not that I think this ever troubled him much—serious monetary losses; and with the critical reception of his last play, *The Boy David*, he had to bear the only important disappointment of his literary career. His health rapidly declined. One severe bronchial attack followed another. His cough racked him. All the while that private hell of insomnia in which he had suffered so long grew steadily worse. 'I CAN'T sleep!' he would complain more and more often, his sunken eyes now so darkly encircled as to look positively bruised. (The last time I heard him mutter those words they were the last words he spoke.) Worst of all, because his parents in old age had lost their memories, he was haunted by the fear that his mind would become clouded before he died.

Appropriately, all this grief, illness and disappointment had to be endured against the jarring background of the slow but relentless demolition of the beautiful Adelphi Terrace. The din, the dust, the devastation were horrible, and each hammer-blow reminded Barrie that very soon now he would be forced to leave his beloved flat. In the last twenty years of his life that large, smoke-grimed, ship-like room had come to mean so much to him. And he had never even begun to tire of the flickering river view that had been a solace through so many pacing nights of sleeplessness.

Not long before his death he wrote to me, 'You can't think what a stage of squalid demolition the Adelphi has reached. Roofs in tatters, windows gone, great holes in walls. At this rate one feels all will be gone in a week or two. Workmen are crawling everywhere with hammers and every blow brings down a chunk. I have seldom seen the outlook so lovely as it is after sunset these nights. All the world a trembling blue except for the lamps. Sad to have to say goodbye to it. . . . Even the light will be taken from us soon as another monster building will be going up. They are debating about it in the House of Lords today and tomorrow, but it is hardly conceivable that commerce will not carry the day.' . . . And later, 'The poor Terrace has now most of its inside torn out and there are more gashes in the walls. None save familiars can do it reverence nowadays and perhaps one ought to look the other way instead of gazing at its shame as I find myself constantly doing from my eyrie. Perhaps I too should have stolen already away. So rapid now is the demolition that in one week many landmarks go. We become like the birds' nests one finds in hedges, half torn away and pieces of egg-shell scattered beneath.'

Hideous rubble of destruction, ceaseless nerve-shattering noise, the impending loss of his home! All this, that shocking act of vandalism, the destruction of Adelphi Terrace meant to Barrie. More, it became to him, I think, symbolic of his own now rapidly crumbling strength—perhaps, too, of the disintegration, the growing chaos of the civilised world.

'The bright day is done and we are for the dark?' Yet, it would be very easy to paint far too sombre a picture of the last years of Barrie's life, which, for all their sorrows, disappointment and ill health, held much happiness, interest—even joy. There were frequent rifts in the gathering clouds of depression, when I remember him at his very best, and gratefully aware of many blessings. Bright among these, a bonus seldom declared by life perhaps after the age of seventy, was the revivifying delight of a great new friendship. With the flashing into his life of Elizabeth Bergner, came that sudden rekindling of inspiration for which Barrie had so long waited; inspiration, which, bursting into blaze, was to plunge him back into that lost heaven of absorption that gave him the sense of being fully alive. Even though the outcome of this final flare-up, the last and, as some thought, the finest of his plays, was to be dogged by ill-luck and, in the narrow sense of the word, to prove a failure, much happiness had gone to its creation. Once again he had known what he called 'the lovely experience— the slinging of sheet after sheet onto the floor,' and whatever the verdict—by no means necessarily final—of the box-office, several of those whose judgment he most valued had glowingly acclaimed his work.

Although Barrie, during this last phase of his life, did not speak of his death, I think he knew it was not far off. He had always had a great distaste for the idea of any biography of himself, but realised that one would inevitably be written. This being so, he decided in 1935 that he would like, by dictating me notes on his life, to give me the material to write the book. To make this possible, it would, he declared, be essential for him to be able to rely on my being at hand all day for at least three months. Unfortunately, the then state of my husband's health made this impossible, and I had to tell Barrie so. He sighed like a drear-nighted December, and away for ever went that possible—or impossible—book.

When I look back across so wide a gulf of time at what, after our last August at Stanway, remained of Barrie's life, it seems short; but, in reality, four more years were still to come, years of which—for the force of his personality increased—I have deeply-scored memories. The most vivid and poignant of these memories centre on the inception, writing and production of *The Boy David*. But, before telling that sad story, I will describe his return to Scotland.

For the August of 1933 Barrie rented Balnaboth, a house in Glen Prosen, some twelve miles north of his native town Kirriemuir, in Forfarshire. Balnaboth, a white-walled, grey-roofed, medium-sized house, stands alone, surrounded by the wild ever-changing beauty of the glen, with the River Prosen, now rushing, now trickling, through its grounds. As an appropriate prelude to a holiday that was to prove anything but peaceful, Barrie was met at the station by a horde of reporters, and for the whole of our stay we were besieged by would-be interviewers and photographers.

There had been a time when Barrie was not in favour with his fellow-townsmen. Angry heads had been shaken over his early book, *Auld Licht Idylls*. What right, Kirriemuirians growled, had 'young Jamie', to poke fun at his native town and their forbears? Many of them had never before read a novel of any kind, and were utterly mystified by the book's queer compound of fact, exaggeration and invention. The mixing up of generations maddened them. So did the twisted topography. Furthermore, they couldn't understand the literary convention of writing in the first person. How dared 'Jamie' pretend to remember events that had taken place long before he was born?

Nor had Barrie been unaware of this local indignation when, with his pockets full of cheques, he went home on a holiday to the town he was making famous as 'Thrums'. 'The Auld Lichts,' he wrote in youthful callousness, or in bravado, to a friend, 'The Auld Lichts shake their heads at me. I could rip some of 'em up to get the notes out of them.'

But pride had long since taken the place of resentment. The prophet had become a prophet in his own country, and Kirriemuir was thrilled by the return of its famous son.

Barrie, too, was excited—not to say disturbed—at finding himself back in the scenes of his boyhood. By impressing upon him, as this perpetually did, the glaring contrast between the past and the present, it seemed to set up within him an almost painful severance. The 'Jamie' of long ago? . . . The 'Sir James Barrie' of today?

> Now times are altered; if I care
>   To buy a thing, I can;
> The pence are here and here's the fair
>   But where's the lost young man?

One difference between the Then and the Now that never ceased to bewilder, even to annoy, the 'lost young man' was the transformation motor cars had brought about in the scale of Forfarshire distances. In his memory Balnaboth was romantically far from Kirriemuir. From one place to the other had been a long day's walk—quite an adventure. Now, of course, a short drive could bring Kirriemuirians to his door. But although Barrie knew this, he still felt it to be a long journey— so much was he back in the past—and this made him think that anyone who took the trouble to come so far ought to be asked to make a long visit. Consequently, luncheon-guests were urged to remain on for tea—some stayed a good five hours—with the result that Barrie became far more tired than was necessary.

All the time Barrie was in Forfarshire this shrinkage of its distances jarred upon him. He never ceased to resent it. Was this, perhaps, partly because the new scale reduced to insignificance the sensationally long walks of his boyhood? At all events, the rapidity with which familiar landmarks, once so widely apart, now flashed past the windows of a car exasperated him. It seemed to diminish—to dwarf the whole landscape. He hated, too, the humiliating fact that he must drive—could no longer walk over the well-remembered hills. Hitherto he had, I think, scarcely realised the insidious change wrought by time in his bodily self, but being continuously reminded of his lost youth reminded him of his present age which, like most of us, he tended to forget.

One way and another, I remember Balnaboth as a curiously fatiguing, exacting time. Barrie's alternations between gloom and glory were difficult to keep up with; he complained of sleeping worse than ever, and the prospect of having in his last week in Scotland to make a speech in Kirriemuir weighed on him out of all proportion. I suppose it seemed more than usually important that he should give his best performance; but, not only did he feel the strain so much beforehand, he was also far more exhausted when it was successfully over than I had ever known him to be after any other public ordeal. Partly, no doubt, because he was older and ailing; but far more, I'm sure, because the emotions re-awakened by his return to his native region and the ever-pressing sense of the pastness of the past had set up an inner turmoil that intensified his usual nerviness.

Despite the weariness, the fever and the fret, I remember many happy days at Balnaboth, and several occasions on which Barrie soared into his best form. And, in retrospect, the month he spent there was transmuted into gold. He forgot all the stresses, strains, emotional pangs; remembered only the delights—the triumphs of his return. In fact, Balnaboth, in his memory, became the very symbol of happiness. In a letter, written to me after we left, he referred to the 'sheer happiness of the days', and, evidently they had done him good, for shortly afterwards he seemed bodily and mentally much better than for some time past.

> This is the land of lost content,
>   I see it smiling plain,
> The happy highways where I went
>   And cannot come again.

This verse kept straying into my head at Balnaboth. Barrie seemed all the time to be searching—searching for something he could never find. His letter makes brief allusion to that search for his old—or rather his young—self, of which, though it was never spoken of, I had been so conscious.

Sept. 1953. I am so glad you did enjoy Glen Prosen; I had similar fears to yours about the experiment, but in a day or two I knew it was to be one of the happiest holidays of my life, and so without a doubt it proved. Fain would I have lingered. For the first time perhaps I was 'sweir' to return to the London that eternally thrills me and has been to me all the bright hopes of my youth conceived. . . . I do love my native region with almost a ferocity of attachment. The houses and its hills and little bridges over the burns had a very steadying effect on me. They were the only things that stood still. All else we saw as in a flashing cinema. I never showed you anything. We were always in cars and a mile in front of whatever I had to say. The only way to have shown you that boy I was looking for of whom you write would have been to steal off in Michael's car in the night-time and to leave it hidden in Caddum Wood while we wandered through a sleeping Kirriemuir. There is a window in one of the mills where I once thought I should have to live my life as a clerk, the window where my father sat for many years. There is the Lozie grounds I did most miserably frequent haunted by the dread that there was nothing for it but to become a doctor. The house in the south-muir opposite

the Window in Thrums is more full of me and I am more full
of it than all else up there. . . . I expect I did go off and make
those nocturnal searchings alone. I daresay it was not Michael
I heard climbing back by the bathroom window but myself.
If so and this was what disturbed my sleep, it was worth it for
it brought serenity in the morning.

* * *

The small number of bedrooms at Balnaboth had made it
impossible to invite more than just a few of the Stanway
'Annuals'—Algernon Cecil, 'Coley', Elizabeth Lucas and
Stephen Gwynne. Peter Davies came with his newly-married,
very decorative wife, Margaret, and their happiness was a
great delight to Barrie. My two sons, the Faulkner boys, and
Jack Davies's son Timothy were all with us. So there was
plenty of 'lawn cricket'; as well as river-bathing for Barrie to
watch, with a new recruit to the band of boys in Dick Rowe,
between whose family and Barrie there were many Forfarshire
links. The garden provided croquet for Barrie, and in the
evenings darts had to take the place of the Stanway shovelboard. His only complaint of the weather was that it was 'too
fine to fish', but, as I suspect his idea that he would still be a
keen fisherman was a delusion, this was probably just as well.

Various other visitors came and went. Amongst them were
my mother, my niece Mary Rose Charteris, Mrs F. Oliver,
Sister Thomlinson and the then Prime Minister, Ramsay
MacDonald, and his daughter Sheila. The boys were thrilled
by the arrival not so much of the Prime Minister as of his
private detective, whose company they found enthralling.
Barrie and Ramsay MacDonald sat up talking until all hours.
The insomnia they shared was, I'm sure, a great bond. I remember the Prime Minister telling me that he could never get
to sleep before four o'clock in the morning, and his handsome
face did look ravaged with fatigue. My most pleasing memory
of his visit was when the inevitable press photographer turned
up all agog to catch two such eminent Scottish birds with one

click of the camera; and in turn, each of the coveted birds came to me to explain in almost identical words, that much as he, of course, hated being photographed himself, he thought 'my host' or 'my guest', as the case was, 'would like us to be done together'. So perhaps he had better submit? With each in turn I cordially agreed that the other would most certainly like it; thus both birds enjoyed a sense of self-sacrifice, and an excellent photograph was procured of the brace of them standing on a bridge dreamily gazing down at the River Prosen.

I have heard Barrie derided for 'liking to be friends with Prime Ministers', a taunt which seems to me to show a singular lack of imagination. The dread of Barrie's boyhood had been that, obliged to become and to remain a clerk in Kirriemuir, he would never reach the city of his dreams, London. Having achieved what seemed so unlikely an ambition, and established himself in London, was it surprising that he should be pleased to find himself sought out by its men of note, among them statesmen whose names, had the course of his life run normal, would have been household words to him and nothing more? What queer brand of an inverted snob would he have been, if this had not pleased him! Prime Ministers had their share in the fulfilment of his boyhood's dreams; and hobnobbing with them sharpened that sense of contrast between his past and his present, which though it could often hurt Barrie, seldom failed to stir his sense of drama. And why, indeed, should anyone be so devoid of interest in history in the making as not to like to know, and judge for himself, those who—for good or for ill—are helping to make it?

Barrie enjoyed being behind the scenes in politics almost as much as he had once enjoyed being behind the scenes at the theatre. And, of course, he had enough humility to be pleased when a Prime Minister asked his advice!

A happy episode in our time at Balnaboth was Barrie's meetings with the Royal Family. One day, the Duke and

Duchess of York brought the future Queen Elizabeth and Princess Margaret Rose to a tea with a birthday cake and crackers. Barrie greatly enjoyed the occasion and played up very well, except for one startling social lapse, the shock of which all but killed one of his guests, a well brought-up British subject. We were all hovering round the door waiting to go out in the correct order, when suddenly Barrie, the host, shot out of the room in front of the Duke of York! Whatever surprise the future King may have felt at so unaccustomed a sight as the back, at close quarters, of a commoner was admirably concealed, and the next day there was a return visit to Glamis—a visit with a sequel. It was Princess Margaret's third birthday, and Barrie had the privilege of sitting beside the heroine of the day, then so tiny that seated at the table her entrancing little face was scarcely above the level of her cup. Each cast a spell on the other, and three years later Barrie wrote for my book *The King's Daughters* a description of their meeting.

Some of her presents were on the table, simple things that might have come from the sixpenny shops, but she was in a frenzy of glee over them especially about one to which she had given the place of honour by her plate. I said to her as one astounded, 'Is that really your very own?' and she saw how I envied her and immediately placed it between us with the words: 'It is yours and mine.'

This childish courtesy made a deep impression on Barrie. The words 'It is yours and mine' sank into his mind, not long afterwards to be joined by another phrase he was told of from the same baby lips. Soon after her third birthday party, the little Princess heard someone speak of him. Swiftly turning her head, she looked brightly up and said instantly, 'I know that man. He is my greatest friend, and I am his greatest friend.'

These two phrases were garnered in Barrie's memory— garnered not to be wasted, for when next he wrote a play both were introduced into its dialogue. The sequel to the Glamis tea-party was that when Barrie met the little Princess again he confessed his act of plagiarism and told her that as she was a collaborator in his play *The Boy David*, she should have a penny for each performance of it.

By the time *The Boy David* was produced, Barrie supposed this little incident long since forgotten. But to his pleased amusement a message came from King George the Sixth to say that if he did not immediately take steps to carry out his promise and pay Princess Margaret her share of the royalties on his play he would be hearing from His Majesty's solicitors. Barrie at once gleefully set to work to write, and with the collaboration of his solicitor, Sir Reginald Poole, correctly to draw up, an elaborately formal Agreement to be signed by Princess Margaret and himself. This mock-solemn Agreement began—

> WHEREAS
> This Indenture made the tenth day of June one thousand and nine hundred and thirty seven BETWEEN James Matthew Barrie so called Author and HER ROYAL HIGHNESS THE PRINCESS MARGARET WITNESSETH as follows: WHEREAS the above-mentioned henceforward to be called the said Barrie did write and otherwise indite a play of short and inglorious life called 'The Boy David' and basely produce the aforesaid play as exclusively the work of his own hand.

This Indenture, the very last thing Barrie ever wrote, was engrossed on parchment and officially stamped, and the plan was that when the requisite number of pennies had been procured from the Bank, he should take them in a canvas bag to the Palace where, by countersigning the document, Princess Margaret would complete the discharge of the debt. Alas, this was never to be. No sooner was the bulging bag of glittering new pennies ready and the date for the ceremony fixed than Barrie was overtaken by his last illness. Thus, sadly, it fell to my lot to deliver the sackful of pennies after his death.

* * *

While at Balnaboth I several times visited Kirriemuir, and so came, near the end of Barrie's life, to know far more of its beginnings. I saw the cottage which for the first twelve years of his life had been his home. Only four rooms, all very small.

I remembered the size of his family. Before Barrie, the ninth child of his parents, was born, two of their children had already died, and his brother Alexander, except for Christmas and some weeks in the summer, was away at Aberdeen University. Even so, with Barrie's youngest sister, there were *nine* occupants of that minute cottage; and of its four rooms, one couldn't be used for living purposes, because until the breadwinner later on found another workshop, it was filled by his hand-loom, and its ceaseless clatter.

A few yards from the cottage stands the very small communal 'Wash House', which used to be shared by all those who lived in the group of dwellings, then called The Tenements, but now grandiloquently described to sightseers as 'Sir James Barrie's First Theatre.'

I saw, too, Strathview, the quite commodious house into which the family moved in 1882, and where Barrie, at that time twelve years old, was later to write so many thousands of words.

Kirriemuir regaled me with memories, some of them perhaps legendary, of Barrie's boyhood. I was told how fast 'little Jamie' had run early one morning in his Glengarry bonnet to see a pig being killed. I heard, too, much of his famous long walks—how he would often trudge thirty miles in one day, and at sixteen years old had once walked twenty-four miles in the morning and then played football that afternoon, after which he had been obliged for some days to 'keep his bed'.

I heard, besides, how early Barrie had shown—and turned to profit!—his extraordinary faculty for vicarious emotion. He used to be paid a small fee to write for some of his elders, who couldn't express their feelings, their letters of condolence. It was even alleged that he sometimes played proxy for mourners. One day when he was six years old, he had, so the story ran, changed clothes with another small boy, who was in deep mourning, but wanted to go on playing games. The bereaved boy had fun at marbles. 'Jamie', conspicuous in his borrowed 'blacks', sat apart and wept. I wonder which child enjoyed himself most.

CHAPTER XIII

LAST HOLIDAYS

BARRIE did not like to be by, in, or on the sea, nor did he
hanker either after an extensive course of sight-seeing, or the
opportunity to hobnob with his fellow-creatures *en masse*. Had
I been told that I should ever see him on a Pleasure Cruise I
simply wouldn't have believed it. In the summer of 1934 this,
however, came about. I had just been very ill with pleurisy,
and the doctors decreed that this year, if there was to be any
shared holiday, it must take the form of a sea voyage. Barrie
heroically agreed to this plan, so at the beginning of August he,
my husband, my two sons, their Nannie, and my friend
Horatia Seymour and I set off on the *Arandora Star* for a nine-
teen days' Mediterranean Cruise. Barrie embarked wearing
an anti-seasick belt and swallowing antidotes in handfuls; but,
though the first days were exceedingly rough, he never suffered
a single qualm and soon became quite a confident seafarer.

Socially, he passed with characteristic rapidity from a phase
of considerable moroseness to one of excessive geniality. For
fear of autograph-hunters his name had been omitted from the
passenger list, and he stubbornly refused to attend the festivity,
hopefully called the 'Getting-Together Dinner'. But he soon
warmed up. Before long he was speaking to strangers, shortly
afterwards metaphorically, if not literally, slapping them on
the back. At the last-night gala, called the 'Breaking-Up
Dinner', he wore a paper cap out of a cracker and blew a tin
trumpet with the heartiest of the professional 'good-mixers'.

He enjoyed playing quoits with all his old dexterity and
throwing rope rings into a bucket. He liked walking round and

round the 'promenade' deck, too, until a certain embarrassment arose. Our fellow-cruisers, at first just one vast indistinguishable throng, had sorted themselves out. We had got onto nodding terms with quite a few, and this made it difficult to know exactly at which moment, after they came into sight, to recognise acquaintances who were walking round the deck the opposite way. To save up your smile seemed churlishly thrifty, but it didn't do to let it be used-up before the meeting was over. If Barrie's smile had to be kept going too long, it tended to turn into a grimace. These repeated, inevitably fatuous, 'Here We Are Again!' re-encounters got so much on Barrie's nerves that, in a desperate attempt to avoid yet another, we would turn sharp on our heels and walk the reverse way round the deck, only to find that—simultaneously—the others had had the same idea!

I shall never forget poor Barrie's horror at his first sight of the 'Lido', where, outstretched by the swimming pool, bodies of tremendous ugliness lay broiling in the blazing sun, not only nearly naked, but thanks to over-cooking, largely raw! There were, of course, some exceptions, but with their distressingly localised corpulence and appalling blisters, most of these sun-worshippers did, indeed, present a gruesome sight; one from which we felt that the public should somehow be protected. What, wondered Barrie, would be the best method? A Selection Committee, with authority to grant or withold a nudity-licence, and compel all who failed to qualify to wear a proscribed minimum?

Despite the shock sustained on the Lido which, once you knew the geography of the boat, could easily be avoided, the cruise evidently suited Barrie. I had never known him cough so little or complain less of sleeplessness. The experience was indeed sufficiently enjoyed to be encored, and at the beginning of August the following year, Barrie embarked on the immense *Homeric* for his second Mediterranean Cruise, accompanied this time by my husband and me, my son Simon, Nannie and her nephew Bobbie Faulkner.

No fear of sea-sickness troubled Barrie on this cruise, nor of being importuned by fellow-passengers. Besides, the vast size of the ship with its numbers of decks made it much easier to keep away from other people, and whenever we felt inclined we could have our meals on a virtually empty deck.

I had never seen Barrie so much moved by anything outside his own mind as by the beauty of Athens, to catch the first glimpse of which he rose before dawn. His ecstasy survived the ferocious heat of the stony precipitous climb up to the Acropolis, and lasted until some time after our descent when, all of a sudden, he was utterly worn out, plunged in black depression and looking alarmingly ill from the heat. But this reaction was very soon forgotten; Athens for the rest of his life glowed in his memory.

Among acquaintances made on the *Homeric* the only ones to become real and lasting friends were Colonel and Mrs Follett and their fourteen-year-old daughter Pauline. One day, as Barrie and I were watching a game of tenniquoits, our eyes were caught, and held, by the beauty of one of the players, a very young girl, whose every movement had the poetry of unconscious, inevitable grace. Lithe, arrow-slim in the crocus-yellow sheath of her swimming suit, she was silhouetted against the dazzling blue of the Mediterranean sky. Her dark hair was blown back from her lovely, eager face. She seemed the very embodiment of joyous youth. Simultaneously, Barrie and I were struck by the thought that this vision looked the ideal Peter Pan—Peter Pan just about to exclaim, 'I'm youth! I'm joy!'

When we came to know Pauline Follett's parents, we learned that she had not only stage ambitions and talent, but even some training, so Barrie, who had long wished to see the part of Peter Pan played by someone as young as this girl, at once decided to recommend her to the management of that year's production. I looked forward to enjoying the play as never before, but to my bitter disappointment, this dream was not realised. Those in control were foolish enough to consider

Pauline's youth and want of an established name a disadvantage, and unfortunately Barrie was not at the time well enough to insist on having his wish carried out.

* * *

Never had I known the see-saw of Barrie's spirits so violent as during our last shared summer holiday in 1936, in Switzerland. The first days at Lucerne were very difficult. Barrie was much distressed by breathlessness, a new symptom which inevitably became much worse whenever we rose to any height in a car or a mountain railway. Socially, too, he was at first at his most suspiciously wary. Then all of a sudden, coming out of a black cloud into blazing bonhomie, he began speaking and paying compliments to strangers. Benignly presiding over the revels he had soon infused the hotel with the Pleasure Cruise spirit. On our last day, such was his effervescence that he could even watch with approval modern dancing, which usually jarred on his nerves. He stood people drinks at the bar, gave and personally presented prizes at the ping-pong tournament, and made a voluntary speech! Naturally, he became wildly popular, and as we left the next day none of his new devotees witnessed the reaction which I need not describe.

From Lucerne we moved on to Gründelwald. Here the hotel was even more lively. Young people abounded, but this time Barrie did not blossom out. He couldn't enjoy any social life. Nor was it much better out of doors. The paths were far too precipitous. The greater altitude made his breathlessness worse. With a sudden, stabbing sense, I realised that he was old.

As the days passed he seemed almost to take an ill will to the mountains—to want to get out of sight of them and shelter all day from the scorching glare of the sun in the inadequate shade of a small wood. Yet, ill as he was, he remained, I'm afraid, sufficiently perceptive to divine how much I longed to be climbing the mountains with my son.

A difficult, saddening, tantalising time. I can't deny that I was glad when the day of departure came. But, on our return journey, Barrie made yet another of his remarkable recoveries. Nor was this by any means entirely because of the direction in which our train was speeding. No, once again, he not only forgave, but quite forgot, all distresses and annoyances; remembered only the good moments—the enjoyment. Switzerland had been a perfect holiday. 'We must go back next year!' . . .

Next year?

CHAPTER XIV

THE BOY DAVID

To tell the story of *The Boy David*, I must go back to the winter of 1934. When I arrived at the flat one morning towards the end of January, I found Barrie neither immersed in *The Times* nor able to pay any attention to his correspondence. He was much too eager to tell me of the impression made on him by Elizabeth Bergner, the brilliant, captivating Austrian actress he had seen the evening before in Margaret Kennedy's *Escape Me Never*. He could talk of nothing else.

Elizabeth Bergner, who had just conquered the London theatre-going world, had played on the Continent several Shakespearean heroines, Bernard Shaw's 'St. Joan', and other leading parts. When, because of the spirit that was taking hold of Germany, she left that country, she had first made films in Paris under the direction of her husband, Paul Czinner, and had then come to London to be starred by the great C. B. Cochran.

At the end of the performance, Barrie, for once more than willing to go 'behind', had been taken by his godson, Peter Scott, to see Elizabeth Bergner in her dressing-room. He had found her as entrancing off the stage as on.

The next evening Barrie took me to *Escape Me Never* and I, too, fell under the spell. I shall never forget my shock of delight when Elizabeth Bergner, entering through the window, first darted on to the stage, looking in her schoolgirl's tunic and beret less than fourteen years old. Vibrantly alive, humorous, harrowing, with some quite undefinable enchantment of her own, she 'held' me through every minute of the play, haunted me afterwards.

A few days later, Elizabeth Bergner came to the flat to see Barrie. He told her he would like to write a play for her. Was there, he asked, any particular kind of part she would choose for herself? Without an instant's hesitation, she said she had always wanted to play David, the little shepherd boy, unconscious of his mighty destiny. The spark was struck. Scarcely had Elizabeth Bergner disappeared down the lift-shaft before Barrie had snatched up a Bible and started to make notes.

I remember Barrie's kindled, teeming look the next morning, and how, the moment I arrived, I was sent out to search bookshops for various works on Jewish history and customs. Laden with books, I came back to find Barrie dashing down notes. ('Barrie in terrific eruption', reports my diary.) The next day I saw that the top sheet of the pile by his inkpot was headed 'Act One'. Before the end of February Barrie had finished the rough draft of that act. Meantime he had become intensely alive, appeared magically rejuvenated. Yet, though he looked years younger, he seemed, I noticed with a pang, driven by a special sense of urgency. Morning after morning I would find him seated at his desk, just perceptibly rocking—a habit of his —from side to side, as he wrote.

Barrie at once told me the subject of his play, but wise after so many events, I begged him *not* to talk about it, and he agreed that for the present this might be wiser.

All I ventured to say was that he must take care to give people no chance to say he had made David too much of a Peter Pan.

The whole of the first act came, it seemed, very easily, but once embarked on the second, Barrie began to groan over the problem of Goliath, and to become, I think, oppressedly aware of the difficulties of the demands he was making upon his Muse —difficulties later on so well diagnosed by Granville-Barker:

The formidable addition to his usual difficulties, the difficulties he was always challenging himself to solve by wedding fantasy to a realism of method, was that in taking a known story to dramatise, he had lost a large part of his liberty—more valuable to him than to most—to adapt character to event and event to character, and both to an imaginative scheme which may grow and change. He has lost the benefit of surprise; we know what is to come. . . . His David and Saul are to be made as actual to us as people we pass in the street, their thoughts and feelings given the currency of our own. Yet something of their legendary status and its glamour must be left them. . . . These figures must be realised and rarefied too. It is no easy task. Nor will the least troublesome part be the question of the sort of speech to put into their mouths.

Towards the end of March, there was, I remember, a phase of despair. Barrie thought he was stuck. But, coming out of the doldrums, he was soon forging ahead. So engrossed was he, indeed, that he could scarcely tolerate the inevitable interruptions of daily life.

The play, which as yet had no title, was still a dead secret. No one, I was adjured, must even know what it was about. After a time Barrie could no longer restrain himself from reading to me passages from the first and second acts, and, in April, he told me that in the third act David was to dream his future, not knowing it to be his own.

'What I have undertaken,' said Barrie one morning, looking, as he spoke, ineffably weary, but very excited—even exalted. 'What I have undertaken requires great sense of the stage, which I have; great daring, which I have; and poetic imagination, which I have not.'

I first read the first draft of the finished play through the swirling mists of a temperature of 104. I remember how the pages ballooned, the wavering lines rose and fell as, defying my protesting hospital nurse, I read straight through all three acts and then wrote a long letter to the author.

Early in June 1934, the first announcement of the play appeared in *The Times*. No title, nor any clue to its subject, merely the fact that Barrie was writing a play for Elizabeth Bergner to be produced in London early next year.

Elizabeth Bergner was 'booked' to appear in *Escape Me Never* in America when its London run finished. There could have been no question of earlier production. Barrie was accustomed to his plays going into immediate rehearsal; any delay, therefore, seemed strange, but he bore it with commendable patience. As things turned out, he had to wait two and a half years!

Cochran, the much-loved 'Cockie', tremendously impressed by the play and quite undismayed by its unexpectedness, longed to produce it at once. But even his zeal could not avail against fate. First, there were Elizabeth Bergner's film commitments; then an almost incredible run of bad luck that caused a series of nerve-shattering postponements.

This long postponement, for which no one was to blame, was a great misfortune. When, at last, the play went into rehearsal, Barrie upon whom old age had suddenly descended, no longer had the strength to produce it. Whether or not his hand had lost its cunning, he was no longer physically fit for the strain of rehearsals. Apart from this calamity, it had been impossible to remain unaware of the adverse effect on the public of the prolonged delay. People had begun to say that there was a curse upon the play and, not only had the repeated postponements given rise to every kind of derogatory rumour, they had also allowed time for many to become irritated by the mystery—always, I thought, a tactical error—in which the theme of the play was still kept shrouded. Worse, many had begun to feel—even to express—resentment that in the first play Barrie had written after a silence of fourteen years, the leading part should have been given to a foreigner. The answer to this grievance was, of course, that but for this foreigner the play would not have been written. This answer Barrie never gave.

Final stroke of bad luck! When, at last, the play was produced, it had to contend with the very worst enemy known to the box office—the opposition of 'Big News'.

The abdication of King Edward the Eighth had just been announced. 'Not only the whole of London,' wrote Dennis Mackail, 'but the whole of Great Britain, was now completely obsessed by something else. If a soothsayer could have predicted these conditions in advance, no manager would have dreamt of presenting a play of such importance in the middle of December, 1936.'

To return to 1934. However badly Barrie's nerves suffered under the strain of the suspense, no word of complaint passed his lips. All through the interminable delay his admiration for Elizabeth Bergner and delight in her company continued as great as ever.

Barrie had during recent years seemed more inclined to films than to plays, but after writing *The Boy David* he resumed theatre-going. He wanted to see the newly-risen or rising stars. I several times accompanied him on his search for the ideal Saul, but it wasn't long before he decided—how rightly —on Godfrey Tearle.

I had always thought it a great pity that Barrie should pay so little attention to the filming of his own plays. He never would have anything to do with this. Nor, when *The Admirable Crichton* was preposterously rechristened *Male and Female*, was he nearly indignant enough to satisfy his secretary. As for the misprint which advertised the film version of *The Twelve Pound Look* as *The Twelve Pound Cook*, this merely made him laugh. Thanks, however, to the glamour of Elizabeth Bergner, he now developed a belated interest in the technical side of filming, and spent many happy hours watching, in an unofficial advisory capacity, the 'shooting' of *As You Like It* in which she played Rosalind.

In the magnificent Forest of Arden at Elstree with its acres of 'real' trees and water, there was, indeed, plenty to amuse onlookers besides the live storks, ducks and geese in the cast. 'Gee!' I overheard an American camera man exclaim, 'Gee! I just CAN'T get this guy Shakespeare!'

*   *   *

It was not until February 1936 that *The Boy David* first went into rehearsal at His Majesty's Theatre. On that very day Barrie heard the news of his sister's death. Grief made him ill.

The doctor was sent for, and forbade him to leave the flat. Nearly a week passed before he was able to go to the theatre to see what the company was making of his play.

Never shall I forget the strain, the tension, of those early rehearsals, nor the impact on the atmosphere of such preter-naturally strong personalities of diverse temperaments as the Author, the Impresario, the Scene-Designer and the Star.

To this day I have only to shut my eyes to see that constella-tion of four. Barrie, looking really alarmingly ill, is plunged in black disappointment verging on despair. He feels every-thing to be wrong but is too ill to know, as formerly he would have known, how to set about putting things right, and his jarred and jangled nerves are, of course, upsetting everyone else's.

At his side, I see Cochran, white-haired now, but in contrast to the author, rosy-cheeked and trim as ever, and, though ill and in perpetual pain from arthritis, everlastingly patient, per-suasive, conciliatory. He is convinced—a conviction nothing will ever shake—that *The Boy David*, the presentation of which he described in his book as 'the most important event of my career', is a thing of beauty, but he is becoming fully aware of the multifarious difficulties of its production.

The vast crowd engaged to play the Israelites and the Philistines look so blatantly, stubbornly, British. How is it to be drilled into movements and gesticulations less glaringly unoriental? And that most awkward member of the whole *dramatis personae*—Goliath? How—whether visibly or invisibly— is he to be presented without bathos? Nor, is it going to be easy to control a little donkey who, though full of demure grey charm, shows singularly little instinct for the stage. Above all, how is Cochran to be given strength to preside over the re-spective artistic temperaments of a dramatist for ever altering his play, a star in agonies of nerves, and a great painter—for the scene-designer is no less than Augustus John!—totally unaccustomed to direction?

Augustus John—an impressive figure splendidly sprawled

across two stalls—is pleased, as well he may be, with the magnificent set he has designed for the battle scene, but sublimely unconcerned as to whether or not it is possible for the contending Israelites and Philistines to clamber up or down his scenery, some of the rocks in which *must*—it had been impressed upon him—be 'practical'.

He surveys the stage of His Majesty's Theatre as though it were, not the setting for a play, but a picture gallery exhibiting a One-Man Show and, so, understandably, resents any suggested alteration that might spoil the general effect of his design. His beautifully painted rocks *look* very well. The question whether the feet of supers can climb them seems to him very trivial. Cochran and Barrie must mind their own business. He hasn't suggested that Barrie should alter the dialogue, or Cochran make any changes in the cast. What right have they to interfere with his job, about which they know nothing!

And the Star? A childlike figure in her long trousers, Elizabeth Bergner looks tormented and is visibly losing weight. So far she is only walking through her part, reading it in an almost uninflected voice from the script. She explains that in the early stages of rehearsal she can never do more than this. Before long, she tells me that she can't bear anyone for whom she cares, and whose approval she values, to attend rehearsals! Is Barrie—Barrie of all authors—then, expected to absent himself from the theatre, and have I got to tell him so?

Hours and hours, days and days, of mounting strain. Then, all of a sudden, Barrie, and with him the whole company, becomes miraculously better. His ability to detect and abolish defects returns. Rehearsals are transformed, Godfrey Tearle shows how magnificent a Saul he is to be. Martin Harvey has been holding up each rehearsal for half an hour over his first entrance, while he debates in which hand to hold the 'sacred wallet'. But it now becomes clear that he will make a most impressive Samuel. His personality is wonderfully right for the part. Best of all, Elizabeth Bergner begins to act exquisitely, to interpret the author's lines to perfection.

At one rehearsal during this lucid interval I remember Barrie in such good spirits that he acted in a Scottish accent both parts in the scene between Saul and Samuel.

But the next day everything was wrong again. Elizabeth Bergner, who told me she hadn't slept all night, declared herself convinced that the part of David ought to be played by a *boy*. Poor Cochran, now in a splint, was in agony of pain. There was renewed trouble over Samuel's wallet. The donkey in a bad attack of stage fright refused to come on at all!

Then, just as Barrie's presence was most needed, he fell ill again, this time with a high temperature. Rehearsals had to go on without him. It looked as if he wouldn't be able to be at the theatre again before the company of more than a hundred set off with its vanloads of scenery for Edinburgh. There, the play was shortly to open, and the advance booking was already many thousands of pounds. Worse was to befall. On Monday March 2nd, Elizabeth Bergner, in great pain, had to leave the theatre. In the middle of the night she was taken to a nursing home. Acute appendicitis was diagnosed. An immediate operation was performed. Poor Cochran had to announce that *The Boy David* was indefinitely postponed. An appalling financial loss was faced with admirable outward composure.

Tongues wagged; rumour rioted. Was it true—I was repeatedly asked—that Elizabeth Bergner was not really ill, but had lost her nerve about the play?

Barrie, outwardly as stoical as Cochran, gave no sign of his own disappointment—appeared indeed—though perhaps smoking and walking up and down his room more often than usual —to have no thought for himself in concern for Elizabeth Bergner, and for several days she was dangerously ill. Then, as anxiety diminished, Barrie, possessor when he chose of an incomparable bedside manner, seemed able to enjoy lavishing his best brand of sympathy on the invalid. Still no sign of self-pity.

For various reasons *The Boy David* did not go into rehearsal

Barrie with Elizabeth Bergner

again for over seven months, when almost the whole of the original company, though this time under a different producer, Theodor Komisarjevsky, reassembled at His Majesty's Theatre for three weeks' rehearsal before they went to Edinburgh. During those three weeks Barrie, disastrously, was very seldom well enough to go to the theatre.

The company arrived in Edinburgh with three clear days for rehearsal before the opening performance. But there was much to cope with—the new stage, the unwieldy number of warriors, Komisarjevsky's extremely complicated lighting-plot, the impracticability of those works of art, Augustus John's rocks, the various artistic temperaments, and the eleventh hour alterations and cuts which the author kept trying to make. Chaos, even more considerable than usual, prevailed at the dress rehearsal.

On the Friday it became clear that Barrie, whose strength was now visibly crumbling, would have to miss the first performance on the following Monday. By Saturday he was hopelessly in bed. That morning I joined him at the Caledonian Hotel. Appalled as I was by his appearance, I was forced to deal him yet another cruel blow. Had I suppressed the news, he would have read it in the papers. I had to tell him of the death of his lifelong friend, the devoted Gilmour.

Barrie was ill throughout the entire fortnight his play was performed at Edinburgh. He had to go out to be X-rayed. Otherwise, he stayed in bed the whole time, except for one evening, when, his waning vitality flickering into brief flame, he arose to dine in high spirits with Elizabeth Bergner, his secretary and the Cochrans.

All through that miserable time he was suffering acutely from pains that either baffled diagnosis or were hopefully called neuritis.

The Boy David was well received in Edinburgh. Elizabeth Bergner transcended even my expectations. 'She reminds you of whichever little boy in your life you have loved most,' exclaimed an entranced woman in the audience. As the *boy* David, Elizabeth was, it seemed to me, perfect; but I thought, as I always had, and as she herself thought, that the adult David—the David of the 'Visions'—should have been played by a man.

Godfrey Tearle's Saul was as fine as anything I've seen on the stage. Martin Harvey, no longer troubled by his wallet, was deeply impressive. When he said, 'Touch not the sacred wallet. I have hacked a King in pieces for less,' there was a note in his voice that made you shiver. Jean Cadell's fine performance admirably carried out the author's emphatic stage direction that there 'must be nothing sentimental about David's mother'.

But good as was nearly all the acting, there was still obviously much that needed pulling together, and the intervals between the visions were lamentably long. Alas, the author was not able to go to the theatre!

One way and another, I associate that fortnight in Edinburgh with nightmare tension, deepening depression, growing foreboding. Poor Elizabeth Bergner, overwrought and sleepless, declaring that she 'loves and reveres' the play, but feels she shouldn't be playing David—that she is too *gamine*. Barrie —strange that I should have called him 'Saul' long before the play had ever been thought of!—exhausted with pain, quite unfit for any exertion, yet Bible in hand, for ever cutting and changing his play.

The brightest break in the dark clouds was a visit from Granville-Barker, who already knew and loved the play. Annoyed and concerned by the tone of some of the London critics who had been to Edinburgh to see the play in advance, he came to judge the production for himself and to have a talk with Barrie, to whom he was devoted.

Granville-Barker was such an expert in the theatre that his renewed high praise of *The Boy David* can scarcely have failed to please and comfort, even if it did not reassure, Barrie. He dwelt much on how intensely moving he found the theme of

the play as embodied in the conflict between David and
Goliath, and in doing so gave in talk, I remember, the gist of
what, after Barrie's death, he wrote about this conflict in his
preface to the published play.

And many of life's conflicts are reflected in it; the conflict between youth
and age; good luck and ill, between the strength of innocence and the
weakening doubt which knowledge brings, and, worst of all, the conflict
not between those who hate, but those who love each other, forced on them
by an overriding fate, kindling conflict within themselves too, and so doubly
bitter. If he amends the story it is to give fuller significance to the theme.
David becomes all but a child, so that he may strangle the lion and the bear
and overcome the Philistines by no possible strength of his own (though—
never to lose touch with reality—it *is* just possible for a stone from a boy's
sling to kill a giant) but because the Spirit of the Lord is upon him. He is
secretly annointed by Samuel and we see age prostrate itself before divinely
gifted youth. In his innocence, David tells Saul the secret, launching the
javelin at his own heart; he conspires against God's will of him in vain.
The wary Saul seeks everywhere for the hidden danger to his throne,
except in the insignificance of that passing shepherd boy—though he, too,
was just such a shepherd once. He even unbars the way for him to do the
deed which was to be his own undoing. The secret out, is not his downfall
only the more certainly destined if the God who deserts him can make this
confiding child his instrument? He could kill him, and will degrade and
embitter the rest of his life by trying. But he cannot kill him. It is one of
life's fundamental conflicts that is here reduced to such deceptively simple
terms and crystallised, as drama should be, into significant action and a
few revealing words.

Granville-Barker declared he could not understand how
'anyone with any sense of dramatic dialogue could fail to
appreciate the play'. In his written analysis of the dialogue,
he praised:

the masterly economy, the equilibrium, the resiliency of it all. Every
speech has its motive, and contributes besides to the advancing of the scene
or the unfolding of the character, with a continuity as clear as a good
drawing or a line of pure melody.

When Granville-Barker turned from *The Boy David* to talk
of the earlier plays he specially stressed how much of a pioneer
Barrie had been. So much, now taken for granted in the

theatre of the day, and so no longer noticed or remarked upon, had, he maintained, in the first place been owed to the 'encouraging influence of Barrie's originality'.

Granville-Barker agreed that the present production of *The Boy David* needed much pulling together and speeding up. Rightly or wrongly, however, it was decreed that whatever changes were decided upon must wait until the company was back in the London theatre.

Alas, when these changes were made, Barrie, though still perpetually cutting and revising his play, was not nearly well enough to go to the theatre. Nor when at last on December 13th, 1936, the long-awaited London First Night came, was there any question of his being able, as of old, to crouch hidden at the back of a box. Instead, I, with a sinking heart, had to telephone to him between the acts to report how the play was going.

At the end of the performance, Elizabeth Bergner, Cochran and I hurried round to Adelphi Terrace. We spoke as encouragingly as we could, but though the theatre had, of course been packed and the applause adequate, that fiddlestring tautness of atmosphere one associates with a really successful First Night had been noticeably lacking; nor did I like the expression on the faces of certain critics.

The tone of the Press next morning confirmed my fears. Some found plenty to praise in the best scenes and admitted 'moments of great beauty', but they complained of the uncharacteristic flatness of certain passages and of the vagueness and slowness of the visions. Above all, they grumbled about the *theme* of the play. Why, they asked, should an author once famed for his power to create, and make convincing, characters so very much his own, go to the Bible for a story to distort? And if he must write a play about David, why have it acted by a woman, and a foreigner at that?

Certain alterations were considered. To my mind, it was a great pity that the magnificently dramatic figure of Saul, so superbly rendered by Godfrey Tearle, should be lost to the play while there was yet a whole act to come, and I could see no valid reason why the 'strong' scene—the javelin and the tent scene—between Saul and David, should not come after, instead of before, the visions and the light pastoral scene between David and Jonathan. Barrie was quite inclined to agree to this, but others were against taking any further risks in the way of change.

Barrie was able to go only once—about a week after the First Night—to see his play at His Majesty's Theatre. He came back terribly distressed by the length of the intervals between the visions, and looking ghastly ill.

After a run of only seven weeks, the ill-starred play came off.

In a letter to *The Times*, Granville-Barker pointed out 'there must be something radically wrong with a system under which sixty thousand people paid to see *The Boy David*, and yet it was branded a failure.' Bernard Shaw, too, wrote to protest. As a fact, the bookings had not fallen nearly as low as the figure at which the author's contract entitled the manager to give notice of withdrawal; but the cost of production was so immense that it exceeded the takings. When Barrie realised this situation he instantly gave Cochran permission to withdraw the play.

No sooner was it announced, on Thursday, January 21st, that the play would come off on the Saturday week than there was a wild rush to the box-office and all the agencies. Every seat for the remaining ten days could have been sold over and over again. Packed 'houses' applauded enthusiastically; thwarted theatre-goers, unable to obtain tickets, clamoured for an extension of the run. Whether this belated enthusiasm would have lasted it is impossible to say, but everyone, the company included, expected a reprieve, and one there undoubtedly would have been. Unfortunately the chance was gone. From the moment it had been decided to withdraw the play the theatre had been re-let. No hope for it. *The Boy David* must come off.

Scores now wrote to say how much they loved the play; others to assure the author that they had only failed to see it because influenza or their children's holidays had kept them from London. Letters came to the flat in bushels. Barrie lay in bed with all his old pains, still undiagnosed, an alarming new one in his chest, and a temperature. He was racked, too, now by yet another sorrow, the newly-discovered fatal illness of his brother-in-law, William Winter.

Barrie uttered no word of resentment. He could talk philosophically, even humorously, about the critics' reception of the work of his old age, but his grief over the disappointment the withdrawal of his play meant for Elizabeth Bergner, he didn't—couldn't attempt to—conceal.

I've heard it alleged that the apparent failure of *The Boy David* shortened Barrie's life. To suggest that his illness was caused by disappointment is, of course, nonsense. The tonic effect of a great success—the delight of giving Elizabeth Bergner the chance to outshine herself—might have brought about a temporary improvement; but, at best, this could only have staved off the inevitable, now fast approaching end, for the cause of his illness was not, as doctors had supposed, mainly psychological or merely muscular, but serious organic trouble. After the curtain fell for the last time on Barrie's last play, there remained to him only four more months of life, months of suffering throughout which, when not actually in bed, he was for the most part either crouched over his fire or wanly prowling round his room mutely bidding farewell—for the destruction of the Adelphi Terrace now compelled him to seek another home—to his cherished view on to the Thames.

Even in this last drear phase, his depression would lift and life take on colour again. That heartrending look of irremediable sadness—of a sorrow beyond all telling—would leave his weary face; and, all of a sudden, he would smile as though he had just glimpsed, or remembered, something of great beauty, or found some long-sought clue. So startling indeed at times was this change that more than once the question, 'What is it?' sprang to my lips.

However ill Barrie might feel, he could never fail to rouse himself to take up his cue in that part for which by nature and by training he had been cast—his part as the expert consoler of others. Less than two months before his own death, my mother died. I shall never forget the gentleness and skill with which, seemingly forgetting all his own sorrow, deep-down tiredness and pains, he set himself, as he alone could, to comfort and support; nor how deeply one could draw on that to some perhaps surprising, fund of practical wisdom always available when needed.

In another vivid memory of that last phase I see Barrie once more at his gayest and most amusing. The occasion only a fortnight before he died, a dinner at my house in Regent's Park, a very small party—besides Barrie, only my husband, my son Simon, Eileen Bigland, H. G. Wells and myself. Barrie and Wells always brought out the best in one another. That night they made us laugh all through dinner, especially by their jokes about the startling new symptoms they had invented to tell their doctor, Lord Horder, whom they were shortly to meet at a dinner at the Garrick Club.

A few days later, Wells, who had evidently been delighted to meet Barrie again, wrote to him: 'I am very much distressed to see the report of your illness in the paper this afternoon. You and I have been in this old literary world together for I don't know how many years, fifty-plus, and all through that time I've had nothing but an affectionate admiration for you and nothing but friendliness and generosity from you.'

*   *   *

The end came with merciful swiftness. On June 11th Barrie's illness took a sharp turn. He was taken to a nursing home. There, after only a week, during much of which he was unconscious, he died without pain.

He was seventy-six. Had he lived longer it would have been as an invalid. I remembered how often in these last months he had asked me to read to him:

> Vex not his ghost; O let him pass; he hates him
> That would upon the rack of this tough world
> Stretch him out longer.

And, in truth, by dying when he did die, Barrie escaped much. He left the world while, dark though the sky had grown, we could at least still speak of the 'war to end war' as The Great War.

He did not have to say good-bye to his view of the Thames by night.

His fears that his mind might fail had not been realised. That dreaded dark epilogue to the long drama of his life was not to be. Far otherwise! Very near to the end, he had recovered all his old happiness in writing. Once again he had known the 'joy of working till the stars went out'.

From the side of the lovely Hill of Kirriemuir, its cemetery looks down on to the little town. While we were staying at Balnaboth, I had seen the plain granite gravestone which Barrie had had made for his family. On it were engraved six names—his mother's, his father's, one brother and three sisters. I had noticed that at the foot of this gravestone a space had been left.

This space is now filled by a seventh name, as plainly chiselled as are the others, and—in obedience to clear instructions—'with no embellishments of any kind'. Neither is there any epitaph, or record whatsoever. Merely the names and the dates.

JAMES MATTHEW BARRIE
1860 - 1937

CHAPTER XV

MOST INDIVIDUAL AND
BEWILDERING GHOST

At the beginning of this book I said that it was not my purpose to attempt a summing-up of so complex a being as Barrie. What, in this final chapter, I *can* attempt to do is to answer some of the questions most often asked about him.

The commonest of these is: Was the man himself as over-sentimental as from his writings he seemed to be?

My diary records that, at our first meeting, Barrie had struck me, not as sentimental, but as saturnine. Neither characteristic is, of course, in the least incompatible with the other. Barrie, unquestionably, had streaks of both. But I soon saw—and twenty years didn't change my view—that his sentimentality was not only superficial, but very patchy. Like most of us—though far more articulately—Barrie had 'soft spots'. Gradually, I learned how these soft spots had been come by, and in so doing, found the explanation for nearly all the passages in Barrie's work that embarrassed me. They had been 'lifted' from life—pulled up by the roots from the soil of his own emotional experience. When Barrie did this he often fell into a not uncommon pitfall of authorship. He projected his own feelings, forgot the need to drag the reader by the sleeve.

For instance, he would quote—and what is more dangerous? —the actual words of some child. Association—*he* could still hear the voice in which they were spoken—made them so funny or so touching to himself. But, taken out of their context, these words lose nearly all point. To some who don't share Barrie's memories, they may indeed convey so little meaning that he might almost as well be writing in a private code.

Nor was it only over children that memories could snare Barrie. When he made a heroine too 'roguey-poguey' as Walkley put it—one may be sure that she has been over closely drawn from life. He has failed to blend realism and fantasy with sufficient art. The transposition has gone wrong. She doesn't get across.

And again, in those passages where what is intended as irony miscarries and, taken the wrong way, brings the blush to many cheeks, it is misplaced reliance on what is virtually a private code that is to blame.

These failures of Barrie's art are not infrequent. Even so, for some—for many indeed—he can't go wrong. Watch them at one of his rainbow plays. The bell rings every time. When they aren't laughing they are crying. Now, look at those differently emotionally wired, for whom the bell does not ring. To them, the very words that touched the others to tears, seem namby-pamby, too whimsical—that hated word can't always be banned—or treacly. They are unmoved; even repelled, perhaps nauseated.

Most of these questionable passages—those that make the queasy writhe, detractors crow—even some devotees uncomfortable—could easily be eliminated. Except for the play and the books about *Peter Pan*, I own the copyright in Barrie's works, so I could myself discharge this novel form of bowdlerisation. But the things which offend some are precisely those that most delight—even console—others; and who am I to judge?

To my mind the essential Barrie is not sentimental. The real sentimentalist refuses to face hard facts. Barrie does not. For all his reputed 'softness', he is no escapist. He faces the most painful truths. The silver coating of his writing covers a core of hard truth, not to be found in the work of many self-styled realists, who for all their brilliant cynicism seem yet naively to suppose that by derision or scolding they can alter human nature. What could be more 'let's face it' than the import of *Dear Brutus*, which is that, whatsoever your chances and your resolves, you can never escape from your nature? Midsummer night magic or no, as you enter the moonlit wood so you will come out of it.

> The fault, dear Brutus, is not in our stars,
> But in ourselves, that we are underlings.

And that tragedy of transience, *Mary Rose*, what other work more mercilessly, however gently, conveys a bitter truth? 'No one, however much loved, should ever come back.'

'Oh for an hour of Herod!' exclaimed Anthony Hope as he left the theatre after the first performance of *Peter Pan*. Some, with no special love of children, may feel inclined to echo his cry. Others, who love children so sensitively that they can't bear to see them, as they think, falsified, may also condemn Barrie's attitude towards them. But here, again, there has been much over-simplification. Because Barrie wrote for, and about, children, and knew how to play with them, he has been labelled as a universal child-fancier. In reality, his liking for children was very far from indiscriminate. It was highly individual. He had to choose his child—hated to be chosen. About some children he could be just as caustic as about their parents, and about no child did he ever lose his sense of humour.

To take a child to a theatre and catch some of his rapture is a great delight. Were the play written by oneself, the delight no doubt would be such that it might well jeopardise one's sense of humour. It never even suspended Barrie's. He didn't want children to take *Peter Pan* seriously. His favourite reaction to his own play was that of the little boy who, favoured by a seat in the author's box, and at the end injudiciously asked what he had liked best, promptly replied: 'What I *think* I liked best was tearing up the programme and dropping the bits on people's heads.'

Nor is there any truth in the theory, derived from misinterpretation of the fable of *Peter Pan*, that Barrie resented the children of whom he was fond growing up. He may have regretted one attractive phase giving place to another—who that ever loved a child has not?—but he never tried to hold a child back.

'One by one,' he wrote to the boys from whom, by 'rubbing them together' he had created *Peter Pan*, 'one by one, as you swung monkey-wise from branch to branch in the wood of make-believe, you reached the tree of knowledge.'

So it should be. So it was.

Barrie's glorification of motherhood has been derided as much as his alleged glorification of childhood. Here again, at times, his pen went wrong when memory took too strong a hold. His impulse, half tenderly, half derisively, to portray some individual woman was uncontrollable; and so, unfortunately, was his tendency to caricature.

Before leaving the perilous subject of 'mothers' I feel I should touch on one point which I never discussed with Margaret Ogilvie's son. In theory Barrie was violently opposed to authors writing about their nearest and dearest. Indeed, to judge from his expressed views, no one more fully shared Wordsworth's abhorrence of 'one that would peep and botanise upon his mother's grave'. How was this oft-declared repugnance consistent with the publication of that greatly loved, but much criticised book, *Margaret Ogilvie*? By his own indictments of this kind of spiritual indelicacy—for that was what *he* seemed to think it—Barrie repeatedly gave me my cue to ask, 'But isn't that just what you did yourself in *Margaret Ogilvie*?' Why did I never ask that question? Had I done so, would Barrie have said that his mother had begged him to write about her? I'm sure she had. I can hear her wheedling him, 'You *will* put me into a book, won't you, Jamie?'

And why ever *not*, if it be in your power, make your mother immortal!

What puzzles me is not that Barrie should have written *Margaret Ogilvie*. The book does not offend me. Besides, I know that, whatever his views about reticence, once Barrie took a pen into his hand something unpremeditated nearly always ran out of it. His subconscious was more than a collaborator. It could, too often did, take control. He might make a myriad notes before he began to write, but he never quite knew what would emerge. What does puzzle me is that, having, as Denis Mackail wrote, 'blazoned his love for his mother through the world,' he should yet inveigh against other writers who, with less success, tried to do the same thing. Was this a genuine blind spot? Or was it a defensive, deliberate shutting of his eyes because deep, deep down he knew—and winced at the knowledge—that he resembled his own creation, Noble Simms, the journalist, to whose writer's mill everything was grist. 'My God!' groaned Noble Simms, 'I would write an article, I think, upon my mother's grave!'

Another frequent enquiry is, 'Was Barrie generous?' May I never be asked a question less easy to answer! He was immensely and imaginatively generous. But very unostentatiously. With the one spectacular exception of parting with all the proceeds—between two and three thousand a year—from *Peter Pan*, he went in far more for spontaneous and secret acts of bounty than for organised charities. He didn't head many public subscriptions, but he gave vast sums away and paid for countless educations. Furthermore, he often—in my experience a rare habit—gave anonymously. The sad thing was that he suffered from the misgiving that, by playing providence in other people's lives, he had at times harmed, instead of benefited, them. He would question the advantages derived from an expensive public school, for which he had paid, or the happiness of some marriage he had made possible. This misgiving, which verged on superstition, gave him almost a sense of guilt. Had he, he asked himself, the Evil Eye? A streak of morbidity? Undeniably, but one for which an early stroke of cruelly bad luck was to blame. Almost his very first act of generosity had had tragic consequences. Soon after he first began to make money his sister, Margaret, became engaged to a very promising young man. To help his prospective brother-in-law,.who was a Free Church minister, to cover the long distances in his scattered parish, Barrie gave him a horse. The very first time this gift horse was ridden it threw its rider and killed him!

Fortunately for Barrie himself, as well as for others, no qualms as to possible ill consequences could check his instinctive generosity. In any emergency he rushed unasked to the rescue. In a more frivolous Fairy Godfather vein, he loved to spend money on giving delightful surprises. He would startle an impecunious friend by the news that he had put money on a racehorse in her name, and the horse had won. Or were she ill, he would send up her temperature by ordering round to the sick-room a sumptuous dinner, complete with waiter, from the Berkeley. This love of giving surprises—surprises bordering on shocks—was a very characteristic trait, of which I had ample first-hand experience. For instance, in the middle of a performance of *Peter Pan*, he contrived, unperceived by me, to spirit away my five-years-old son, Simon, and waft him wholly unrehearsed into the play. One moment the little boy was at my side in the box; the next, resplendently attired as one of Napoleon's marshalls, he stood cross-armed on the deck of the Pirate Ship.

Was Barrie conceited? Many have asked that question, though what exactly in this—or indeed in any—context is meant by that word I never know. As inevitably as a tall man must know that he is tall, and the winner of a race must know that he can run, so Barrie must have known that he could write. But writing is a gift, and Barrie couldn't possibly feel self-satisfied about a gift. I can't pretend that the word 'conceited' ever crossed my own mind in connection with Barrie, but on consideration I should say that, if he were proud of anything, it was not of his gifts but of his diligence. The number of hours he had worked at a stretch, the number of words he had written in a week, was his nearest approach to a boast.

No degree of modesty—false or real—could have blinded Barrie to the fact that he had craftsmanship, but if he ever spoke of technique, it was in a disparaging way. He must have realised, too, that he had individuality, but since this, besides being perilously close to idiosyncrasy, was inescapable, he knew that it was a fetter as well as a wand.

Very early in his life, Barrie had proved to himself—as well as to others, some of whom had been so sceptical—that he could earn enough money with his pen to keep, not only himself, but a host of dependents. This must have been a satisfaction. But if success had given him a certain self-confidence, he never even began to lose his deep underlying humility, and an abashed—almost guilty and certainly exaggerated—sense of the part that, what he called, 'luck' had played in his success.

I have been asked if Barrie was liable to anger as well as to melancholy.

Fits of depression were much more common than annoyance, but now and again nervous distemper would discharge itself against some human target. A gust of resentment could make him temporarily unreasonable—even unjust—in his diatribe against some real, or supposed, offender. But, distressing though this derangement might be, it was as superficial as the scum on the surface of a deep lake. Barrie's considered, as opposed to his hasty, judgment, was always wise, kindly and remarkably just.

It did not need much discernment to see that the way to treat Barrie's fits of resentment was to give his grievance its head—to agree that the offender's conduct was monstrous and join in the attack. Could you bring yourself to do this, Barrie would at once react and, veering round, defend the object of his own abuse. Yes, those were the right tactics—and how easy to employ them had I not been so fond of him!

Remaining exasperatingly fair-minded, I would feel compelled to reason with him, when at that moment—as any fool could see—rationality was the last thing wanted. Nor did he ever care for argument for argument's sake. What he craved was sympathy. That could always soothe and lure him back to reasonableness.

Was there any way of reaching Barrie when, Saul-like, he glowered in gloom and you felt 'league-sundered by the silent gulf between'? Yes, one infallible way—to turn the tables; be in trouble yourself and tell him so. Then, forgetting himself, he would rush to the rescue—lay himself out to understand, advise, console, sustain. Once his imaginative sympathy was stirred, he would spare no effort to help. And who was ever better equipped to soften grief—or sublimate it? Equally, were the trouble not sorrow, but merely diffidence, no one could do more to dispel a bad attack of this intermittent malady, and lure the sufferer back into cheerfulness. Whenever Barrie chose—and he often did choose—to treat despondency, he could 'retrick' other people's 'beams' as deftly as his own.

When, as not seldom now, my mind travels back into the past, one specially vivid picture of Barrie rises before my eyes. I see him, as I so often saw him, crouched over his Adelphi hearth, busily engrossed in mending the log fire on its great mound of ashes. The persistence and skill with which he would ply the giant bellows, and their ally, the long steel prong, until the dying embers blazed into flame again, had become to me symbolic of the patience, persuasion and tact with which he would set himself to revive the self-confidence of anyone for whom he cared. No one knew better how to rekindle hope and courage when they sank low. No one was more glad to do it.

For the rest of my life the scent of wood smoke will make me see that wide cavernous hearth and, on his knees beside it, Barrie—'most individual and bewildering ghost'—patiently, intently, fanning grey ashes into flame.

INDEX

ACHESON, Katie, 147
Adams, Maud, 127
Adlard, Eleanor, 121
Admirable Crichton, The, 37, 127, 205
Allahakbarries, The, 15, 122-5, 132, 137, 156
Allen, Rev. H. B. ('Priest'), 155, 169, 173, 181
Amundsen, Roald, 130
Anderson, Mary, 124
Armstrong (W. W.), 142
Ashford, Daisy, 32
Asquith, Herbert, 17, 44, 57, 61, 64, 102, 114, 147, 187, 196-7, 215
    Herbert Henry, *v.* Oxford and Asquith, Earl of
    'Margot', *v.* Oxford and Asquith, Countess of
    Michael, 17, 44, 64, 91, 93, 137, 142, 163, 165, 172, 182, 191, 196-7
    Simon, 44, 64, 88, 91, 93, 154, 160, 162-3, 165, 173, 181, 196-7, 215, 222
Auld Licht Idylls, 187

BALDWIN, Earl, 2
Balfour, Earl, 146, 172
Bancroft, Sir Squire, 68, 71
Baring, Hon. Maurice, 28, 35, 95
Barnard, Dorothy, 151
Barnes (Cambridge Don), 162
Barrie, Alexander, 115, 195

Barrie, David, 52
    (father), 13
    Lilian (niece), 115-16
    Margaret, 222
    (mother), 13
Barrymore, Ethyl, 127
Bax, Arnold, 32
'Beb' (Herbert Asquith), 164, 180
Beech, Stella, 159
Bergner, Elizabeth, 186, 201-5, 207-10, 212, 214
Bibesco, Princess, Priscilla, 177
'Bibs' (Countess of Plymouth), 164
Bigland, Eileen, 112, 215
Birrell, Rt. Hon. Augustine, 15, 40-1, 150, 159, 161-2, 169, 172, 180, 184
Blackwood, Lady Patricia, 144
Bonham-Carter, Cressida, 173
    Laura, 173
    Mark, 173
    Lady Violet, 136, 173
Boucicault, Dion, 162, 166
Boy David, The, 31, 38, 64, 118, 185, 187, 194, 201-14
Bridgeman, Maurice, 136
Bright, R. Golding, 29
Brown, Harry, 40-1, 43, 46-8
Bute, Marquis of, 66

CADELL, Jean, 34, 210
Campbell, Mrs Patrick, 5-6, 60-2
Cannan, Mrs Gilbert, 157-8
Captain Hook at Eton, 80-1

Cave, Lord, 140, 165
Cecil, Algernon, 153, 191
  Lord David, 144, 157, 162, 166
  Lady Guendolen, 153, 166
Charteris, Ann, 93, 177
  Hon. Evan, K.C., 41-3
  Hon. Guy, 151, 166
  Hugo, 92
  Laura, 93
  Hon. Martin, 91, 93, 159
  Mary Rose, 93-4, 182, 191
  Hon. Yvo, 13
Chesterton, G. K., 174-7, 182
  Mrs G. K., 175, 182
Churchill, Clarissa, 172
  Lady Guendeline, 172
  Peregrine, 172
Cochran, C. B., 201, 204, 206-9,
  212-13
Cockerell, Sir Sydney, 169
Coles, E. H., 151-2, 169, 172-3, 191
Collins (H. L.), 81, 142, 166
Colvin, Sidney, 67
Compton, Fay, 34, 36
'Courage', famous speech on, 69-70,
  96, 103, 117
'Critics' Circle, The', 34
Czinner, Paul, 201

Darling, Diana, 157
  Lord Justice, 157
Davies, Arthur Llewellyn, 10
  George, 13
  Geraldine, 151
  Jack, 13, 151, 191
  Jane, 151
  Margaret, 191
  Michael, 13, 135
  Nicholas, 13, 57, 128, 135, 146,
  157, 159-60
  Peter, 13, 57, 191
  Sylvia Llewellyn, 10, 156

Davies, Timothy, 151, 191
Dear Brutus, 3, 21, 93, 127, 219
de la Mare, Colin, 174
  Jinny, 162
  Walter, O.M., 162, 174, 176-7
Desborough, Lady, 162, 174
  Lord, 174
Devonshire, Duchess of, 177, 179-81
Dickens, Charles, 59
  Miss, 31
Doyle, Sir A. Conan, 15, 171-2
Draper, Ruth, 166
Dufferin, Brenda, 3-4, 40-1
  Marquis of, 144
  Marchioness of, 144
Duke-Elder, Sir Stewart, F.R.C.S.,
  72
du Maurier, George, 152, 156
  Gerald, 10
Dynasts, The, 106

Edinburgh University, 20, 25, 78
Edward VIII, 204
Elizabeth, Princess (now Queen),
  112, 193
Escape Me Never, 201, 203
'Esther', 147-8, 179
Eton College, 80-1, 146

Farewell, Miss Julie Logan, 64, 134
Faulkner, Bobbie, 154, 165, 191, 197
  Dick, 154, 165, 172, 191
  Harry, 154
  'Nannie' (Miss Mabel), 154, 170,
  179, 196-7
  Tib (Mrs H. Faulkner), 154
Fight for Mr Lapraik, The, 26-7
Flying Carpet, The, 111
Follett, Colonel, 198
  Mrs, 198
  Pauline, 198
Forbes, Norman, 34

Freyberg, Major-General Bernard, V.C. (now Lord Freyberg), 7, 41-3, 68-72, 103-4, 144, 159
Lady Freyberg, 144, 159
Frohman, Charles, 20-1
Furse, Charles, A.R.A., 21

GALSWORTHY, John, 2, 68, 75, 162-5, 169-70, 180-1, 184
Mrs, 170, 180-1
Garland, Mr, Mrs and Miss Hamlin, 157
Gillette, William, 127
Gilmour, T. L., 96-101, 123, 157, 184, 209
Godfrey Marten, Schoolboy, 119
Gore, Lady Winifred, 182
Granville-Barker, Harley, 64, 84, 159, 161-2, 202, 210-13
Helen (Mrs), 161-2
Great Ormond Street Children's Hospital, 177
Greenwood, Frederick (Editor), 25
Greenwood Hat, The, 64, 99-100, 123, 170n
Gregory (J. M.), 82, 126, 142
Grey, Mrs Jose, 166
Grosvenor, Beatrice, 173
Rosemary, 173
'Grum, Mrs', 153-4, 159-62, 164, 172-4, 177

HAIG, Earl, 67-8, 70-2
Haldane, Lord, 152
Hamilton, General Sir Ian, 6
Hardy, Mrs (first), 107
Mrs Florence, 108-9, 169, 171-2
Thomas, 59, 67, 104-11
Hartington, The Marquis and Marchioness, 177
Hartley, L. P., 174
Headlam, G. W., 157

Hendry (H. L.), 82
Henley, W. E., 14, 21
Herbert, A. P. (Sir Alan), 127, 169
Hobbs (J. B.), 82, 126
Hope, Anthony, 184, 219
Horder, Lord, 215
Horner, Sir John and Lady, 63
Housman, A. E., 2, 59-60
Hunter, Mrs Charles, 178

Ibsen's Ghost, 181
Irvine, Principal Sir James, 68, 71-2, 117
Irving, Sir Henry, 87, 127, 161

JACKS, L. P., 169
James, Henry, 37
Hon. Mary, 160
Jardine (D. R.), 126
Jerrold, Mary, 34
John, Augustus, O.M., 206-7, 209
Journey's End, 83

KARSAVINA, 32, 165
Kennedy, Margaret, 201
King's Daughters, The, 193
Kipling, Rudyard, 2, 75, 184
Komisarjevsky, Theodor, 209

LAMB, Charles, 170
Last, Harry, 136, 143-4, 155
Lawrence, D. H., 19
(Editor), 177
Letters of J.M.B., The, 73
Lewis, Eiluned, 63
Lady, 156
Lister, Francis, 88
Little Minister, The, 21
Little White Bird, The, 20, 33
Lorraine, Robert, 12
Lucas, Audrey, 119, 131, 144
Elizabeth (Mrs E. V.), 112-14, 119, 151, 157, 171

Lucas, E. V., 28, 68, 112, 119, 136, 141
Lyon, Lady Mary, 158
Lytton, Hon. Anthony, 158
  The Lady Hermione, 158
  Pamela, Countess of, 1, 158
  Earl and Countess of, 63

MacCarthy, Desmond, 34-5, 161-2, 165
McCartney (C. G.), 166, 174
MacDonald, J. Ramsay, 2, 173, 191
  Sheila, 191
Mackail, Denis, 8, 11, 33, 40, 98, 159, 204, 221
  Diana, 159
  Margaret, 165
Maclean, Ian, 182
Macnaughton, Hugh, 136
Maid in Waiting, 180
Mailey (A. A.), 82, 142, 166
Manchester Guardian, The, 35
Margaret Ogilvie, 13-14, 220
Margaret (Rose), Princess, 193-4
'Margot', *v.* Oxford and Asquith, Countess of,
Marsh, Sir Edward, 144
Martin Harvey, (Sir John) 207, 210
Mary, Queen, 145-6
Mary Rose, 33-6, 38, 45, 71, 83, 88, 105-6, 163, 219
Mason, A. E. W., 41
'McConnachie', 66, 72
Memoirs of Mrs Patrick Campbell, 61
Meredith, George, 104
Mew, Charlotte, 109
Meynell, Viola, 73
Moore, George, 64, 177-80
Morrison, Rt. Hon. W. S., 174, 181
  Alison, 174, 181
My Lady Nicotine, 23, 115, 159

Nannie, *v.* Faulkner, Mabel, 'Nannie'
Nansen, F., 130
Nash, Paul, 32
National Observer, The, 141
Navarro, M. de, 124
  Mme de, *v.* Anderson, Mary
Nichols, Robert, 67, 167-8
Northborne, Lord, 160
Nottingham Journal, The, 25, 97
Number of People, A, 144

Ogilvie, Hon. Bruce, 177
Oliver, Fred, 41, 43, 63, 184
  F. S., 79
  Mrs (Fred), 191
O'Neil, Norman, 34, 154
Osborne, Lady Guendolen (afterwards Lady Guendolen Cecil), 136
Oxford and Asquith, Countess of, 165-6, 168, 173
  Earl of, 21, 40-1, 67, 92, 167

Pall Mall Gazette, The, 20
Partridge, Bernard, 122-3
Peake, The Lady Joan, 159
Pershing, General, 41
Peter Pan, 20, 53, 83-4, 129, 156, 160, 177, 218-22
Ponsford (W. H.), 82
Poole, Sir Reginald, 177, 194
'Porthos' (St. Bernard dog), 20
Preston, Harry, 63
Prew, James, 143, 145, 180
'Princess Elizabeth Gift Book, The', 112
Punch, 119

Quiller-Couch, Foy, 165
  Sir A.T., 33

R.A.D.A., 38

Raleigh, Lady, 136
Philippa, 136
Professor Sir W., 5, 27, 35, 138-40
'Rhodes Scholars', 78
Robb, James, 117-18, 184
Robey, George, 12
Rosebery, Earl of, 97, 101
Rowe, Dick, 191
Royal Literary Society, The, 75, 80

Sapcot, Mrs, 147
Scott, Captain, 70, 102, 130
Peter, 29, 201
Seaman, Owen, 167
Sentimental Tommy, 52, 54, 150-1
Seymour, Miss Horatia, 162, 166, 196
Shall We Join the Ladies?, 37, 45, 146
Shaw, George Bernard, 2, 37, 61, 75, 78, 161, 201, 213
Shields, Sir Douglas, 111-2, 162
Shropshire Lad, The, 59
Smith, Charles Turley, 119-22, 124-31
Snowden, Philip, 173
Sons and Lovers, 19
Stanley, 'Mrs', 46, 50, 58, 126, 130
Stevenson, R. L., 8, 37, 45, 68-9, 104, 169
St. Andrews University, 66-73, 79, 117
St. James's Gazette, The, 25
St. Joan, 201
Story of J.M.B., The, 11, 27
Strickland, Sara, 30

Tearle, Sir Godfrey, 205, 207, 210
Terry, Ellen, 68-9, 71, 94
Tess of the Durbervilles, 109
Thesiger, Ernest, 34
Thirkell, Angela, 166

Thomlinson, Sister Mildred, 114-15, 191
Thompson, Joseph, 102, 122
Times, The, 19, 32, 34, 39, 57, 74, 119, 144, 201, 203, 213
Tonks, Professor, 41-2, 178
Toole, J. L., 181
Tree, H. Beerbohm, 20
Trollope, Anthony, 57-8
Truth about the Russian Dancers, The, 32
Twelve Pound Look, The, 21, 205

Ulysses, 59

Vanbrugh, Irene, 162-3
Voltaire, 37
Voyages of Captain Scott, The, 130

Walkley, A. B., 32, 34, 37, 157, 218
Walpole, Sir Hugh, 74, 77
Warner (P. F.), 75
Watson, Marriott, 123
Wedgwood, Eliza, 156
Wells, H. G., 16, 75, 181-2, 215
Wemyss, Earl of (author's father), 6, 89-90, 92-3
Countess of (author's mother), 16-17, 91-2, 95, 215
'Wessex', (Thomas Hardy's dog), 108-11
What Every Woman Knows, 21, 87, 174
Wheel, The, 93
When A Man's Single, 182
Where was Simon?, 85-92
Whibley, Charles, 5, 14-16, 24, 41-3, 45, 59, 68, 72, 80, 113, 136-7, 150-1, 162, 169, 173
White Company, The, 172
White, Maude V., 174
Wilson, President Woodrow, 41, 43

Winter, Margaret, 151, 162, 184
    William (Jun.), 151
    William (Sen.), 151, 184, 214
Wood, Judy, 154
    Stanley, 156
Woodfull (W. M.), 126
Worthington (T. S.), 160

Wyndham, George, 176
    Miss Olivia, 41, 43

YORK, Duke and Duchess of (after-
    wards George VI and Queen
    Elizabeth), 193
Young Visiters, The, 31-2